# THE BLACK WATCH

# The Black Watch

## The History of the Royal Highland Regiment

## Eric and Andro Linklater

**BARRIE & JENKINS**
COMMUNICA - EUROPA

Filmset and printed by Jolly & Barber Limited
Rugby, Warwickshire

*To the memory of my father*
ERIC LINKLATER

# Contents

# List of Illustrations

Black and White

# Acknowledgements

It would be impossible to write such a history without the help of the Regiment, but I am enormously grateful for the profusion in which that help came, and most especially to Colonel Rusk D.S.O., M.C. and Mr James MacMillan F.S.A. at The Black Watch Museum for their advice and encyclopaedic knowledge, and for their permission to study and quote from numerous diaries, letters and other unpublished documents in the Museum's possession; to the Officers, Non-Commissioned Officers and Private Soldiers of The Black Watch, past and present, for interviews, letters, journals and reminiscences; and to the Colonel of the Regiment, Lord Ballantrae K.T., G.C.M.G., G.C.V.O., D.S.O., on whose splendid history *The Black Watch and the King's Enemies* much of my information of the Second World War is based, and who originally suggested that I should complete this work after the death of my father.

I wish to thank the following for permission to quote from copyright material: Leo Cooper Ltd for a passage from Michael Brander's *Scottish Highlanders and Their Regiments*; Oxford University Press for two extracts from Brigadier Sir Howard Kippenberger's *Infantry Brigadier*; William Collins Ltd for three extracts from the first volume of John Connell's *Wavell*. I am grateful to The Black Watch Museum for most of the illustrations used in this book; to the photographer Dr Findlay; to the Imperial War Museum for Plates 19 to 26; to the York and Lancaster Museum for Colour Plate IX; to the Scottish United Services Museum for Colour Plate III; to Heinemann Educational Books Ltd for the map of the Western Front, taken from the *Military Atlas of the First World War* by Arthur Banks, and to Cambridge University Press for the map of the Peninsular Wars, taken from the *New Cambridge Modern History Atlas*, edited by H. C. Darby and Harold Fullard. I must thank the Public Record Office and the National Army Museum for much courteous assistance.

Andro Linklater

# Preface

*by Lord Ballantrae*

It is now some years since I was invited by the publishers to suggest an author for a new and definitive history of The Black Watch. I was a little shy about asking Eric Linklater, for I knew that he had several books on the stocks; but he wrote back by return of post to say that there was no book to which he would sooner set his hand, although (he said) it might well be his last. And so it sadly proved to be. Having begun work on it with characteristic eagerness, and frequent bulletins to me reporting this or that new discovery among our archives, he began to falter. Illness closed in on him, and he died in Aberdeen, whose University he had graced fifty years earlier, in October of 1974.

Before going up to the University, by dint of a mammoth lie, he had served on the Western Front as a private soldier in the Regiment for more than a year before his 18th birthday. The deep furrow across his bald pate, corresponding with the furrow in the steel helmet which hung in his successive homes, was an honourable scar indeed. Literary fame, and the fact that he stood head and shoulders above every other Scottish writer of his generation, had not dimmed his passion for The Black Watch. He had been especially thrilled when he was elected Rector of his old University during the Chancellorship of that greatest of all Black Watch soldiers, Lord Wavell.

If you ask any bunch of, say, twenty Jocks how many of their fathers have served in the Regiment, the hands of at least half of them go up (and, incidentally, 90% of them come from the regimental area of Perth, Angus and Fife); if you ask the same question of a group of officers, the figure will be three-quarters. The present Commanding Officer of the 1st Battalion as I write is another Duncan Cameron, a collateral descendant of the Duncan Cameron who emerges so sympathetically from these pages. His predecessor's father and brother were in the Regiment; and *his* predecessor had a brother killed in the Regiment in Crete in 1941, and a great-uncle in it as well. And so it goes on; and, let us hope, will go on going on.

It was partly in this tradition that I was inspired to ask Eric's younger son Andro to take on from where Eric had left off. I am heartily glad that I did, for in my view he has done the job superbly. I know some of the considerable difficulties from my own experience: since, many years ago, Lord Wavell as Colonel of the Regiment ordered me to write a brief history for the use of recruits. For the first 75 years of our existence there is little manuscript material; from about 1800 onwards we are rich in diaries and letters almost to the point of embarrassment, and selection becomes a difficult matter. The task of unravelling the various reincarnations of the 2nd Battalion, and of pursuing the ramifications of numerous battalions on numerous fronts through the two world wars, is really baffling: yet what we have here is a masterpiece of clarity, as well as magnificent reading.

By the time this book appears in print, I shall have finished my happy period of seven years as Colonel of the Regiment. It is my final privilege to thank the Linklaters, father and son, for the great service they have done us; and to welcome Eric's last book and Andro's first. And so I sign myself, for the last time:

Ballantrae,
Colonel, The Black Watch

CHAPTER I

# The Raising of the Regiment

In the early years of the eighteenth century there lived in the Highlands of Scotland a scattered society that, without industry or roads, existed on a primitive husbandry, a minimal commerce and cottage crafts, in a habit of life indifferent to any thought of material improvement because there was no prospect of change. It was a static society, built upon the clan, and the clan was essentially a military companionship. Its disabilities were obvious, but it was cohesive, it drew strength and a measure of comfort – a sense of security – from the general belief that all in the clan, from its Chief to the poorest cottar, were related by common descent from a distant and perhaps legendary ancestor.

On the coastal fringe between the Highlands and the North Sea there were two small towns, Aberdeen and Inverness, and two villages of appreciable size, Elgin and Dingwall, in which English was spoken because English was necessary for trade, and the area enjoyed some commerce with the continent of Europe. Within the Highlands the great majority of people spoke only Gaelic, their ancient tongue. Their chiefs, however, and those near in relationship to them, spoke both English and Gaelic, many were fluent in French, and more than a few knew Latin: it is probable that all who could find an opportunity to travel abroad had done so, and in their families a regard for education was warmly fostered.

The Highlands exported fish, black cattle, and mercenary soldiers. Fish, caught on the west coast, were shipped to Glasgow; by unmade but well defined drove-roads black cattle were driven to Lowland markets and thence, if there was demand, to England; the soldiers found employment in the armies of Sweden and Russia, Denmark and the Netherlands, and to call them mercenaries does not denigrate them, for to earn their pay they put their lives to risk. Since the time of Joan of Arc, under whose banner they marched, Scottish soldiers had fought for France, and the *Garde Ecossaise* had a long and distinguished history. In the seventeenth century the Thirty Years War opened a wider market than ever before, and Donald Mackay, Lord Reay, recruited 3,600 men for Christian IV of Denmark, while 10,000 Scots are said to have served under Gustavus Adolphus of Sweden. No one knows how many lived and came home to Highland glen or Lowland pasture, but Dugald Dalgetty – whose immediate begetter was Walter Scott – cannot have been the only survivor, and a military traffic, long continued and widely spread, may well explain a curious paradox: despite the notorious poverty of the High-lands, the Highlanders seem always to have possessed arms in plenty.

During the later decades of the seventeenth century small companies had been enlisted, by governmental authority, for police duties in the north, but there is no detailed or consecutive record of what they did. It is probable, however, that not all were trustworthy, for after the collapse of the Jacobite rebellion in 1715 the remnant three companies were disbanded, and not until 1725 was 'The Highland Watch' revived under a name that became more widely known. The new force owed its being to the lively imagination and shrewd judgment of General George Wade, an Irishman.

Ordered to make a thorough investigation of the state of the Highlands, and to disarm the clans, Wade did more than that and built metalled roads that reached from Dunkeld in Perthshire to Inverness, that swept past Loch Tay and, through the Great Glen, marched from sea to sea. Whether he disarmed the clans as effectively as he believed is by no means certain: a previous attempt had been evaded, and Wade himself admitted, not only that old worn-out weapons had been exchanged for the Government bounty while better pieces were prudently concealed, but that the import of obsolete muskets from Holland, and their dutiful surrender, had apparently proved a sound speculation. His roads, however – roads and forty stone bridges – remained as enduring evidence of a singular and exceptionally energetic genius.

He also gave life to a human institution, that has lasted longer than his roads, when, in a report written in 1724, he recommended:

> That companies of such Highlanders as are well affected to His Majesty's Government be established under proper regulations, and commanded by officers speaking the language of the country, subject to martial law, and under the inspection and orders of the Governors of Fort William and Inverness, and the officer commanding His Majesty's forces in those parts.
>
> That the said companies be employed in disarming the Highlanders, preventing depredations, bringing criminals to justice, and hinder rebells and attainted persons from inhabiting that part of the kingdom.

In consequence of that recommendation the enlistment of six such companies was authorised by George I on the 12th May, 1725; and because, at Wade's insistence, they wore a uniform tartan – and that tartan was dark – they became locally known as *Am Freiceadan Dubh*, and subsequently, in a more widely known language, as The Black Watch. They wore 'the Government tartan'; they may well have regarded themselves as a clan sanctioned by legal authority, and from Wade's report it is clear that they were raised specifically for service in the still troubled Highlands.

The kilt of that time – woven of the Government tartan – was a more voluminous garment than the *feileadh-beag* or little kilt of to-day. It was a combination of kilt and plaid, twelve yards long, belted round the middle and so disposed that the lower part, neatly folded, hung to the top of the knee-cap while the upper part, thrown across the left shoulder, was held there by a brooch: though cumbersome, it had the advantage of becoming a blanket at night. A short jacket was worn and, before the adoption of regimental scarlet, was of green, blue, or black cloth. A flat blue bonnet and a large purse or sporran, perhaps of goat-skin; brogues and gartered hose; a dirk with knife and fork tucked into the sheath; and a pair of small steel pistols might complete the costume, but usually the soldiers carried more than that.

Usually they carried a heavy musket and bayonet, a cartridge-box and a broadsword; and it is not surprising to learn that on the line of march many were accompanied by gillies who shared the burden of their ponderous armament. The soldiers of *Am Freiceadan Dubh* – of those six independent companies – were the sons of well-to-do or well-regarded families. They were used to the attendance of gillies, and while all enjoyed the privilege of bearing arms in a country where the wearing of a sword and possession of a musket were intolerably forbidden, there were many who acknowledged a sense of duty to the Protestant religion whose continuance the Jacobite rebellion had threatened, and so to the Hanoverian Government that so manifestly supported the Protestant Church. Not all the soldiers of The Black Watch were Whigs – there had been recruiting in Perthshire and Lochaber, where Whigs were in a minority – and neither the Frasers who filled a whole company, nor the Grants of Speyside were disposed to favour one party or the other; but half the regiment, and probably more, were Campbells from the west and Munros from the east, who were Whigs beyond dispute.

In 1739 the status of the independent companies suffered a change, their range of employment was enormously enlarged, and they lost their independence. A Royal Warrant dated the 7th November – three days after Britain's declaration of war against Spain – authorised the formation of a new Regiment of Foot and required the Earl of Crawford, its nominated commander, to raise 'by Beat of Drum or otherwise' four additional companies to give the regiment a strength of about seven hundred men. In May, 1740, *Am Freiceadan Dubh*, now labelled the 43rd of Foot and wearing jackets of scarlet with buff facings, assembled in a field near Aberfeldy and were inspected by their Lieutenant-Colonel, Sir Robert Munro of Foulis, Chief of his clan. For some time the Regiment remained in Scotland, on duties the same as those of the independent companies, but early in 1743 when Britain, already at war with Spain, was involved in the War of the Austrian Succession, The Black Watch was ordered to London, ostensibly to be reviewed by the King on Finchley Common. But rumour spread quickly, and spoke of a farther destination. Flanders seemed probable, the West Indies were a darker possibility.

Many, if not most of the men – even after the original six companies had become the 43rd of Foot – may have believed that the terms of their enlistment still held good, and the fact that for three years, in their new scarlet jackets, their duties had been the same as before must have reinforced that belief. That there was much disquiet in the ranks, before the Regiment left Scotland, is suggested by a statement that some of the officers tried to allay anxiety by assuring their companies that as soon as the King had seen them they would turn about and march home again. It is possible, on the other hand, that disquiet was no graver than barrack-grumbling until the Regiment had crossed the Border and met a recruiting party of The Royal Scots.

The Regiment left Dunkeld towards the end of March, and after it had crossed the Firth of Forth the *Edinburgh Evening Courant*, of the 4th April, reported with admiration, 'They are certainly the best-looked Foot Regiment in the service, being generally tall, well-bodied men, and very stout.'

South of the Border their route lay through Newcastle and York, and somewhere they encountered a party of Royal Scots who were marching north. The Royal Scots, the First of Foot, were immeasurably older in experience than the Highlanders, and it may be that when the latter said they were going to London to be reviewed by the King – and then would go home again – why, the veterans of Pontius Pilate's Bodyguard shouted with laughter and told them, 'It's Georgia and Jamaica you're going to! You'll be broken up and drafted, and you'll be dead of fever in three weeks.'

The West Indies had, indeed, a more dreadful reputation than any theatre of active war, and among many reports of the squalid danger of service there – danger undignified by conflict with a visible foe – there is one, in the *Scots Magazine* of May, 1742, that records the death, between the 26th October, 1740, and the 26th February, 1742, of some 260 officers 'besides the Lord Cathcart, Commander-in-Chief, and 10,000 private men'. To simple Highlanders – men who, for most of their lives, had rarely been beyond sight of Ben Wyvis or Ben Cruachan – the thought of Jamaica meant not only death in exile, but degradation, for transportation to the colonies was punishment commonly reserved for malignants and the worst of criminals. When they reached London, moreover, they were disappointed and angered to learn that the King had not waited to receive them. George II had gone to Flanders, and on Finchley Common the Regiment was reviewed by General Wade. He showed warm approval of its appearance and its exercises, and a great crowd attended the parade. But neither the King nor the Prince of Wales was there, and the soldiers had been cheated. Resentment grew, and with it grew a dark suspicion that they were about to be cheated again.

So, then, the history of The Black Watch is opened by mutiny. For more than two hundred years it would serve, in many parts of the world, with discipline that leapt again and again to a flame of valiancy, but mutiny opens the story, and unlike other regiments that have suffered such disgrace and resolved to forget it, the mutiny on Finchley Common has been remembered with a lively sympathy.

It was on the night of the 17th May that rather more than a hundred men, armed and obdurate, gathered in the darkness of the Common and indignantly set out to march home again. Their plan was to lie hidden by day and march by night, and by the 21st they had gone almost as far as Oundle in Northamptonshire. But their purpose was discovered before they had started, Dragoons were mobilised for pursuit, and the rebels, deeply disappointed by their realisation that most of the Regiment had chosen to obey orders, began to lose heart. They had left London seventy miles behind them, but Scotland was a long way ahead.

They were in a strong position in a wood when General Blakeney, in command of the pursuing cavalry, sent a Captain Ball to demand their surrender. They would surrender if they were promised a free pardon, they said; and Ball reported their terms. The General refused to negotiate, and the rebels, still confident that they had a case which authority could not ignore, laid down their arms. In London again, they were imprisoned in the Tower, and before their court-martial were persuaded to plead guilty: a plea that prevented any attempt to excuse their intemperate action by reference to the terms of their original engagement and their belief that the Government was still bound by those terms. Three men were condemned to death, and the remainder drafted to regiments in Gibraltar, Minorca, Georgia, or the Leeward Islands.

The three who were shot were Corporal Samuel MacPherson of Laggan in Badenoch, Corporal Malcolm MacPherson of the same parish, and Private Farquhar Shaw of Rothiemurchus. Among the rebels the two MacPhersons were the only non-commissioned officers, and their stripes implied their greater guilt; while Shaw is said to have shown some violence in resisting arrest. It can hardly be disputed that the Government was ill-advised in demanding the death penalty for three men of a regiment unaccustomed to the obligations of general service, and as intemperate as the rebels

PLATE I    *The Finchley Common mutineers, 1743: Private Farquhar Shaw shot in the Tower.*

PLATE 2  *Corporal Malcolm MacPherson, shot for desertion.*

PLATE 3    *Corporal Samuel MacPherson, shot for desertion.*

PLATE 4    *Piper MacDonnel, transported to Georgia for desertion.*

22

themselves in imposing, on many others, the virtual sentence of death-by-exile. Two years later Charles Edward Stuart, the Young Pretender, landed in Moidart, and to his standard at Glenfinnan rallied a few hundred clansmen. Among those who gathered to his cause were Lochiel's Camerons, and of the mutineers sent into exile nine were Camerons. Early adherents of the Prince were the Stewarts of Appin, and four of the mutineers were Stewarts. Cluny MacPherson, Chief of his clan, was one of Charles Edward's most faithful supporters; as well as the two Corporals who were shot, fifteen MacPhersons had joined the rebels on Finchley Common. Also among them were MacGregors, MacIntyres, Grants, Robertsons, MacDonalds, and Frasers: all of them belonging to clans that supported Charles Edward. It is impossible to avoid a belief that the Hanoverian Government's vindictive punishment of the mutineers did much to encourage, fortify, and enlarge the menace, to itself, of the Jacobite rebellion of 1745.

In the regimental annals of the British Army there is nothing more remarkable than the fact that two years after its mutiny The Black Watch, in its first continental engagement, behaved with exemplary dash and discipline, and emerged from the lost battle of Fontenoy, as the rearguard of an undeservedly beaten army, with all the assurance of men who were still masters of the field.

Mutiny is not lightly forgotten, and the Regiment cannot easily have forgiven the execution of the two MacPhersons and Farquhar Shaw. All but the Finchley rebels had embarked at Greenwich with no graver complaint than a demand for some badly needed shirts, and they were on foreign soil, for the first time, when they heard of the sentences pronounced by a court-martial that showed no mercy other than allowing twenty-six very young soldiers a mitigated exile in Gibraltar or Minorca. The news cannot have done much to hearten and encourage men who were now committed to a continental war of which the origin and motives – even, indeed, the necessity – must, to all but a very few, have been utterly obscure. The only way in which The Black Watch could be fashioned as a fighting force, informed by purpose and enthusiasm, was to give it regimental pride; and the court martial had made that uncommonly difficult. But commanding the Regiment was Sir Robert Munro of Foulis, and he, a man of outstanding and remarkable character, found appropriate but unrecorded means by which to overcome what may, at first, have been a mood of sullen ill-humour – of grudging response to every order – and create instead a spirit and a temper that came out from a lost battle not only with undiminished pride, but with a pride that flaunted itself.

The Regiment's first Colonel was the Earl of Crawford, a distinguished soldier but only a titular commander. He was succeeded by Lord Sempill, of whom the Regiment saw little or nothing. It was Sir Robert who trained The Black Watch and led it into battle, and he – aged sixty-one when Fontenoy was fought, and burdened by an extreme corpulence – was a man of wide experience, high intelligence, and unfailing fortitude. He had first seen foreign parts in 1705, and as a Captain in The Royal Scots had served with distinction under Marlborough. Returning to Scotland in 1712 he was elected Member of Parliament for Wick Burghs, and served his constituency for thirty years. A minor historian of the time described him as 'a gentleman of calm wisdom, determined courage and unassuming piety, sincere in friendship and full of compassion'; and a later writer declared that 'such was his influence over the soldiers under his command and their admiration of his character, that his spirit and high sense of honour pervaded the whole regiment'.

There appears to be substance for that encomium in a letter from the Elector Palatine in which he thanked King George II for 'the excellent behaviour of the Highland regiment', whose soldiers, according to popular report, neither drank to excess nor used bad language. It may be, of course, that privates of The Watch, when they expressed their deeper feelings, used the Gaelic tongue, which has unsuspected riches and was little known abroad; but, beyond question, their behaviour at Fontenoy was exemplary.

The French, as so often before, were the enemy against whom an allied army was advancing, and the French were commanded by that masterly old soldier of fortune, the Marshal de Saxe. He, after occupying most of west Flanders, had laid siege to the important fortress of Tournai and was forced to cover his siege when the British and their allies, attempting to relieve Tournai, moved cautiously in from the east. He prepared and fortified a position of which the right wing lay on the village of Antoing by the river Scheldt. From there his line ran east along a ridge for two miles to Fontenoy, and there turned north; the village of Vézon – east of Antoing and beyond Fontenoy – was also held by the French. Between Antoing and Fontenoy were three heavily fortified redoubts, Fontenoy was strongly held, and from it to the Forest of Barry ran two lines of entrench-ments, occupied by twenty battalions of infantry, and behind them cavalry. But Saxe was cautious as well as thorough, and he had bridged the river to assure means of retreat should retreat become necessary. He was old, and suffered from dropsy; he felt too ill to ride, but not too ill to win a battle; so he was carried about the field in a litter. To comfort and succour him – for he had enemies on his own side, as well as dropsy – the French king, Louis XV, and the Dauphin had ridden hurriedly to be present at the battle.

Commanding the Allied Army was the young Duke of Cumberland who, at the age of twenty-four, was already so fat that he was said to have some difficulty in mounting a horse. Unquestionably brave, he was, as Carlyle described him, 'a man *sans peur* at any rate, and pretty much *sans avis*'; a judgment substantiated by the course of battle. His allies were Hanoverian, Dutch, and Austrian: the Dutch were commanded by the Prince of Waldeck, who had little knowledge of war and seemingly no inclination for it, while the Austrian cavalry, few in number, were led by Count Königsegg, formerly a brilliant soldier but by 1745 rather too old for active service.

It was on the evening of the 9th May that Cumberland approached the French position, and saw ground broken by woods and copses, and beyond them a wide plain and a gentle slope towards Fontenoy. On the 10th he drove in the French outposts, and with the Dutch and Austrian commanders rode forward to reconnoitre while a company of The Watch under Captain Grant skirmished with French light troops on the edge of the village of Vézon; Cumberland wasted no time in putting his new boys to the test, and had no cause for complaint.

Early in the morning of the 11th the Allies formed up in front of Vézon, facing Fontenoy, with the woods of Barry on their right; the Dutch, on their left, extended the line to Peronne. The Allies numbered about 46,000, against whom Saxe – after leaving 20,000 or more before Tournai – may have deployed as many as 52,000.

There is a popular story that, at some phase of the battle, a Guards officer politely invited the French to fire first, and though that story may be doubted – doubted rather than denied – there is no doubt whatever that Fontenoy was fought – *sans avis*, it may be –

with an extravagant gallantry and in a blaze of colour. Uniforms were elaborate: blue or buff facings on red coats, gold and silver lace, tall pointed caps that gave ten inches of added height to the Grenadier companies, and bandsmen in theatrical finery. It is difficult to avoid a feeling that the soldiers were too well dressed for the occasion – that in their handsome costumes they faced death with too much effrontery – until one remembers that British armies have always been grudgingly maintained, and most of the red coats were probably old and faded. Here and there was a pristine scarlet, and in comparison with modern war Fontenoy was outrageously picturesque; but Britain's habitual regard for economy, in the matter of its armed services, did something to reduce the colour of its army to a stained and workmanlike hue.

Cumberland's original intention was to send in his cavalry in a bold, far-swung onslaught from the right, but that was foiled by his discovery that the Forest of Barry was more thickly defended than he had supposed; and thereafter his tactics were simple, direct, and ineffective. The British and Hanoverian infantry formed-up in line opposite the open space between Fontenoy and the woods, and the battle began with an attack, by Guards and Highlanders, on a French outpost at the tongue of the woods. Though deeply entrenched, the French were thrown out, but the strongly manned Redoubt d'Eu was the cause of more trouble. On the left the Dutch, with great caution, advanced towards Antoing and Fontenoy, but they had no heart for what lay ahead, and quickly retired. Between Fontenoy and the woods there was little cover, and to move troops forward would expose them to enfilade fire from both sides: from Fontenoy, that is, and the Redoubt d'Eu. A brigade commanded by Brigadier-General Ingoldsby was ordered to take the redoubt, but was poorly handled and achieved nothing. The Highlanders were in the brigade, and when Cumberland saw them unoccupied, he himself – or so it has been said – galloped across and led them to support the Dutch in a new attack on Fontenoy. The Dutch were no more enthusiastic than before, the Highlanders trotted ahead and took some French trenches, but were left exposed to overwhelming counter-attack when the Dutch again retreated. Cumberland withdrew them and added them to the main assault of his British and Hanoverian infantry, who were advancing in the solemn splendour of the parade ground despite the cannon-balls that came in, from either side, to harass the progress of their scarlet ranks. On the left the massive defences of Fontenoy were still intact; on the right the Redoubt d'Eu menaced his other flank; but Cumberland pressed forward, through a doubly enfiladed gap, and his infantry, with drums beating and colours flying, approached their enemy in the pomp of an heroic discipline.

It was, presumably, in this phase of the battle that Sir Robert of Foulis sought leave of Cumberland to order his soldiers in what is said to have been their own style of fighting. It was a style – if report is true – that was based on economy, on respect for human life, and the fact that rapid fire was unknown in the eighteenth century: the flintlock musket called Brown Bess was an excellent weapon, but it had to be loaded with precision, aimed with care – it was almost five feet long – and fired with deliberation; and the French musket was certainly no better. The rate of fire permitted soldiers to lie down when the enemy were seen ready to discharge – rise, aim, fire and lie down again before their opponents could discharge their next volley – and the efficacy of that curious and improbable drill seems to be demonstrated by the fact that The Black Watch, though engaged from start to finish of the battle, emerged with few casualties. Also remarked, and gratefully remembered, was

PLATE 5    *The chaplain at Fontenoy, 1745. Painting by W. Skeoch Cumming, 1897.*

26

their Colonel's behaviour: Sir Robert's corpulence made it difficult for him to lie down, and almost impossible to get up without assistance; so he, while his Highlanders obediently lay prone, remained an erect and conspicuous target, and by the grace of God – or so it was believed – escaped injury.

The theatrical character of the battle – vividly advertised by the brilliance of opposing uniforms – is emphasised by a scrap of dialogue, quite probably authentic, that has survived the erosion of time. The British and the Hanoverians had crossed the perilous gap that was enfiladed from both sides, and there was a brief pause as the Guards Brigade and the Garde Française came face to face. Lord Charles Hay of the Grenadiers ran forward, took off his hat, and shouted to the French, 'We hope you'll stay there till we come up to you, and not swim across the river as you did at Dettingen.' Then, turning to the Grenadiers, called for three cheers; and having cheered, the British line, company by company, fired volleys that almost obliterated the leading French regiments. The Regiment du Roi was said to have lost 33 officers and 345 men to the Coldstreamers' fire, and the old Marshal de Saxe, in momentary fear of defeat, was carried from his litter to a horse, lifted to the saddle, and with a couple of troopers on either side rode about to restore order.

In massive counter-attack he sent in horse, foot, and guns, and the British and Hanoverian infantry, bled too deeply in the deadly gap, were incapable of effective resistance and reluctantly retreated. The battle, so theatrical in some of its aspects, could not conceal, behind its bright uniforms, a dark and bloody realism. Each army lost between seven and eight thousand men, a doleful score to which the Dutch contributed little, and when Cumberland admitted defeat and decided to retire he had only two regiments that still seemed capable of disciplined and effective action in that most difficult of martial exercises, a fighting withdrawal: The Black Watch and Lord Howard's 19th of Foot, subsequently known as The Green Howards. They showed so aggressive a temper, and fired to such good effect, that the French were unable to interfere with the retirement, and perhaps had no great wish to do so. The retreat was ordered in exemplary fashion by Lord Crawford – who had commanded a brigade of Household Cavalry in the battle – and he, in the most flattering way, thanked the two regiments by assuring them that they had gained as much honour as if they had been the victors.

Cumberland, too, appears to have been favourably impressed by his new regiment. One of the Highlanders was reputed to have killed nine men with his broadsword, but as he swung to assault a tenth his sword-arm was lopped off by a cannon ball. Cumberland, who had been watching him, proposed to reward the Regiment for such valorous homicide. 'Tell me what you want,' he said, and the Regiment asked him to pardon an unfortunate man who, having carelessly allowed a prisoner to escape, had been sentenced to be flogged, which would have been a disgrace to them all. It is a pleasant story, and may be true.

In a pamphlet published in Paris, soon after the battle, an anonymous French author wrote: 'The British behaved well, and could be exceeded in ardour by none but our own officers, who animated the troops by their example when the Highland furies rushed in upon us with more violence than ever did the sea driven by tempest. . . . In short, we gained the victory, but may I never see such another!'

The Highlanders who fought at Fontenoy were not committed to another battle, in their own country, eleven months later. Fontenoy was fought in May, and in August Charles Edward Stuart, the Young Pretender, raised his standard at Glenfinnan and in

September routed Sir John Cope at Prestonpans near Edinburgh. That was the prelude to invasion of England, the retreat from Derby, the unrewarding battle of Falkirk, and the Prince's calamitous defeat at Culloden. Scotland had been stripped of troops to meet the demands of war abroad, and when the Jacobite flag took the breeze at Glenfinnan Johnny Cope commanded no more than two regiments of dragoons, who were somewhere in the Lowlands, a regiment of infantry in Aberdeen, another in the forts of the Great Glen, a third in Edinburgh, and a dozen or so dispersed companies in the midlands. Many regiments were hurried home from Flanders, to join the army that General Hawley was about to march into Scotland, but The Black Watch joined a division stationed in Kent to repel the French invasion that was anticipated. It was, presumably, policy rather than compassion that kept them in Kent. Some three hundred men of the Regiment had near relations serving in the Jacobite companies that fought for the Prince, and loyalty to the Hanoverian throne – so conspicuously demonstrated against the French – might have been strained beyond endurance had brothers and cousins challenged from opposing ranks.

Sir Robert of Foulis became Colonel of the 37th Foot, but did not live long to enjoy his promotion. At the battle of Falkirk, in January, 1746, his new regiment fled when the Jacobites charged, and Sir Robert and a younger brother who stood with him to fight it out, were killed by Lochiel's Camerons. They were buried in the churchyard of Falkirk, and their funeral was attended, not only by the 37th Foot, but by many from the Jacobite army.

# CHAPTER 2

# Ticonderoga and the West Indies

At Fontenoy The Watch lost two officers and thirty men killed; three officers, two sergeants, and eighty-six men wounded. Nearly nine hundred men were still fit for service, and when the Government decided to send an expedition to North America they and several other regiments embarked at Portsmouth for Cape Breton. They did not go far before meeting adverse gales that drove them home again; and as if to advertise the difficulties of engaging in offensive operations overseas – when ships had to find a favourable wind to fill their sails – a second attempt was defeated in like manner, and so was a third. A new objective, and destination, was quickly found – too quickly to promise success – and, with less than adequate intelligence of the enemy's strength and dispositions, Grenadiers and Highlanders led an assault on L'Orient. The French retreated, but when darkness fell the expedition made hurried preparation to re-embark, for belated discovery had been made of the very large force which the garrison of L'Orient could summon to its aid. So from Quiberon the Highlanders sailed to Cork, marched from there to Limerick, and in February, 1747, returned to Cork in pursuance of an exercise with which all soldiers have grown familiar, and which cannot – if politeness must be observed – be given the soldiers' name for it. The exercise was continued by a return to Flanders, to reinforce a British army still fighting in alliance with Austrians and Dutch, where the Regiment saw little service but early in 1749 covered a British withdrawal and re-embarked for Ireland.

There, by reduction of a regiment previously numbered the 42nd, The Black Watch moved up one in the numerical table of seniority, and acquired the ordinal which was to distinguish it, as clearly and as fondly as its Highland name, for the rest of its service. Sir Robert of Foulis had been succeeded in command by his younger brother John, who died in 1749, and to follow him came Lieutenant-Colonel John Campbell, later the 5th Duke of Argyll. The Regiment remained in Ireland until 1756, and established very friendly terms with the natives of a country that has usually resented the presence of British troops. Remarkable also is the fact that crime – 'crime' in the military sense – was almost unknown, and for many years there was no instance of corporal punishment, though in other regiments flogging was a regular and common occurrence. It was said, indeed, that if the private men of a company discovered in their ranks a person, obnoxious to themselves and likely to cause trouble, they would club together to buy his discharge; and it is known that great regularity was observed in the welcome duty of public worship.

During those years of peace in Ireland, and what seems to have been a placid, easily accepted discipline, the old quarrel between England and France had found fresh fuel in North America, where France, in the hope of confining English settlements to the Atlantic coast, had built forts from Quebec down to New Orleans. The French were dashing, brave, and imaginative, but the English had all the material advantages: they had the sea-power which let them maintain military aid to their colonies, and opposed to some 60,000 French settlers in Canada there were, perhaps, a million English, Scots, Welsh or Irish colonists to the south. The French, however, were more enterprising and successful than the British in enlisting the sympathy and assistance of the Red Indian natives of the country, and they were quicker to learn the necessary tactics of irregular warfare in the heavily wooded, vast spaces of the American continent.

War reached the continent – almost casually, as now it seems – when the unfortunate General Braddock landed in Virginia in command of two weak battalions, mobilised the provincial militia, and raised a few recruits despite the apathetic temper of the colonists. Slowly he marched towards the Monongahela and Fort Duquesne, 120 miles away, but his untrained troops had no chance against the French and the Indians who surprised them not far from the Fort. Braddock was mortally wounded, his little army defeated with heavy loss of life.

In the following year a larger expedition was mounted, and in June, 1756, the 42nd landed in New York. The Commander-in-Chief was the Earl of Loudon, whose gift for inaction was perhaps the outstanding feature of his general ineptitude. David Stewart of Garth – sometime Colonel in the Regiment, and its earliest historian – says of him: 'The General was so occupied with schemes for improving the condition of his troops, that he seemed to have no time for employing them against the enemy, and allowed a whole season to pass away, without undertaking a single enterprise.' His idleness was much appreciated by the commander of the French army, the Marquis de Montcalm, who, says Stewart, 'carried on, with great activity, an irregular warfare, by skirmishes and detached in-cursions, exceedingly distressing to the inhabitants, and destructive to the British troops'.

The forts of Ontario, Oswego, and Granville fell in succession, and the 42nd, condemned to idleness by an idle commander, were quartered in Albany where they did nothing until the following year, when 'they were drilled and disciplined for bush-fighting and sharp-shooting, a species of warfare for which they were well fitted' – though their ardour and impatience 'often hurried them from cover when they ought to have remained concealed'. At long last, when summer was approaching, a plan was made to attack Louisburg on the southern shore of Cape Breton island, and in June, with some 5,000 men, Loudon sailed to Halifax where he was joined by as many more, who had lately come from England. In Halifax he learnt that a French fleet of seventeen ships of the line, with attendant frigates, had put in to Louisburg, and to Loudon that seemed sufficient reason for postponing or cancelling his projected assault. Opinions differed, however, and there was some angry debate before his decision was accepted, and he returned to New York. Montcalm, on the other hand, besieged and took Fort William Henry on the upper Hudson, and so acquired virtual command of Lakes George and Champlain. For the time being the campaign in America had come to an end, and everywhere the French had been successful, the British had failed.

A recruiting campaign in Scotland had raised seven hundred men for The Black Watch, on whose arrival the Regiment numbered rather more than 1,300. Lord Loudon's unfailing incompetence had, after three years, come to the notice of Parliament – where the Prime Minister, the Duke of Newcastle, had accustomed Members to his display of a similar disability – and Loudon had been recalled. General Abercromby assumed command of the army in America, which was reinforced, and at home Pitt became Secretary of State. General Braddock, dying near Fort Duquesne, had said, 'We shall do better next time' – and on both sides of the Atlantic there was now a renewal of confidence. There would be action on several fronts, and Abercromby planned an assault on Ticonderoga, where in 1755 the French had built a fort, of earth and timber, which acquired importance because it commanded a portage on the river-line between Canada and the English colonies: it stood on a neck of land between Lake George and Lake Champlain, rather more than two hundred miles north of New York.

Abercromby had an army of more than 15,000 men, of whom some 6,000 were regulars, the rest provincial militia, and an artillery train. The fort, between the two lakes, could be assaulted only on one side – there was deep water on the other three – and that was stiffened by entrenchment and a tall rampart, fortified by three batteries, and guarded by a formidable and perhaps impassable abatis: great trees had been felled and hauled into position in front of the rampart so that they lay, piled one upon another, like a prostrate forest with all its sharpened branches pointing to the enemy. On Lake George, however, there was a fleet of boats, the soldiers embarked, and landed near the fort unopposed. They marched on the 6th July, and a French advanced post was abandoned without a shot being fired. But in thickly wooded country the guides lost their way, there was an unexpected skirmish, and though a French detachment was driven back with considerable loss, an officer of great charm and virtue, Colonel Lord Howe, was lamentably killed. The advancing columns were withdrawn to their landing place, and the attack was resumed on the following day.

Abercromby's decision seems to have been precipitate. By prisoners he had been told that the French General Lévi, with 3,000 men, was advancing to the support of Ticonderoga, whose garrison already numbered about 5,000. An Engineer officer whom he sent to reconnoitre reported that the entrenchments were incomplete, and attack might be attempted with some prospect of success. To anticipate Lévi, then, Abercromby decided to attack without waiting for his artillery train, and his doomed infantry were launched against what proved to be an impregnable position. The 42nd and the 55th of Foot were in reserve, but when the forward battalions were held up – by fire and the entanglement of a prostrate forest – the Highlanders of The Watch were moved by impatience, a mounting indignation, a furious compassion, and charging into the felled trees used their swords to lop off the sharpened branches, and some came close enough to the rampart to hack footholds and climb it. Bayonets waited on the other side, and the attack lost impetus with the loss of half its strength; but still the Highlanders demanded access to the enemy, and died rather than abandon that ancient right. Three times had Abercromby to command their Colonel – Colonel Grant had succeeded him who became the 5th Duke of Argyll – before Grant could persuade them to withdraw, and when they did they left on the field more than half their private men, and two-thirds of the officers, either dead or desperately wounded.

Stewart of Garth, one of the most admirable and likable of all the officers who have served The Watch, has left a sound and perennially interesting comment on the occurrence or persistence of a mood or temper which may occasionally result in extravagant losses, but sometimes in unexpected victory. Judiciously he writes:

This impetuosity of Highland soldiers, and the difficulty of controlling them, in the most important part of a soldier's duty, has been frequently noticed and reprobated. To forget necessary discretion, and break loose from command, is certainly an unmilitary characteristic; but as it proceeds from a very honourable principle, it deserves serious consideration, how far any attempt to allay this ardour may be prudent or advantageous to the service. . . . It is easier to restrain than to animate.

In front of that untaken fort – in that forest of fallen trees – the 42nd lost 8 officers, 9 sergeants, and 297 men killed; 17 officers, 10 sergeants, and 306 soldiers wounded. The battle, however, was regarded not as a disaster, but as a triumphant display of Highland gallantry. Though it achieved nothing it showed an heroic temper, and without an heroic temper an army is worth very little. Heroism, of course, tends to be extravagant: that has to be admitted. But Fontenoy and Ticonderoga were the opening chapters in what was to be a long story, and without them it might have been a poorer story.

Among those killed was Major Duncan Campbell, who had foreseen his fate three years before; it is a story which deserves to be told for, among the instances of second sight in the Highlands, there are few so well-attested. Walking on the slopes of Ben Cruachan in the summer of 1755, Major Campbell had encountered a panting, frightened figure, who begged to be sheltered from the friends of a man whom he had accidentally killed. Moved by his distress, Campbell promised him help. 'Swear it on your dirk,' the fugitive insisted, and, stung by his doubt, Campbell angrily replied, 'I swear by the word of an Inverawe, which never yet failed friend or foe.'

He hid the man in a cave, and returned to Inverawe, where he found armed men searching for the murderer of his own foster-brother. Bound by oath, he kept his silence, but for two nights while the murderer lay hidden in the cave, Campbell saw the blood-boltered apparition of his foster-brother, and heard it say, 'Inverawe, shield not the murderer. Blood must flow for blood.' On the third day the murderer departed, but his victim's shade was not yet at rest, and that night it appeared with the words, 'Farewell Inverawe till we meet at Ticonderoga.'

That was the story Campbell told to his brother-officers during the Regiment's sojourn in Albany, and he begged them to tell him if they recognised the name. It was unfamiliar to them, for the excellent reason that the place was then more generally known as Fort Carillon, but when Colonel Grant did learn its Indian name, he persuaded the other officers to say nothing of it. Nevertheless, when Campbell joined them on the morning of the fight, he declared, 'You have deceived me. He came to my tent last night. This is Ticonderoga. I shall die today.'

Recognition of the Regiment's high temper came quickly, and in two aspects. Pitt, who had 'sought for merit wherever it might be found, and found it in the mountains of the north', authorised again the enlistment of 'hardy and intrepid men' who – as he told Parliament – would 'conquer for you in every part of the world'. He ordered, that is, the raising of a second battalion of the Highland regiment, which now became The Royal Highland Regiment 'as a testimony of His Majesty's satisfaction and approbation of its extraordinary courage, loyalty, and exemplary conduct'. The approbation was announced before London had heard of the desperate fighting at Ticonderoga, and was the more gratifying because it did not depend on the fanatical courage of a single day.

The 2nd Battalion, embodied in Perth in October, 1758 – with few exceptions all the recruits were Highlanders, 'hardy and temperate in their habits' – embarked for the West Indies, and 'the old regiment', having suffered so severely, was not employed again in that year. But now the war in North America was prosecuted with vigour, and other Highland regiments played their part with the distinction that was expected of them. Fraser's Highlanders were part of a formidable expedition, commanded by Brigadier-General Wolfe, that by the exercise of skill and fortitude took possession of Cape Breton and the town of Louisburg, destroying in that process a powerful French fleet.

Under Brigadier-General Forbes, in an army of some 6,000 men, Montgomery's Highlanders marched from Philadelphia to Fort Duquesne, where Major Grant, of Montgomery's, announced his advent with pipes playing and drums beating. A lively conflict ensued, in which Grant was taken prisoner and some 200 of his regiment killed or wounded. But General Forbes, unperturbed, pressed the advance and the French re-treated, leaving ammunition, stores and provisions for the victors. Fort Duquesne was renamed Pittsburgh, and gradually embarked on a history dominated by coal, iron, and steel, the French suffered other reverses, and their Canadian colony was now manifestly vulnerable.

Only a few months after its formation the 2nd Battalion of the 42nd had its baptism of fire in the French islands of Martinique and Guadeloupe. Part of an army almost 6,000 strong, under Major-General Hopson, it landed without serious opposition near Port Royal in Martinique, but after minor success withdrew because it needed heavy guns to maintain its position, and the Commodore of the fleet which carried the army would not expose his ships to dangers that could not be mastered. As an alternative it was decided to attack Guadeloupe, where at first there was little resistance except from a lady of high temper called Madame Ducharney, who had armed her Negroes and encouraged them to fight with some determination. Lieutenant Maclean, of the 42nd, lost an arm but remained on duty, and, says Stewart, 'was particularly noticed by the French ladies for his gallantry and spirit, and the manner in which he wore his plaid and Scottish regimental garb'.

Highlanders and Royal Marines landed from boats to assault a well-defended Fort Louis, and used their bayonets to good effect. But bayonets were no defence against fever, and before very long almost a third of the army lay dead or in hospital with Yellow Jack. General Hopson died, and command passed to General Barrington, who maintained the offensive with great energy, and on the 1st May the French, who had fought gallantly since the end of January, were obliged to surrender. The 2nd Battalion had made a good beginning. Less than a year before, its soldiers had known no stranger landscape than the hills of Perthshire or Argyll, no danger larger than winter snow might bring; and now it had survived, not only shot and shell, but the superstitious fear that the heat of the sun and the malignant heat of fever can beget.

Now the scene of action is again Canada, where General Amherst was preparing a renewed assault on Ticonderoga, with General Prideaux at Niagara to guard against attack from the west, while General Wolfe from lower Canada would take Quebec. From its winter quarters on Long Island the 1st Battalion of the 42nd joined the force under General Amherst in June, 1759. At Fort Edward he commanded four regiments of the line, nine battalions of provincial militia, with artillery; and when the 2nd Battalion of the 42nd arrived from the West Indies his force numbered nearly 15,000 men. It was notorious that Ticonderoga was formidable in defence, but hardly had the siege begun when the French commander, convinced that he could not hold the fort, set fire to its buildings and withdrew to Lake Champlain. The French, as it seemed, were now unwilling to risk a major engagement, and Amherst pursued them to the lake. There they had a small fleet of ships, and Amherst prudently decided to postpone battle and build a brigantine that would mount 18 guns, and a sloop to mount 16: it was early August when he reached the lake, and by early October his ships were afloat. There was a minor mishap when a smaller vessel, carrying an officer and twenty men, was captured by the French, but what halted the operation was hard frost. The lake froze, and Amherst's army returned to Ticonderoga and wintered there.

With marvellous skill and sublime determination Wolfe had taken Quebec – his great victory had cost him his life, at the age of thirty-two, as it did Montcalm – and now Montreal was France's last stronghold in Canada. In May, 1760, both battalions of The Black Watch marched across country from the Hudson to Oswego on Lake Ontario, where Amherst assembled his whole army in early August. The 1st Guards and the 1st Battalion of the 42nd embarked as the advance guard, and sailed to the head of the St Lawrence. The main army followed; Fort Lévi was quickly taken, and the river proved more dangerous than the French. One day, in wild white rapids, a corporal and three men of the 42nd were drowned, and three days later eighty-four men, of various regiments, lost their lives when their boats were wrecked. But the advance continued, the advance guard reached Montreal on the 6th September, and on the same day a force commanded by General Murray reported its arrival below the town. On the following day Colonel Haviland reached the south bank of the St Lawrence, having marched from the northern end of Lake Champlain; and co-ordinated punctuality let the three forces promptly set about the investment of Montreal. The Marquis de Vaudreuil, Governor-General of Canada, seeing no prospect of help, surrendered the town, and with it all Canada and what remained of his army. Ten battalions became prisoners of war, and the reward of victory was a country larger than China, though rather less populous.

# CHAPTER 3

# Royal Highlanders and Rebel Americans

To General Amherst came orders in 1761 to send a considerable force to the West Indies, naming in particular the 42nd because the Highlanders' 'sobriety and abstemious habits, great activity, and capability for bearing the vicissitudes of heat and cold, render them well qualified for that climate, and for a broken and difficult country'. With other regiments, both battalions sailed to the Barbadoes, where Major-General Monckton was in command. Early in January, 1762, eighteen regiments embarked in a fleet commanded by Rear-Admiral Rodney to effect the capture of Martinique. There was some brisk fighting, but it was not prolonged, and a spirited French counter-attack was repulsed; the enemy began to retire, 'the Highlanders, drawing their swords, rushed forward like furies, and being supported by the Grenadiers under Colonel Grant and by a party of Lord Rollo's Brigade, the hills were stormed, the batteries were seized, and numbers of the enemy, unable to escape from the rapidity of the attack, were taken.' Such is the account of the action, published by the *Westminster Journal*, and the consequences of French capitulation, which followed almost immediately, were extremely gratifying: Britain acquired possession of all the Windward Islands. But the conquerors of Martinique were now faced with a more difficult task.

War had been declared against Spain, and their next objective was Havana, capital of Cuba and the commercial centre of Spanish America. It was a handsome city with a magnificent harbour, and its importance was emphasised by its military strength – it was said to be impregnable – and its recurrent wealth when its cellars were filled with cargoes of gold and silver from Mexico and Peru. In command of the expedition mounted against it was the Earl of Albemarle, sometime aide-de-camp to the Duke of Cumberland, and commanding the invading fleet of nineteen ships of the line, eighteen frigates, and more than a hundred transports, was the veteran Admiral Sir George Pocock. Accompanying Albemarle were his two brothers, Augustus Keppel, a Commodore, and William, a General.

To prevent the British fleet from entering the harbour, the Spaniards sank three of their ships of the line across its mouth, but troops were successfully landed and preparation was speedily made to erect batteries against the lofty fort called El Moro. That proved difficult, for the heat of midsummer was excessive and on the rocky approaches to El Moro it was impossible to find cover. Both soldiers and sailors, it was said, died of thirst, heatstroke, or sheer exhaustion as they dragged their heavy guns uphill, and in a siege that lasted from the 7th June until the 12th August more men died of disease, or exhaustion, than by bullet or bayonet. Albemarle commanded an army of about 11,000 men, of whom 345 were killed, 640 wounded, and 672 fell mortally sick. The 42nd seem not to have been

PLATE 6   *General John Reid, commander of the 42nd at Martinique and twice wounded there. In 1756 he composed the regimental 'Highland March' to which later were added the verses of 'In the Garb of Old Gaul'.*

closely engaged, for the battle casualties of the two battalions were only a dozen men killed and wounded, though some eighty officers and men died of what can only be called other unnatural causes.

The Spanish garrison had fought bravely and was reduced to barely 800 men before it capitulated. The survivors were allowed all the honours of war, and embarked for Spain while the victors happily counted their prize-money. Havana was said to have been worth three million pounds sterling, and the fleet and the army divided, in equal shares, prize-money amounting to £736,185 2s. 4½d. Albemarle got nearly £123,000, and each of his brothers took £6,816. A private man's share was £4 1s. 8½d. A few months later Havana was restored to Spain, and though its capture had been regarded as a great triumph – 'It was,' said Edmund Burke, 'the most decisive conquest we had made since the beginning of the war' – only the Keppels got or enjoyed any large and lasting benefit.

The 42nd, now reduced to a single battalion, embarked for New York, where it landed in October, 1762, and for that winter was quartered in Albany. In the following summer it learned how to fight Red Indians, who themselves had learned the advantage of tribal union. Several tribes in alliance had attacked the British forts between Lake Erie and Pittsburgh, and to relieve Fort Pitt the 42nd, with detachments from two other regiments – in all they numbered less than a thousand – marched under command of Colonel Bouquet. After some lively skirmishing, in thickly wooded country, they feigned retreat to lure the Indians from cover, and punished them heavily. The Regiment wintered at Fort Pitt, and in 1764 was again employed against the Redskins: it marched many hundreds of miles, it became as expert in forest-war as its opponents – perhaps better than they – but when it returned to Fort Pitt it was only a shadow of the regiment that had left Scotland in 1756. A decade of service in the West Indies and North America had taken a heavy toll, but when it was under orders to return home, and those who wanted to remain in America were given leave to volunteer for other regiments, many did so. By the colonists they were highly regarded, as is testified by the *Virginia Gazette* in its issue of the 30th July, 1767:

> Last Sunday evening the Royal Highland Regiment embarked for Ireland. Since its arrival in America it has been distinguished for having undergone amazing fatigues, made long and frequent marches through an unhospitable country, bearing excessive heat and severe cold with alacrity and cheerfulness. . . . It has ensured to us peace and security; and along with our blessings for those benefits it has our thanks for that decorum in behaviour which it maintained here, giving an example that the most amiable conduct in civil life is in no way inconsistent with the character of the good soldier.

The men, as it seems, were wholly admirable, but the officers not entirely faultless. They lacked ambition, says Archibald Forbes in a very lively history published in 1896: 'Probably no regiment in the service has produced fewer general officers than the Royal Highlanders. And this simply because the officers of this regiment have for the most part chosen to remain in it and perform regimental duty in preference to being detached as aides-de-camp, staff officers, and other votaries of non-regimental service. The pride of the officerhood of The Black Watch has been to regard it as a family which lives in itself and for itself.'

That is a bold claim which might be challenged by other Highland regiments, notably by The Gordon Highlanders who, in the latter half of the nineteenth century, were notorious for their belief that soldiering meant regimental soldiering and nothing else. But Archibald Forbes is indisputably right in emphasising the tribal or familiar nature of the regiment: raised as a Government clan to wear the Government tartan, it has always had a sense of inherited relationship that sets it apart from all but a few others which, by some benign accident, also enjoy that privilege.

In October, 1767, the remnant of the 42nd landed in Cork, and promptly sent recruiting parties to the Highlands, which raised it to its established strength before the beginning of June; and of its new recruits only two had been born south of the Tay. In the following year the Regiment was authorised by Royal Warrant to bear 'In the centre of the Colours the King's cypher within the Garter, and Crown over it. Under it *St Andrew* with the motto *Nemo me impune lacessit*.' With some concern, however, it was observed that the men had now a rather shabby look. Their jackets were the colour of old bricks, and after a year's service jackets were cut down to serve as waistcoats; kilts looked no better, for most of them had been tailored from two-year-old plaids. Government stockings were so shoddy that men bought their own, and bought, too, ostrich feathers to beplume the bonnets for which parsimonious officialdom allowed no better adornment than fragments of bearskin. In 1769 the 42nd was posted to Dublin and there, by the Colonel's bounty, the soldiers were given waistcoats of white cloth and white goatskin sporrans which looked better than cut-down jackets and purses of bald badger-hide. In North America, in the Redskins' country, officers had eschewed unnecessary decoration, but now they brightened their coats with gold lace, and sergeants, at their own expense, wore silver lace. Sergeants exchanged their halberds or Lochaber axes for carbines – it was, one imagines, a welcome exchange – and private men were gratified by the issue of a musket shorter in the barrel than their old Brown Bess by three and a half inches.

For eight years the Regiment remained in Ireland and throughout 1771, when it moved from Dublin to Belfast, it was employed in aid of the civil power, and this unpleasant duty was renewed in 1772: in some parts of the country there was dispute between Catholics and Protestants, in others between landlords and their tenants. The Black Watch was uncommonly successful in mitigating the hostility evoked by police action – there were Gaelic speakers on both sides, though their Gaelic showed some difference – but more remarkable, perhaps, was its stubborn retention of the character which had marked the independent companies from which the soldiers were, in a sense, descended. In language, habit, and behaviour they were naturally conservative. Their manners were those of a well-conducted village – there was no crime in their companies – and their stature, at a standard height of five feet seven inches – in the grenadier company they were taller – was well above the average of the entire army. The men appear to have lived well, and were able to save a little money which they spent on improving the faded uniforms in which a careless Government was content to clothe them.

Their peaceful engagement in Ireland came to an end in 1776 when the colonists of North America embarked on a War of Independence. Their war had valid reasons – political, economic, and psychological – of which the most influential were probably geographical and strategical. At a time when sea voyages were long and uncertain in their outcome, the colonies were very far from London and their administration was difficult; a successful war against the French in Canada, moreover, had removed a military threat of which the colonists had always been acutely aware. By defeating the French the British had unimaginatively removed that threat to their daily lives which the colonists most sorely feared, and thereby given them the freedom to meditate rebellion. But politicians who expect gratitude have always been disappointed, and when the ministers of George III were disappointed it was, as usual, his soldiers who suffered.

On the 1st May, 1776, the Regiment, under the command of Lieutenant-Colonel Thomas Stirling, embarked at Greenock in company with Fraser's Highlanders. A few days later the convoy was scattered by a gale, and the *Oxford* transport, carrying a company of the 42nd, was captured by an American privateer. The soldiers were taken aboard the privateer, and a prize crew took over the transport. But the Highlanders overpowered the Americans, seized the ship, and sailed her to Jamestown in Virginia. They were again unfortunate, for Virginia was now under rebel power, and for the second time they became prisoners. They were tempted with the promise of lavish gifts to renounce their allegiance and adopt the American cause, but stoutly they refused the proffered bribes and drank the King's health. For two years they remained captive, but then were exchanged and rejoined the Battalion.

The other transports crossed the Atlantic without misadventure, and on the 3rd August the 42nd and Fraser's Highlanders joined the army of Sir William Howe on Staten Island. Boston had been evacuated, but George Washington, the American Commander-in-Chief, failed to hold New York, was defeated at Brooklyn on the 27th August, and again at White Plains on the 28th October. Colonel Stirling had been tireless in training his men for what would now be called jungle warfare – much of North America was very thickly wooded – and the 42nd, though closely engaged with the enemy whom they had lately defended against the French, suffered only minor losses. The British, however, were unfortunate in being commanded by a General who lacked confidence and enterprise: Howe was a poor soldier who failed to take advantage of the Americans' unreadiness for serious war, and gave Washington time to recruit and train, organise and inspire, an army sufficient for the historic duty he had accepted.

After the fighting at White Plains the 42nd was engaged in a curious assault on a hill-top fort that impeded communication between New York and the country east of the Hudson River. The Hessians – a large force of German mercenaries – were to deliver the main attack, while the Highlanders made a feint on the east side of the fort. They disembarked from a flotilla of small boats and found the hill precipitous: it was so steep, indeed, that the bullet which killed Lieutenant MacLeod entered the back of his neck, descended in an almost perpendicular line, and lodged in a buttock; and a piper, shot dead as he started to play, went tumbling down from the top of the hill to the bottom. But brushwood grew thickly in crevices of the rock, the soldiers pulled themselves up, and having gained the summit turned the intended feint into reality and charged. Two hundred of the enemy immediately threw down their arms, and when the remainder saw the massive approach of the Hessians from the other side, they surrendered to the number of 2,700. The Black Watch lost eleven killed and about seventy wounded.

During the season of skirmishing that followed, the Highlanders of Fraser's Regiment, commanded by Colonel Maitland, chose to distinguish themselves by the addition of a red plume to their bonnets. 'Such was the origin,' David Stewart declared, 'of the red feather subsequently worn in the Highland Bonnet . . . In 1795 the feather was assumed by the Royal Highland Regiment.' The earliest evidence of the Red Hackle therefore coincided with the birth of the American Republic, a birth which could not long be protracted after the battle of Brandywine, for, although Washington was again defeated there, a major factor in his ultimate triumph was made evident. Serving in his army were the Marquis de la Fayette and other French officers, for both France and Spain had declared war on Britain, in support of the Americans, and because folly and maladministration in Westminster had disastrously weakened the Royal Navy, Britain lost command of the sea and was unable to supply an army fighting so far from home. Washington had his troubles – there were rivalry and dissension in his army, there was occasional treachery – but for British Generals the problems were more severe, and the British Generals were less able than Washington to deal with them. They took several years to lose the war, but lost it was at last, and Cornwallis – most skilful of British commanders in all that untidy fighting – was forced, by French blockade, to surrender in October, 1781.

The Regiment, however, remained in or near New York for another couple of years, until the war found official conclusion, and then removed to Halifax in Nova Scotia, and from there, in 1786, to Cape Breton. No records survive of how the Highlanders occupied their time between 1781 and 1789, when they returned to England, and there is no scrap of evidence that they were either depressed by defeat or impressed by their participation in a war that was to have momentous consequences for the world. Perhaps the most abiding memory of those years in America was of a grievous insult to the regiment when the Inspector General of Infantry sent out a draft of 150 men of a sort that The Black Watch could by no means accept: 'refuse of the streets of London and Dublin', 'depraved and dissolute' – so they are described by the kindly and tolerant Colonel Stewart of Garth, and when half of them, clearly unfit for service, had been sent to hospital, the other half was transferred, by means unknown, to the 26th of Foot. But The Black Watch could not forget the insult, and continued to be angry long after it had forgotten its little battles in a momentous war.

Another lasting memory was of the loss of the broadsword and pistols which the Highlanders had lately carried – or so it seems – only by bounty of their Colonel. It was decided, by some obscure authority, that these were unnecessary – if not an encumbrance – and the Regiment was deprived of them. But in thickly wooded country pistols were manifestly useful, and there were many who sturdily believed that the broadsword was far superior to the bayonet. The sword could cut as well as thrust, and psychologically it was certainly a better weapon. The argument was, of course, largely academic, and all who were conservative by temper would inevitably – and perhaps rightly – have voted for the sword.

CHAPTER 4

# Red Hackle and Yellow Jack

The Regiment embarked for England in August, 1789, and after wintering in Tynemouth marched to Edinburgh in May, 1790: it had been on foreign service for fourteen years. It now found recruiting difficult, for there was trouble in the Highlands, where crofters and cottars were being evicted to make room for the sheep that were so much more profitable. George Gordon, Marquis of Huntly, came to the rescue, offering himself and an independent company of very fine young men that he had lately raised: it was a gesture which will seem strange to those who remember the urgent rivalry that, in later years, invigorated regimental feeling in The Gordon Highlanders and The Black Watch. The Regiment, thus fortified, spent some unhappy months marching about Ross and Cromarty where, without using force, it maintained an uneasy peace; and the following winter was no more pleasant, for the French revolution had encouraged mischief-makers in the Lowlands, and there, too, it had to prevent – with tact and patience – unseemly violence. Not until war was declared against France was the Regiment released from police duties.

Then ensued one of those seasons, of frustration and orders that about-turn, during which private men and commanding officers are at one in their detestation of the remote authority that compels them to exhaust their native goodwill in purposeless activity. The Regiment saw some action not far from Ostend, but suddenly was withdrawn to England to join an expedition prepared against the West Indies; and in Portsmouth strategy took a new turn. A landing on the French coast was considered, and the Regiment got as far as Guernsey, but no farther; and presently returned to Portsmouth. Then it re-embarked for Flanders, where France had mobilised an army of more than 200,000 men and the Allies – particularly a corps commanded by the Duke of York – were sorely in need of reinforcement. The Black Watch was one of ten regiments, under command of the Earl of Moira, that now promised help, but though they boldly and briskly marched from Ostend to Malines, where they joined the Duke, they were condemned to a miserable winter, cold as Siberia, and a strategy grimly governed by inferiority of numbers and a reiterated compulsion to withdraw. In the Netherlands they met, quite unexpectedly, a sullenly hostile population, and 'the misery of the succeeding retreat to Daventer,' writes Colonel Stewart, 'was such as had not then been experienced by any modern army, and has only been exceeded by the sufferings of the French in their disastrous retreat from Moscow.'

The policy of withdrawal – or, more plainly, the continuing necessity of retreat – took the Duke's army as far as Bremen, where the Germans welcomed it with great warmth. Nothing had been achieved, but The Black Watch had demonstrated its hardihood and the admirable protection that the kilt affords to marching men. In that dreadful winter there were regiments that lost as many as three hundred men from disease

41

or exhaustion, but between June, 1794, and re-embarkation in April, 1795, The Black Watch had suffered, from sickness or death in battle, the loss of only twenty-five. And when they returned to England they were honoured by the award of a decoration they still wear.

On the 4th June, 1795, when quartered at Royston in Hertfordshire, the Regiment, on ceremonial parade, fired three rounds in honour of George III's birthday, and a box containing red feathers was opened. The Commanding Officer made an explanatory speech in which he said that the red feathers were an award for gallantry, and the officers and men of the The Black Watch pinned to their feather bonnets the bright addition of a Red Hackle.

The account of that ceremony is accepted as historically true, and until fairly recently it was also believed that the gallantry, so celebrated, had been observed during a skirmish at Geldermalsen in the Netherlands, where a regiment of Light Dragoons, momentarily demoralised, had galloped off, leaving two field guns for the French; with admirable promptitude an attack was mounted by The Black Watch, men harnessed themselves to the guns and recovered them with the loss of one dead and three wounded.

That story is now generally discredited, for though there are two vivid records of the incident, by pensioners of the regiment, which Archibald Forbes quotes in full, it appears that neither was written until many years after the event, and in Colonel Stewart's history, published in 1822, there is no mention of the affair. It must be added, however, that Stewart makes no mention of the parade at Royston and the distribution of the 'Red Vulture feathers' which were certainly a reward for distinguished conduct, and, one would think, for conduct in the campaign so lately concluded and otherwise so bleakly un-distinguished.

Twenty-seven years later the Regiment's exclusive title to the Red Hackle had to be asserted with all the authority of the Horse Guards. Other regiments had shown a desire to decorate their bonnets with a scarlet plume, and on the 20th August, 1822, the Adjutant-General firmly informed commanding officers that 'The Red Vulture feather prescribed by the recent regulations for Highland regiments is intended to be worn exclusively by the Forty-Second Regiment'. It was not for the first, nor indeed for the last time, that the War Office had had – or would have – to correct or clarify the regulations it promulgated.

Major-General Sir Ralph Abercromby, who in the Netherlands had commanded a brigade under the Duke of York, was in 1795 given command of an army of some 25,000 men destined for service in the West Indies. As a General he was enlightened, and much liked, ever intent on the welfare of his troops; the ships allotted for the voyage were exceptionally well-appointed. They were, however, no match for the weather. A fleet of nearly three hundred put out from Portsmouth, but quickly lost the *Impregnable*, their flagship, which ran aground. The fleet was recalled, but a single transport failed to observe the signal, sailed on, and after a pleasant voyage reached Barbados on Christmas Day. The others were less fortunate. They again weighed anchor on the 15th November, and before sunset all were clear of the Isle of Wight except the *Middlesex*, an East Indiaman aboard which were 500 men of the 42nd. She was disabled when the frigate *Undaunted*, crossing her bows, carried away her bowsprit; she put back for repairs, and a few days later the rest of that vast fleet were scattered and driven back by a furious gale from the south-west that wrecked several ships and drowned many men.

Violent weather continued for some weeks, but on the 9th December a re-assembled fleet again put to sea, and again met storms so furious that not until the end of January 1796, did a fleet, now numbering only fifty ships once more put out from Portsmouth; others sailed as opportunity offered from many different ports, and a few, having survived gale after gale, had already reached the West Indies. Some found unexpected harbours, and a transport that berthed in Gibraltar, landed five companies of The Black Watch under Lieutenant-Colonel Dickson; and there they remained. The East Indiaman *Middlesex* reached Barbados on the 9th February – more than a month before the Commander-in-Chief – and put ashore her five companies of The Black Watch in good health, for which David Stewart gives due praise to General Abercromby for the care he had taken to supply the ships with fresh vegetables and medical officers.

When Admiral Christian arrived, towards the end of April, an attack was mounted on the island of St Lucia, and the Highlanders had the distinction of serving in a brigade commanded by that brilliant soldier, John Moore: he, the son of a Glasgow doctor who corresponded with Robert Burns and incited him to autobiography, would in a later year devise that new system of drill and movement which became the model for British infantry, and laid the foundations of the superiority it evinced in the arduous campaigns of the Spanish Peninsula. There was some brisk fighting in difficult country, but the French garrisons surrendered before the end of May, and for the second time within two years St Lucia changed hands. While fighting continued – or a prospect of fighting – the troops were unaffected by the pernicious climate, and The Black Watch sent very few to hospital; but three days after the French had surrendered they were trooping in, and sixty went sick within a week.

St Vincent was their next objective, where the 42nd and The Buffs quickly drove the enemy from a series of redoubts. The French capitulated, on terms, but several hundred of them, instead of behaving obediently as prisoners of war, broke their engagement and found refuge in the woods. They were immediately pursued, but the country was almost incredibly rough – tall, steep ridges divided by precipitous ravines, towering forests, impenetrable undergrowth – and operations were difficult and prolonged against an enemy who, while ingenious in attack, could remain invisible behind curtains of tropical vegetation. The French – assisted by some 5,000 Caribs and Negro Irregulars who were pleasingly known as 'Brigands' – maintained a sporadic resistance from June until September, but David Stewart, who himself was actively engaged, observed with manifest satisfaction that the climate of St Vincent was so much better than that of St Lucia that, on St Vincent, 'the deaths among the troops did not exceed one third of their number; while, of the four regiments in St Lucia, which consisted of 3,890 men, there were only 470 fit for duty at the end of thirteen months. The service,' he continues, 'was rendered more destructive by the want of every comfort. A pound of salt pork, a pound of flour, and a glass of new rum formed the daily allowance. There were no tents or covering, except such huts as the soldiers erected to screen themselves from the rain.'

In those days the soldier faced the hazard of storm and shipwreck before he could confront his country's enemies; and if he survived Atlantic gales, he might find that his country's human enemies were almost negligible in comparison with the enmity of a climate that bred lethal fevers, or with the remarkable ignorance of foreign conditions that the military bureaucracy in London habitually revealed. It is recorded that from May, 1796, to June, 1797, 264 officers and 12,387 soldiers had died of Yellow Jack or other diseases, but their 'venerable commander' – Sir Ralph Abercromby was in his sixty-fourth year – enjoyed vigorous health, and operations continued.

Trinidad promptly surrendered when an attack was launched against it in 1797, but a subsequent attempt on Puerto Rico met with no success, and the invading force sensibly re-embarked. The 42nd, due to go home, renewed its strength by addition from the 79th Highlanders who had served for two years in Martinique and were allowed to exchange into The Black Watch, which then returned stronger, in a numerical sense, than when it left England, and landed in Portsmouth without a sick man aboard. It was, of course, only half a regiment – the other half was still in Gibraltar, whither appalling weather rather than strategic need had directed it – and when re-united the Regiment was about 1,100 strong; but, says Stewart, 'the moral feelings of the troops were sensibly deteriorated'.

To early historians of the Regiment its moral or social character appears to have been of as much interest as its military achievements, which were not conspicuous. In half a century of service its only major battle was Fontenoy, and in its other memorable action, at Ticonderoga, nothing was gained but a reputation for impassioned bravery. In the West Indies it had conducted itself in exemplary fashion, but there – as in Canada and the American War of Independence – it had engaged only in minor battles, and the Regiment itself seems to have thought lightly of what it did, though what it did was always done well. Archibald Forbes has commented on the curious fact that not until 1909 did The Black Watch solicit battle honours for Havana, Martinique, or Guadeloupe, though other regiments proudly displayed them. The Black Watch – or so it seems – was satisfied with its own assessment of its behaviour, and perhaps pre-occupied with an inherent need to maintain certain standards and – quite positively – its individuality.

That is made evident by David Stewart in his comment on the substantial reinforcement which The Black Watch had accepted in September, 1795. Several Highland regiments, raised in the previous year, were disbanded and their soldiers drafted. Some came to the 42nd, and 'although these drafts furnished many good and serviceable men, they were, in many respects, very inferior to former recruits. This difference of character was more particularly marked in their habits and manners in quarters, than in their conduct in the field, which was always unexceptionable'. Worse was to follow, for when that half of the regiment which came from the West Indies re-joined the other half in Gibraltar, 'the cheap and free indulgence in wine permitted in the garrison affected the conduct of a considerable proportion of the men'. Spanish wine had no ill effect on their health, for in a year on The Rock only eleven died out of a total strength of nearly 1,200; 'but the moral habits of many evinced a melancholy change'.

Fortunately, however, the Highlanders moved to Minorca, where 'their habits and conduct were in a great measure restored by the excellent discipline of Brigadier-General Oakes'. There was little resistance to their landing, and a numerous Spanish garrison surrendered without serious fighting; having, as Fortescue says in his magisterial *History of the British Army*, 'been cowed into surrender by rapidity of movement and the confidence of bearing shown by Lt. General Sir Charles Stuart', whose success – so Fortescue continues – has been absolutely forgotten because his victory was bloodless, though 'it forms one of the most striking examples in our history of the powers of impudence in war.' Stuart, an outstandingly able soldier, was expected to command the considerable British force, now assembling in Minorca, for Britain's widely expanding strategy in the Mediterranean, but the army was disappointed, and sorely saddened, by his untimely death in May, 1801. He was succeeded by an officer whom The Black Watch knew well, and under whose command the regiment would win, at Alexandria, a fame that far exceeded the early reputation it established at Fontenoy. But to make clear the necessity of that battle will require a little explanation.

CHAPTER 5

# Alexandria

At that time, dominating the political scene was Napoleon Bonaparte, who in 1798 had invaded Egypt, taken Cairo, and quickly completed the conquest of Lower Egypt. On the 1st August, however, Nelson surprised the French fleet at anchor in Aboukir Bay, and with a supreme tactical genius and measured audacity proceeded to destroy it: out of thirteen ships of the line eleven were taken or sunk, as were two out of four frigates. Napoleon and his army became, in effect, prisoners in Egypt. Within that prison, however, they remained unsubdued; Napoleon repressed insurrection in Cairo, invaded Syria, and was only checked in his progress by Captain Sir Sydney Smith R.N., who inflicted a costly defeat at Acre. In compensation, the Turks were twice defeated, and when political and personal considerations persuaded Napoleon to return to France, the army, which he stealthily abandoned, continued to be a formidable proposition.

By 1800 the Tsar of Russia was friendly with Napoleon, and if the First Consul could unite the northern powers against Britain, the British Fleet might have to be withdrawn from the Mediterranean, allowing France to reinforce its army in Egypt, and enlarge its menace to India. 'Nor was it possible,' says Fortescue with merciless accuracy, 'to foresee what arrangements the autocrats of France and Russia, the one absolutely unprincipled and the other insane, might not concert for the partition of Turkey.'

In Gibraltar, Sir Ralph Abercromby received orders to gather and embark an army of 15,000 infantry, and effect liaison with the Turks for the invasion of Egypt and defeat of the French. Issuing the orders was Henry Dundas, Secretary of State for War, who thought that Abercromby would have an easy task, and whose information about Egypt, the French, the Turkish allies, and Britain's numerical strength, was as erroneous as his opinions.

In later years the 42nd helped to transform Gibraltar into a naval base, but in 1800 there were no facilities for the urgent repairs which were required by Abercromby's fleet of transports, and so, through inclement weather, the leaking vessels were nursed to Malta where, in the dockyard at Valletta, some semblance of health was restored to them. That achievement was balanced by the unhealthiness of the army, which long confinement in the transports had exacerbated. It was not until the end of the year that the fleet eventually anchored in Marmorice Bay on the west coast of Turkey, an anchorage which, Stewart observed, 'was not less remarkable for its security and convenience, than for the magnificent scenery of its surrounding mountains'. There the magnitude of Abercromby's task began to be revealed, for his Turkish allies promised greatly but performed little, his own forces had been reduced by a tenth through sickness, and it now appeared that, once landed in Egypt, the army's drinking water would have to be supplied from the ships, which if dispersed by storms would condemn the soldiers to die of thirst. This information Dundas had not thought fit to pass on to Abercromby – an omission which provoked that remarkably patient man to comment, 'There are risks in British warfare unknown in any other service.' Such intelligence as he did receive was not reliable, and a particularly gross error was the estimate of the French numbers at 12,000 regulars, when the true figure was two-and-a-half times as great.

However, his was a sanguine temperament, and accepting the inconstancy of weather, allies and politicians as hazards beyond his control, he worked to reduce the possibility of failure in the crucial operation of transferring the soldiers from their ships to the beach, by assiduous training, and by the precision of his orders. Three lines of landing craft would carry in the soldiers and artillery; while in the boats, the men were forbidden to speak, stand up or load their muskets; when the Grenadier companies went ashore, they would hoist their colours, and the other companies would fall in on their left. Yet it must have been obvious to all that the expeditionary force was about to challenge a formidable enemy, in circumstances that gave the enemy every advantage.

Not until the 23rd February, 1801, did the fleet put out from Marmorice, and on the 1st March, 'the coast of Egypt was descried, presenting in its white sandy beaches, and tame uninteresting background, a remarkable contrast to the noble elevations' of the country from which it sailed. Time had been wasted waiting for Turkish reinforcement, during which the French had been usefully strengthened. Nor, when the fleet came to anchor in Aboukir Bay, was the weather as tame as the landscape. For a week there were such angry gales that landing, on a beach some six miles away, was manifestly impossible, and the French were given time to fortify their defences.

On the northern horn of the bay was the Castle of Aboukir where guns were mounted which could enfilade the beach, and the southern horn was similarly guarded by the artillery in a block-house. At the centre of the bay was a high sand-hill, and John Moore, now a Major-General commanding the Reserve, decided that this should be his objective. When the gale abated, on the 7th March, the landing craft were ready to go and, at 2 a.m. on the following morning, put out in a silence broken only by the splashing of oars. There were fifty-eight flat-boats in the leading line, and when, in daylight, they came within range of the French guns, they met a furious cross-fire that in shallow water was reinforced by grape and case-shot. But the sailors rowed steadily on – soldiers and sailors cheering when they met musketry as well as case-shot, and springing ashore formed up in line. Moore led his brigade against the central sand-hill, and his soldiers, without firing a shot, climbed that steep and treacherous slope, and at the point of the bayonet drove the French from the shelter of their trenches.

To his left, the remainder of the Reserve – the 42nd and 58th – were assailed by cavalry as well as infantry. The 42nd were the first to land, and, says Fortescue, 'formed under heavy fire and repulsed the horsemen by their volleys. The Highlanders then advanced, with the 58th in support, and drove the infantry opposed to them out of the sand-hills, and captured three guns.' The Guards, on their left, were in some confusion, after two of their boats had been sunk, but with the help of the 58th another cavalry attack was repelled, and on the left of the line The Royal Scots and the 54th drove off a battalion of French infantry. The landing had been achieved in an operation of the utmost daring, most skilfully ordered; and in Fortescue's opinion 'the finest performance of the day was that of the 42nd Highlanders, who, after suffering heavily in the boats, were so steady and so perfectly formed upon landing that they beat off the attack of the French cavalry.' They lost 21 killed, 156 wounded, and the battle for Alexandria was by no means over. Heavier fighting lay ahead.

Not until evening was the whole force disembarked, and after advancing for a couple of miles Abercromby halted for the night. The army lay on the narrow strip of land between the sea and Lake Aboukir, facing west towards Alexandria, eleven miles away, with its right flank on the sea. Palm trees grew from the sandy desert, and to Abercromby's vast relief it was found that water lay near their roots: a little digging would assuage the soldiers' thirst, and the grim thought that he was still dependent on the ships could be forgotten. Marching was hard, however, for he had very few horses, and such transport as there was had to be manhandled through the sand, as had the guns. There was rough weather on the 9th and 10th and the army had to wait, for stores and supplies, until the wind went down. The French General Friant gathered in his outlying detachments, except those at Rosetta and the garrison of Aboukir Castle, and, when he was joined by General Lanusse, was able to cover the approach to Alexandria with a force of some 5,000 men and twenty-one guns.

The British advance was resumed on the 12th, with the Reserve brigade under John Moore on the right, the Guards in the centre, and three other brigades on the left. The French cavalry withdrew, and the main body of their army established itself in a commanding position known as the Roman Camp, not far from the western end of Lake Aboukir. Friant had to guard his line of communication with Lower Egypt, and ensure a passage for General Menou, his Commander-in-Chief, when Menou should choose to advance from Cairo. Abercromby made camp about a mile and a half from the enemy, and gave orders to march at five o'clock on the following morning, his purpose being to turn Friant's right flank. His guns – no more than sixteen pieces – were painfully hauled, by sailors, to the head of his parallel columns, where his advance guard consisted of the 90th, the Perthshire Light Infantry, and the 92nd, The Gordon Highlanders, mustered only a few years before, whose first battle this would be. The whole army numbered about 14,000, and in its slow advance it suffered heavy losses from the fire of the horse-drawn French artillery. The advance guard, however, pressed on, and to the French it seemed that the two battalions were unsupported. Friant ordered a general advance, by horse, foot, and guns, but the 90th and 92nd withstood the attack with a disciplined valour beyond all praise. Casualties were grievous, but their accurate and steady fire dismayed the enemy.

Action became general when Abercromby's centre and left-hand columns began to deploy, and the French fell back. On the right the Reserve brigade gained the heights of the Roman Camp, which the French abandoned; a dashing attack by Dillon's regiment on the extreme left allowed the left wing to draw level; and the whole army moved half a mile forward into the plain that lay west of the Roman Camp. There Abercromby halted his line and summoned General Hely-Hutchinson, his second in command, and John Moore for a consultation. The French now occupied the fortified heights of Nicopolis, their main position in front of Alexandria, and it has been suggested that Abercromby, who was very short-sighted, failed to see how formidable it was. He proposed to turn both flanks, with Hutchinson attacking on the left and Moore on the right; but from the heights of Nicopolis

PLATE I    *An eighteenth century engraving of 'A Piper of a Highland Regiment'.*

PLATE II (over page)    *'The Black Watch at Bay' by W. B. Wollen* R.I. *The Regiment turning back the French Lancers' charge at Quatre Bras.*

PLATE III   *'An Officer of the 42nd' by Edwards Dayes; painted in 1780.*

the French guns poured in so damaging a cannonade that Hutchinson halted his brigades and asked for further orders: Hutchinson's eyesight was as defective as Abercromby's, and he failed to see the possibility of assaulting the southern face of Alexandria itself. On the plain the troops endured the battering of the French guns, and towards evening Abercromby abandoned his attack and withdrew to the Roman Camp. His army had suffered 1,300 casualties, and the French losses were no more than 500. No one gained anything from the engagement except the 90th and 92nd, who were rewarded with the battle honour of Mandora: a redoubt that stood near the scene of their gallant action.

Abercromby's weakness was, of course, the direct consequence of Henry Dundas's incompetence, who had sent him, with insufficient strength and no reliable information, to essay a task of such appalling difficulty that no one, less dedicated to duty, less impervious to fear, would have launched his reckless but brilliantly executed assault on the beach. Now – still unaware of the enemy's numerical strength – he set about strengthening his position, and from the fleet got a welcome reinforcement of heavy guns. The soldiers acquiesced in new, laborious duties, and daily the sick list grew longer; ophthalmia and fever had reduced his force by almost four thousand since the landing. Aboukir Castle surrendered – that was welcome news – but now, at last, Abercromby realised how inferior in strength he was to the French, and was accordingly puzzled as to what he should do. The right wing of his army occupied the ridge on which the Roman Camp was situated, while further back the left was extended across the desert floor in echelon. The core of the defence – for further advance seemed impossible – was the Roman Camp, and for its greater protection, a redoubt was constructed on a spur some small distance in front of it, and the command of the entire ridge was committed to the charge of John Moore.

On the 19th March, General Menou, the dilatory French Commander-in-Chief, arrived in Alexandria with reinforcements that raised the strength of his army there to 10,000 men, of whom 1,400 were cavalry, and a sufficient number to man forty-six guns; and now he decided to take the initiative. The surprise Menou anticipated, however, was foiled by Abercromby's opportune order warning his troops of the possibility of a night attack. In the early hours of the 21st March, Moore heard sharp firing break out on the left of the line, followed a little later by a crescendo of musketry on the right. Guessing that the earlier shooting was a feint, and that the main force of a French attack must be directed at the ridge, he galloped back to the Roman Camp, where he found the forward redoubt under heavy fire. The left wing of the 42nd had already reinforced its defenders, but Moore now ordered the right wing and the 28th – The Gloucesters – to move forward as well. They had no sooner advanced to the redoubt than it was discovered that a French brigade, hidden by the smoke and murk of early dawn, had infiltrated and now stood between the redoubt and the Roman Camp.

In the ranks of the 42nd was Private Andrew Dowie, who left a vivid description of the action.

> The morning being very calm, and not a breath to carry our smoke away, a French regiment passed on our right and formed in our rear. This being observed by Major Stirling, who hearing the officers dressing their line in the French language, instantly ordered the right wing to the right-about, gave them a volley and charged. We pushed them forward at the point of the bayonet, and in spite of every effort on their

part we forced them towards the ruins of the Roman Camp, where they made for a breach in the wall, and choked themselves like cattle forced in at a gate. By this time it was daybreak; the carnage was terrible – in fact they were almost annihilated. The major then ordered us all out of the ruins to support the left wing.

Dowie's account omits the participation of The Gloucesters, which earned them the privilege of wearing a cap badge fore and aft, but throughout the day both regiments fought side by side.

When both wings of the 42nd were re-united, they faced to the front to meet and break the advance of another of Menou's battalions, and now, with the day and the possibility of victory growing brighter by the instant, the Highlanders threw themselves in pursuit of the enemy. A colour was captured*, but in the morning light the Regiment was revealed to be scattered on the level ground in front of the ridge, a natural target for cavalry. The French horsemen charged the broken groups, but with stubborn courage the men held together under sergeants and junior officers, and withstood the shock, breaking the squadrons into disorder, and under fire from the ridge the French eventually rode back the way they had come. 'The 42nd,' wrote Fortesque, 'stands pre-eminent for a steadfast-ness and gallantry which would be difficult to match in any army.'

The Regiment re-grouped on the high ground near the redoubt, which was now hemmed in on three sides. The Roman Camp itself was under attack, and, as ammunition ran short, the British fire began to slacken so that it must have seemed to Menou that a final galvanic thrust by the cavalry would break Abercromby's hold on the ridge. Seeing the charge, Abercromby called the 42nd back to the rear of the redoubt, but the horsemen swirled past their bayonets, and the General himself was surrounded. Private Dowie remembered seeing 'Sir Ralph engaged with three of the enemy, cutting before and behind like a youth of twenty. One of our grenadiers named Barker, having spent his ammunition, charged his piece with loose powder from his cartouche, fired his ramrod, and killed one of them, while Sir Ralph struck down another, and the third made off.' However the General was already mortally wounded by a bullet which had lodged in his femur; another round had struck him on the chest, but he refused to leave the battle-ground until it became obvious that Menou, his last effort repulsed, was withdrawing his army, leaving a thousand dead upon the field and another two hundred as prisoners. The British had lost 243 men killed, but the losses of the 42nd were disproportionately high; after this, their third battle since landing at Aboukir Bay, they had only 315 unwounded men.

A week after the battle, Sir Ralph Abercromby died when his wound became gangrenous. He was a man of the highest distinction, a classical scholar, and of so profoundly liberal a temperament that he had refused to serve in North America against what he considered to be the justified revolt of the colonists. Though he spoke out boldly against political ineptitude, he was utterly loyal, and when the Government was in difficulty it was Abercromby who was summoned to help. Like Wolfe, and later Moore, he

---

*This standard belonged to the 3rd Battalion of the 21st Light Infantry who called themselves 'The Invincibles'. It was lost in the subsequent cavalry charge and recovered by another regiment. The Alexandria Medal issued by the Highland Society commemorated the incident. See page 45.

PLATE 7  *Aquatint of Sir Ralph Abercromby receiving his death wound, 1801.*

died when victory was certain, for the spirit of the French army never recovered from their defeat.

In successive small actions, Hutchinson, Abercromby's successor, reaped a large harvest of French prisoners, so that by June the only remaining resistance in Egypt came from the garrisons in Cairo and Alexandria. Cairo soon capitulated, but the French in Alexandria, under the direct eye of General Manou, held out until the end of September, before they too surrendered. One day before the news of this last setback reached London, Napoleon accepted the generous peace terms offered by the British government: his army in Egypt was destroyed, his allies' fleet had been sunk by Nelson at Copenhagen, and in the East his friend Tsar Paul of Russia had been assassinated. For the moment, therefore, peace offered greater rewards than war.

For the Regiment, the battles at Aboukir Bay and Alexandria won them a fame far exceeding that earned at Fontenoy or Ticonderoga, and the victory of Alexandria was of incomparably greater significance than those gained in the forests of North America or the feverish heat of the West Indies. As a mark of distinction the Sphinx was added to the Regimental arms, and among the soldiers themselves, the date of the victory became a festival to be celebrated with as little restriction on high spirits as Red Hackle Day in more recent times. To contemporaries, Alexandria was a famous occasion, but in the light of the later campaigns against Napoleon, it may also be seen as a watershed in the Regiment's history.

# CHAPTER 6

# The Peninsular Campaigns

When the government first authorised the employment of Highland soldiers in foreign service in 1743, it had taken a calculated risk. The towering reputation established by The Black Watch at Fontenoy and in North America served not only to vindicate that risk, but to justify the authorities in raising a plethora of Highland regiments. Of regular troops, thirty new corps or second battalions were gazetted by 1802 when the Peace of Amiens was signed, and of Fencibles and Militia, perhaps as many as fifty new regiments came into being. An area whose population was no more than 700,000, could not sustain such a large military establishment. Although some of the new regiments were broken up after a dragon-fly life, and their men drafted to other corps, the sheer number of competitors in the recruiting area gradually forced the Regiment to find more of its recruits in Southern Scotland, among the hinds and farm-servants displaced by improving landlords in the Lothians, and in the streets and closes of the industrial south-west. There was a different character to these men, which was eventually reflected in the Regiment.

When the uneasy peace ended in 1803, the 42nd, in common with other regiments, raised a 2nd Battalion under the 1797 Militia Act. The militia were conscripted, the names being chosen by ballot from the parish roll. Substitutes, however, were permitted, and while a wealthy man might buy his own if he did not wish to serve, the less well-off paid insurance to a society which guaranteed to produce a substitute if their name should come up. Perth's flourishing insurance trade may be said to date from this period, for there were several societies active in the city, and many of the 2nd Battalion's recruits were substitutes. One such later published an account of his experiences as 'An anonymous private of the 42nd', a vivid and not entirely reliable record, which is nevertheless worth reading for the light that it throws on the changed character of the Regiment.

The private's reasons for preserving his anonymity quickly became apparent in his narrative. He was paid £10 down, and was promised a further £10 when he joined a regiment. His principal reason for choosing the 42nd was that the recruiting officer had 'twenty bottles of whisky paraded on the table', more it would seem than any other regiment. With the help of the recruiting sergeant, he lightened the table's burden, spent his down payment on reinforcements, and passed his first week of service in a drunken stupor. Then he was sent with a detachment of other recruits to join the 2nd Battalion at Weely Barracks in Essex. At that time the 1st Battalion shared the same barracks, and the veterans of Egypt suffered from a monstrous, desert-begotten thirst, which even the new recruit found awesome, and it quickly exhausted his remaining bounty.

This was a pattern of behaviour common enough in the rest of the army, but strange, until that time, to the 42nd, whose soldiers for the first half-century of the Regiment's existence could scarcely be prevailed upon to drink their daily rum ration, preferring to take it at most twice a week. Stewart of Garth singled out the half-battalion stationed at Gibraltar in 1795 for comment on their drunkenness, and that would seem to be when it first became widespread. Certainly by the beginning of the new century, even the Colonel, Dickson of Kilbucho, was known as a toper of such generous appetite that one of his men, sentenced to be flogged for drunkenness and already strapped to the halberds, was said to have shouted to him 'Hey Kilbuckie, you're no going to let them flog an auld drunken loon just like yourself?' According to legend, Colonel Dickson had him released at once. It is not immediately clear why a previously abstemious regiment should have taken to drink, but it may not have been coincidence that the change came when the Highland society which first gave the Regiment its character was gradually being destroyed.

Despite the difficulties of recruiting there, the majority of the 42nd still came from the Highlands, and so many were monoglot Gaelic speakers that hospital mates, for instance, were required to be bilingual, while the anonymous private, being a Glaswegian, derived lofty amusement from 'the difficulties our Highlanders had to understand the common people, for some of my comrades knew no language but the Erse'. The private, however, was only one of a large infusion of Lowlanders who now entered the Regiment. The 1st Battalion had discharged many of its longest serving soldiers in 1802, and only numbered about 400 when it came to Essex. Its strength was brought to more than 900 by transfers from the 2nd Battalion, and its new Major, David Stewart, noted that there were some 230 Lowlanders on the roll.

Militia battalions were raised for service only within the United Kingdom, and so, when the 2nd Battalion left the barracks in 1804, the journey took them no further than Ireland. The Battalion was commanded by Lord Robert Blantyre, an officer who exacted the highest standards of discipline from all ranks. When Captain Smith was discovered to be improperly dressed, the Colonel placed him under arrest, and was in no way moved by the Captain's despairing plea that 'your Lordship will not insist on my putting on the uniform of the 42nd, as my health is certainly too delicate to bear the kilt'. No kilt, no commission, the Colonel ruled, and the delicate Smith duly arranged a transfer. His brother officers took their duties more seriously, and there is a slightly long-suffering note to the anonymous private's comment that 'there were no officers more strict on cleanliness than our own'.

His fellow-privates were addicted to gambling, particularly at whist and all-fours, which he at first found shocking, claiming that he always kept his Bible in his haversack, but there it would seem it remained, for soon he too was gambling, and on the Sabbath. Their official life was taken up by parades and manoeuvres. It was a simple regime. Mondays and Fridays, each corps exercised separately, Tuesdays and Saturdays, they exercised by brigades; the General's Parade came on Wednesdays, with some 15,000 men appearing at The Curragh. Thursday was a rest day, except for those corps which had failed to satisfy the General the day before. On Sunday they attended Divine Service.

For two years the 2nd Battalion maintained its routine and reputation for smartness, but in 1806, the officers briefly relaxed. There were no parades, duties were excused, drunkenness was forgiven. The purpose of the Saturnalia was to induce the men to volunteer for the regular army. A £10 bonus was offered, but the real attraction was the introduction of a limited seven-year service, where previously there had been no choice but to sign on for life. Most of the Battalion volunteered, and 120 men, including the anonymous private, were sent to join the 1st Battalion, while the rest remained in Ireland.

The 1st Battalion had sailed for Gibraltar in October, 1805, and it was to be garrisoned there for three years, in which time it lost 31 men to fever, and its pigtails to Army Regulations. Twenty-eight deaths a year was the average rate for a regiment in the Mediterranean – a horrific figure which puts the 42nd's loss in perspective, and suggests that it was indeed a well-ordered garrison. Certainly the anonymous private was suitably impressed by the strictness of the Colonel, James Stirling. Typically, however, he was even more struck by the insatiable thirst of the regulars compared to the militia.

The loss of his pig-tail made less impact, but Sergeant Anton, serving in the militia, was grateful for its abolition. 'The tying was a daily penance,' he wrote. 'Daubing the side of the head with dirty grease, soap and flour, and the back was padded and pulled so that every hair had to keep its place.' Satisfying as the result might be to a sergeant-major's ruby eye, it was a feast for the barracks mice whose appetites put many a good soldier on defaulters' for parading with a half-chewed queue.

One day in three, the men worked on the New Mole, which helped to make a safer anchorage for the Navy, and these being 'king's works', they were paid an extra 9d above their 1/- a day. So far as the anonymous private and his friends were concerned, it was all drink money, since there was nothing else to spend it on, and no other recreation available. It was a tedious life, and nothing is more evident than the Regiment's exhilaration when it left the Rock in the autumn of 1808 to join Sir John Moore's army in Portugal. Compared to the static existence of a garrison, the start of what became known as the Corunna campaign seemed idyllic.

> In the beginning of October we commenced our advance, taking with us no commissariat, and moving after the fashion of troop marches in Britain; sergeants getting billets for the men of their companies, where, after dismissal, our rations of bread and beef and a pint of port wine were served to us; thus happy went the soldier's life, for the weather was pleasant and our duties light. [Private Gunn's account; unpublished.]

Sir John Moore's responsibilities were of a different order. Alone among the continental nations, Spain and Portugal still resisted Napoleon's armies and diplomacy, but the British government was reluctant to give more than token aid to their resistance. Moore's instructions, contained in a letter from Castlereagh, the Foreign Secretary, were 'to employ a force of not less than 30,000 infantry and 5,000 cavalry in the North of Spain, to co-operate with the Spanish armies in the expulsion of French troops from that kingdom'. Since the enemy numbered over 200,000, the success of the British expedition was heavily dependent upon the performance of their Spanish allies.

The cavalry and 5,000 infantry were to be disembarked under the command of General Baird at Corunna, in the north-west corner of Spain, so Moore's most urgent priority was to unite his army. With winter drawing in and Napoleon marching on Madrid, speed was essential, and indeed Moore left Lisbon before wagons could be found for the commissariat. But his position was at once made doubly precarious. The roads to the north were too narrow and boulder-strewn for his artillery, and it had to be

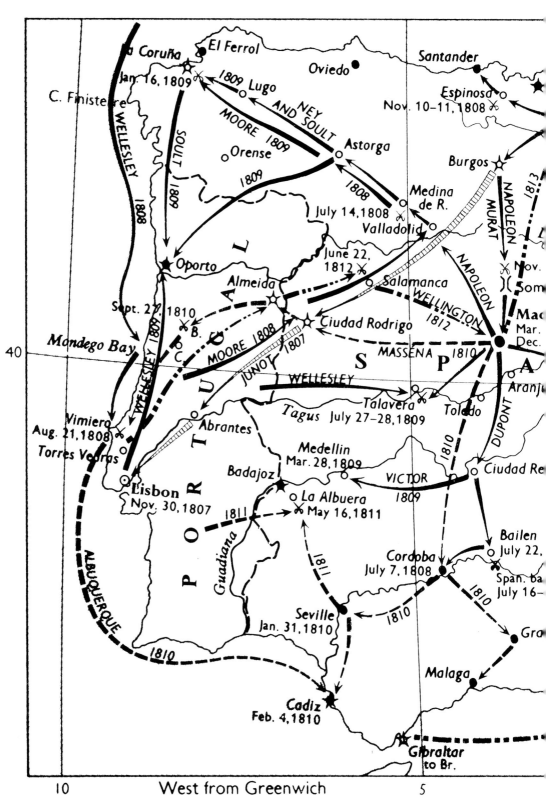

*The Peninsular War: 1807–1814, Courtesy Cambridge University Press.*

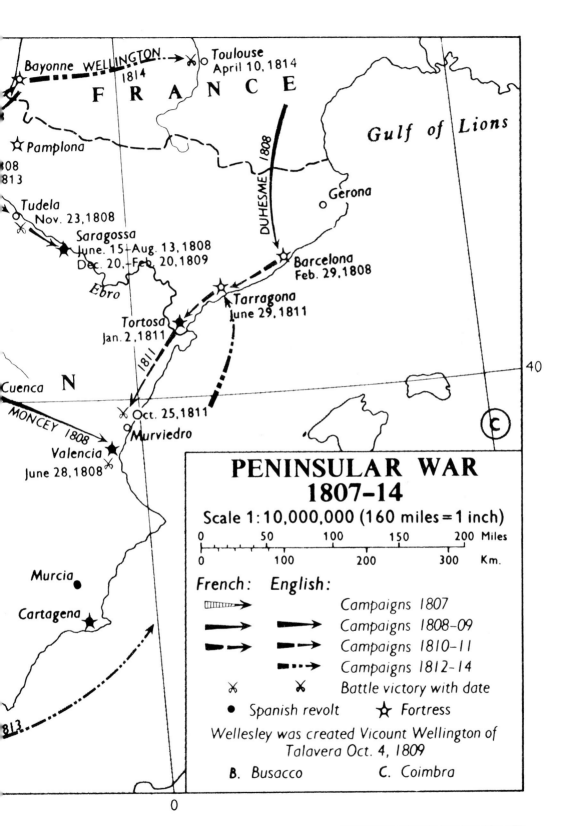

Bayonne WELLINGTON →✗ ○Toulouse
1814 April 10, 1814

F R A N C E

Gulf of Lions

☆ Pamplona

'08
'813

Tudela
Nov. 23, 1808
✗

Saragossa
June. 15–Aug. 13, 1808
Dec. 20, –Feb. 20, 1809 ★

DUHESME 1808

○ Gerona

Barcelona
Feb. 29, 1808 ☆

Ebro

☆ Tarragona
June 29, 1811

Tortosa ★
Jan. 2, 1811

1811

Cuenca N

MONCEY 1808

✗ Oct. 25, 1811
○ Murviedro

Valencia
June 28, 1808 ✗

★

40

Murcia ●

Cartagena ★

813

## PENINSULAR WAR
## 1807–14

Scale 1 : 10,000,000 (160 miles = 1 inch)

0   50   100   150   200 Miles

0   100   200   300 Km.

French:   English:

→   → Campaigns 1807

→   → Campaigns 1808–09

→   → Campaigns 1810–11

→   → Campaigns 1812–14

✗   ✗ Battle victory with date

● Spanish revolt   ☆ Fortress

Wellesley was created Vicount Wellington of
Talavera Oct. 4, 1809

**B.** Busacco     **C.** Coimbra

0

PLATE 8  *Major-General James Stirling of Craigbarnet. Volunteer in the 42nd in 1777.*
*Commanded in Gibraltar and Portugal.*

sent eastward first towards Madrid, before swinging north to rejoin the General at Salamanca.

The rest of the Lisbon force arrived at the rendezvous in early November, and during the month of waiting for the guns, Moore learned that three Spanish armies had been almost entirely destroyed by the French. He thought seriously of retreating to Lisbon, but allowed himself to be dissuaded by the British Minister at Madrid. Instead he decided to unite with Baird, and then either act in co-operation with the Spanish General Romana, leading an army of 60,000, or to try to tempt Napoleon from his siege of Madrid by threatening his line of communication. It was typical of Moore's ill-fortune that by the 5th December, when he moved north from Salamanca, neither course was possible. Madrid had fallen on the 4th, and Romana's men were too demoralised to constitute an army at all.

His despatches show that Moore was always conscious that, unless he had the assistance of a large and effective Spanish force, he would be forced to retreat to the coast whenever the French chose to concentrate their overwhelming strength against him. From the journal of the anonymous private in the 42nd, it is equally clear that no such thought ever crossed his mind; in anticipating battle he anticipated victory, whatever the odds might be.

On the 15th December, a captured despatch revealed that 100 miles to the north was a small French force under Marshal Soult, entirely unaware of their presence in the area. Four days of forced marches brought Moore to Mayorga, where at last he met Baird, and on the 22nd December, the united army was within a day's march of 18,000 Frenchmen. Then, as they lay poised for the very action, almost the only action, for which Moore's unsupported force was suited, a succession of reports flowed into headquarters, bearing the information that Napoleon was advancing rapidly from Madrid with 80,000 men; the last report showed him to be only four days' march away. Caught between 100,000 of the enemy, Moore had no choice but retreat, and he ordered his divisional commanders to inform the troops.

The 42nd, now in Baird's division, took his news badly. The men stood transfixed for several moments, said one of their officers, 'and at length their disappointment broke out into a murmur. . . . Indeed the effect of this counter-order on our soldiers was the most extraordinary, and from the greatest pitch of exaltation and courage, at once a solemn gloom prevailed throughout our ranks. Nothing was heard but the clang of firelocks thrown down in despair, which before they guarded as their dearest treasure.' They returned to quarters he noticed, 'in a sullen silence'.

The path of retreat ran westward across a plateau, fording the river Esla, and then, at Astorga, began to climb into the mountains. In open country Moore ran the risk of Soult driving in his right flank, and so Baird's division was detached to guard that side, while Moore himself remained with the rearguard of Paget's cavalry and Craufurd's light infantry. The two remaining commanders, Hope and Frazer, started with their troops immediately. They crossed the Esla at Valderas on Christmas Day which was celebrated with lethal results to discipline. Moore and the rearguard followed a day later. Twenty miles north Baird's division found that incessant rain had flooded the river, so that the Regiment was forced to cross 'with our kilts above our weams', according to the private, and one of their two baggage wagons had to be abandoned, which was far more serious. They saw no sign of the French, but when they reached the Leon-Astorga road it was choked with the remnants of Romana's army which Soult had brushed out of Leon.

Behind them, Napoleon realised, as Moore had done, that if the British were trapped before they reached the mountains, they could be utterly destroyed, and he pushed his troops to their limit. In the snow-bound Escurial Pass they baulked, but the Emperor led them through in person rather than be delayed. His furious energy was matched by Moore, however, and on the last day of 1808, the British rearguard marched out of Astorga with Napoleon just 15 miles behind. The prize had escaped, and the Emperor returned to Paris, leaving mundane pursuit to Soult.

At Astorga, Baird's flank guard had rejoined Moore's army to find that in the two leading divisions discipline had almost disappeared. 'The misbehaviour of the troops which marched by Valderas,' wrote Moore in a General Order, 'exceeds what he could have believed of British soldiers. It is disgraceful to the officers and strongly marks their negligence and inattention.' Drunkenness, endemic in the army, now reached epidemic proportions. Men looted houses for wine, and broke into the stores which were intended for the divisions in the rear. Their officers, dispirited and resentful of the order to retreat, made little effort to restrain them. On 1st January they reached the snow-line, and the Highlanders' buckled shoes, supplied under contract – the cheapest contract – began to disintegrate. Private Gunn, issued with new shoes on the 29th December, was in bare feet by the time the Regiment reached Villafranca on the 3rd January. To add to his misery the 42nd was halted near 'a storehouse full of biscuits, pork, shoes, etc., where we saw men busily employed breaking into the casks and throwing their contents into the river. There was naturally a slight murmur amongst our people when it was found that none of the many useful articles were to be served out.' Gunn wrote with masterful restraint. However, he managed to persuade a man of the 50th who had looted a cask of shoes to sell him a pair, and the Regimental pioneers secured some barrels of pork, past which the Highlanders marched, each one sticking his bayonet into a lump of meat.

The army now suffered a terrible ordeal in the bitter weather. The anonymous private, detailed for provost's guard on the 4th January, discovered, when he rejoined the Regiment, that the army's path was marked by 'dead horses and mules, baggage of every description, men, women and children who could not keep up'. The pregnant wife of a pay sergeant in the 42nd fell behind here, had her baby with the French advance guard, and rejoined the Regiment at Corunna. Indeed Soult's men were so close behind that in the passes before Lugo, the army's pay wagon was rolled over a precipice to prevent it falling into enemy hands. At Lugo, Moore decided to offer battle, and at once the morale of his men soared, but when Soult declined the occasion, and supplies ran short, the retreat had to continue. Moore now pushed his troops hard in order to gain the time he would need to embark his army without interruption. In foul weather they marched through the day and night until 11 a.m. on the 9th January when they arrived at Bretanzos.

Here the contagion of disorder which ravaged the two leading divisions reached back into Baird's troops. Throughout the retreat the breakdown of supplies periodically forced the Regiment to forage for supplies in empty houses, and at Villafranca some men had stumbled on a butt of wine which rendered them *hors de combat*, but otherwise the troops had held together. At Bretanzos, however, the anonymous private estimated that only 150 men came in with the Regiment. The night before, the division had halted briefly during a violent thunderstorm, and Baird had ordered the men to bivouac where they could, with the result that his entire division became scattered. But Bretanzos marked the end of the nightmare. From there the land sloped down to the sea and, for the first time since the retreat began, no mountains blocked the path. During the day 1,500 stragglers passed through the rear-guard, and the Regiment's order was restored by the time it came to Corunna on the 11th January.

That day provided the final disappointment for Moore, because the transports which he had ordered from Vigo, round the coast, had not yet arrived. 'Had I found the transports here,' he wrote in his final despatch, 'the embarkation would easily have been effected, for I had gained several marches on the French.' By the time the ships came in on the 14th, the French had made up the distance.

To fight this unsought action, the General placed Baird's division in the focal spot, a low range of hills about three miles in front of Corunna. On their left, Hope's division filled the space between the hills and the sea, and the broken ground which stretched back from Baird's position to the outskirts of Corunna was lightly guarded by dismounted cavalry under Paget. In the rear the town itself was protected by Frazer's division, the one that had suffered most during the retreat.

On the 16th January, the French cannon started to fire on Baird's troops, and the guns, which were situated on peaks overlooking the British position, seem to have been ranged particularly on the commanders. The 42nd suffered heavily, for it was situated in the middle of the range, between the 4th and 50th Regiments, and Moore placed himself close to them so that he could see both the valley separating the two armies, and the ground on his right. Soon after the bombardment began, two snakes of infantry came down from the French position and entered the valley. The smaller turned towards Hope's division between the hills and the sea, but deciding this was a feint Moore turned his attention to his right flank on which a cloud of *tirailleurs* under Marshal Jourdain were advancing with their customary shouts of 'En avant – tuez – tuez.' The 4th Regiment was ordered to draw back, forming a right angle to the main position, and now, faced by a line of troops where they had hoped to enfilade, Jourdain's sharpshooters quickly dispersed.

The main brunt of the attack was delivered by the larger column of infantry, which had entered the valley opposite the 42nd's position. Directly below the Regiment was the small village of Elvina, and when the column reached its walls, it divided to pass either side, and then halted to deploy. Baird had been wounded by a cannon-ball, and it was Moore, taking direct command, who gave the 42nd its order to advance, sending it off with two words which recalled the last occasion that he and the Regiment had fought together: 'Remember Egypt,' he said, and the order must have added fire to the ferocious charge that followed.

The men had been lying on the ground, and Private Gunn recalled that 'on standing up, a strange sight met one's gaze; close to us was advancing a line of sturdy Frenchmen, too close in fact for our volley to have full effect. Both sides were, I think taken by surprise, but our opponents more so, for all that were able to do so went to the right about, pursued by us down the hill.' In the tumultuous rush 'ilka man gat his birdie', wrote the anonymous private, 'and many of us skivvered pairs front and rear rank. I think I see the grizzly fellows now, running and jumping as the Highlanders, laughing and swearing, stuck the pointed steel in their loins. We followed them down the hill in the rage and wrath of the Highlanders.' The French were bundled off the slopes and into the village of Elvina before the rush was halted. As reinforcements came up, the French pushed the 42nd back to the edge of the village, but there the 42nd took up a strong position behind walls and ditches, from which they could not be removed. The Elvina position was vital, and as the French fought to break the Regiment's hold, Napier, commanding the 50th, waited impatiently on the ridge above them. He had no orders, but decided at last to follow the advice of his second-in-command, 'You cannot be wrong to follow the 42nd.' Despite Napier's personal example of charging into the village, the 50th came to a halt beside the 42nd at the edge of the village.

To fill the places vacated by the 42nd and 50th, Moore brought the Guards up from the back of the hill. When they appeared over the crest, some of the 42nd's Light Company, whose ammunition was spent, began to retire, thinking they were to be relieved. Moore sent them forward again, but as he rode back up the hill, a cannon-ball struck him and tore open his shoulder and chest. A private helped his staff to lift him to the shelter of a wall, then other men from the 42nd under the command of a sergeant found a blanket and started to carry the General back to Corunna. A surgeon saw him, but was sent to attend other wounded men. An officer came up with a wagon, but Moore refused to be transferred to it on the sergeant's assurance that his men would 'keep the step and carry him easy'. It is not hard to believe that Moore heard in the sergeant's voice the accent of his own boyhood, and, approaching so near to death, found it as comforting as the man's promise. Over the long miles to Corunna they kept the step, while behind them the last French reserves closed in on Elvina. The 42nd and 50th broke that attack like the others, and as evening came, the French began to retire from the village.

They buried the General early in the morning, and by then half of his army was embarked. During the remainder of the day, the rest were hurried on to the transports, so that many regiments, including the 42nd, were split up between different ships. Each sailed when she was filled, and gales soon scattered them across the Bay of Biscay. When these ragged, shoeless soldiers began to come ashore at Plymouth and Portsmouth, their appearance created widespread alarm. It was assumed that they must be the survivors of a catastrophic defeat, and *The Times* gave voice to the general feeling, when it described Moore's campaign as 'a shameful disaster'. It had been neither shameful nor disastrous, for victory was never possible. But to have sustained the will to fight through a long retreat was a triumph, and in that the 42nd could justly claim a share.

In the battle the Regiment had lost 35 killed and 111 wounded, but the retreat had been more deadly; 99 men were eventually marked 'missing in Spain'. If this number should seem high, it may be compared with the 6th Regiment, which lost 400 men on the retreat, with the 9th which lost 300, and with Soult's army of which 25 per cent of the men were in hospital. Among the survivors the ordeal created a close bond, and for some time Regimental duties were made as easy as possible, but despite this dispensation another 19 men died of fatigue and illness. 1809 was a sad year in the Regiment's history, for harsh as it had begun, worse was yet to follow.

In the summer the threat of invasion brought the 42nd to Moore's old training camp at Shorncliffe, where it practised repelling the expected French hordes. Instead they became the invaders, when in July they were sent on the ill-considered expedition to Walcheren. 40,000 troops were put ashore near Flushing to wrest control of the river Scheldt from the French, and within six weeks 4,000 were dead of malaria and typhoid fever, and 11,500 were in hospital. The Regiment's toll was in proportion, but even after its return the damage continued. In March, 1810 Major Macara of the 1st Battalion wrote to Major Dick serving with the 2nd Battalion, 'We have lost about 130 men since the Regiment returned from Walcheren, and have only about 200 fit for duty, and even those are looking as yellow as a kite's foot.' Nor was that the end, for three years later Wellington still found the Walcheren troops more sickly than the rest. But for the time being the 1st Battalion was left to gather itself together in peaceful garrisons, ministering to its shivers with wine and the quinine derived from Peruvian bark.

Macara's correspondent, Major Dick, was the extremely gallant son of a most ambitious doctor, and from 1809, when the 2nd Battalion sailed from Ireland to join Wellesley's forces in Portugal, both father and son had scope to exhibit their particular qualities. On the long ridge of Busaco, where the British hurled back the assaults of Massena's columns, the Major so distinguished himself that he was awarded a medal for his valour, while the Doctor began an artful campaign to persuade 'Old Daddy' Stirling to retire and sell his colonelcy to the Major. When this failed, the Doctor pressed Colonel Farquharson to sell his commission, promising to pay a higher price than normal for it, but Farquharson proved as hard to move as Wellington, now ensconced behind the lines of Torres Vedras. Neither budged until the spring of 1811, when Wellington emerged from his fortress to besiege Almeida, and Colonel Farquharson showed signs of coming round, encouraging Dr Dick to believe that he had a first option on the colonelcy. His optimism was as delusive as that of Massena who now sought to envelope Wellington's besieging army from the rear.

On the morning of the 5th May Massena's troops attacked Wellington's position at Fuentes d'Onoro, and in the dawn mist over-ran the right wing, isolating the 7th Division. Craufurd's Light Division was sent out to rescue them, and in a superb display of military manoeuvre brought them back across the open plain. Retiring slowly in column and square, they withstood a series of cavalry attacks, but some of the enemy's horse burst past them, sabred an advanced post of the Guards, and charged on the rest of the British line. There they were met by the 42nd who, with controlled fire and long bayonet, put an end to the sortie. It was a neat and disciplined action in a confused and bloody struggle, and Wellington recognised its merit by decorating the Colonel, Lord Blantyre.

Commanding another battalion, Major Dick had again distinguished himself, and borrowing some of his courage, the Doctor now wrote directly to the Commander-in-Chief, suggesting a brevet promotion for his boy. Wellington's refusal was worded so charmingly and with such flattering reference to the Major's worth that the Doctor was convinced that field promotion was no more than a battle away. He had need of that comfort for his chance of purchasing a permanent commission for his son disappeared when the 1st Battalion sailed for Lisbon in April, 1812. The wretched Farquharson, who had presumably been conducting a secret auction, now ceased his swithering and sold his commission. The buyer was Major Macara.

The new Colonel took command of a Battalion 1,110 strong, of whom 365 had been transferred to it from the 2nd Battalion. Reduced to no more than a cadre, the 2nd Battalion returned to Scotland where it continued to recruit and train men for the 1st until the peace of 1814. It left with the good opinion of Wellington who wrote that 'on every occasion it conducted itself in a manner worthy of the Distinguished Regiment of which it forms a part'. And Lord Blantyre, who of course was biased in the matter, thought that 'it looked much the fitter of the two Battalions'.

In the winter and spring of 1813, the two great fortresses of Ciudad Rodrigo and Badajos were captured, and the way was opened for a general advance into Spain. It began in triumph with Marmont's rout at Salamanca on the 21st July, when, after three weeks of chess-like manoeuvring, the French left wing extended too far, and Wellington snapped at the chance. It was said by the French that the battle was lost in forty minutes. Pakenham's division appeared round the shoulder of a hill, and, with the sun behind them, took the French so entirely by surprise that they could only loose off one volley before their formation was smashed. The 1st Division, in which the 42nd served, was on the far left of Wellington's line, and did not come up to the action until nightfall, when the French were withdrawing. There was some bitterness in the Division, since they had also been in reserve at Ciudad Rodrigo and Badajos, and they complained that justice had not been done them. Wellington agreed that they had been ill-used, and promised he would see them righted at the first opportunity. That proved to be Burgos, but it is doubtful whether the Division thought itself righted even then.

After Salamanca Wellington marched into Madrid, where the Spanish gave him the keys of their capital, and the British awarded him a Marquessate and one hundred thousand pounds. Perhaps the glory perturbed his judgement, for when, in September, he advanced on Burgos, he left in Madrid 100 heavy guns, and took with him only three 18-pounders, some howitzers and the 1st Division.

The castle of Burgos was raised above the surrounding country by a hill, and was protected on its southern side by a double line of walls and a gorge. To these material defences could be added the indomitable spirit and ingenuity of its commander, General Dubreton, whose qualities rendered the fortress more formidable than Ciudad Rodrigo. Its weakest point was a fortified hill which lay just outside the southern walls, and was connected to them by a causeway which ran across the gorge. Wellington's Chief Engineer, General Jones, proposed that the outpost, named St Michael, should be stormed on the night of the 19th September, and the responsibility for its capture was allotted to the Portuguese, while the 42nd were to carry the scaling ladders, and provide covering fire.

The entire Regiment volunteered for these duties; a company was selected for each, and the remainder were detailed for a diversionary attack in the gorge beneath the castle walls. Private Gunn, selected for the diversion, described the experience of advancing in bright moonlight which enabled the French to see them clearly. 'We pretended to be moving very stealthily to draw their attention to us, and they appeared to use just as much cunning in never letting on that they saw us, but just as we arrived within a short distance of them, they opened a terrific fire. I never saw such a blaze.' Behind them the ladder and firing parties tried to take advantage of the diversion. General Jones wrote:

> Portuguese troops allotted to the escalade were preceded by a company of High-landers carrying the scaling ladders. The Highlanders coolly raised the ladders against the escarpment, and the attention of the garrison being much occupied, they mounted to the upper staves almost without opposition, but the assaulting party, notwithstanding this stimulating example, would not enter the ditch.

Recovering from their surprise, the defenders bayoneted the leading Highlanders as they reached the top, while below them the Portuguese still hung back. But this struggle now pulled the French from their posts by the gorge, and Major Somers-Cocks of the 79th, gathering the diversion group and the Light Companies of two other Highland regiments, stormed into the rear of the outpost, and the St Michael position was soon firmly under British control.

It was the last success which sheer gallantry could bring in the siege. For five sunless weeks the Regiment laboured to make fascines and gabions, to dig trenches with inadequate tools, and to man these defences against the fire and daring assaults of the defenders. But without a proper siege-train or a sufficient number of guns to make a fair-sized breach in the walls, it was all labour in vain. Two of the heavy guns were put out of action, and ammunition for the third was so scarce that ninepence was paid for each ball found and brought to the artillery. The anonymous private summed up trenchantly: 'You might as well have sent the boys of the grammar school to take Edinburgh Castle with pop-guns.'

Late in October, a French army of 80,000 men approached, and the besiegers crept away from Burgos, with the wheels of the wagons muffled in straw. In many ways the retreat from Burgos can be compared to the retreat from Corunna – the same extravagant drunkenness, the same chilling rain, and behind them the same Marshal Soult – and again, the 42nd seemed to be less susceptible than others to the general riotousness in which a British army retreated. The anonymous private, who in 1809 prided himself on his ability to 'fall in with two loaves and a pigskin of wine', found no such windfalls on this occasion. Major Dick, commanding the Battalion in Mascara's absence, was a stern disciplinarian, who tolerated no excesses, and when the Regiment reached Portugal, he had several men flogged and half a dozen corporals reduced to the ranks for ill-discipline. The nature of their crimes can be gauged by the case of the anonymous private, who had put up corporal's stripes at Burgos just a month before. Now a man in his section was discovered to be wearing trousers instead of the kilt, and the short-lived corporal was reduced to the ranks. Later he was promoted again, and later still reduced again, to end his career as he began it, anonymous and private.

The career of the Dick family, however, at last took a happier turn. An election was pending in Perthshire where the victor of Barossa, Sir Thomas Graham, was standing as a Whig. Dr Dick controlled two votes in the constituency, and was wooed by both sides. Determined to make his votes count, and remembering that Wellington was a Tory, the Doctor wrote to his son, 'His Lordship will be much more likely to recommend you for promotion if he knows that your nearest connexions can give two votes for or against the cause he espouses.' The Major received his promotion, and the Tory squeezed in with the Doctor's votes, but it would be a very wizened cynic who could believe it was more than coincidence. The Doctor's hint that his votes could be bought was rendered superfluous by the son's behaviour at Burgos, which had again attracted the notice of Wellington. He was awarded his third medal of the campaign, and in November given brevet rank as Lieutenant-Colonel.

Colonel Macara returned from leave while the Regiment was in winter quarters. It was a hard winter with snow on the ground, and the men's health had still not recovered from the Walcheren fever. No less than 147 men died between December and March. The hospitals were full, and when Private Gunn fell sick he was simply laid out on the floor of a barn, and even there he was better off than the most serious cases. They had been put in an open loft above, where the snow drifted in and covered them. As the toll mounted, unrest in the Regiment began to grow, and an unrelated incident served to bring it out into the open.

An Irish corporal named McMorran was courting a Portuguese girl, presumably with little success, for he began to suspect that an officer in his company, Lieutenant Dickenson, had discouraged the girl from seeing him. After a long interview with her, McMorran arrived late on parade. Dickenson announced that he would be reduced to the ranks, and then ordered him to fetch his musket and come out on parade. He brought his weapon from his hut, and approached the officer. The anonymous private was watching: 'When a soldier goes to speak to an officer with a musket in his hand, he comes to the recover, the next moment to the present to fire.' The Corporal did so, but then shot Lieutenant Dickenson through the head. It was the most terrible crime that could be committed in the army, and the sentence was appropriate. McMorran was hanged, shot and his body was hung in chains for three weeks. The ill-feeling in the Regiment now broke out in an ugly scene involving the Adjutant. Lieutenant Innes 'was regarded as a bit of a tyrant', according to the anonymous private, and when he went into the hut occupied by McMorran's friends, he was surrounded. The men refused to disperse and threatened him with the same fate as Dickenson if he did not make their lives easier. Innes, who had been accustomed to the stricter conditions of the 2nd Battalion, wrote to his former commanding officer, Lord Blantyre:

> I was much surprised on joining to find the Battalion in a worse state of discipline than I had ever expected. They appeared to be under no command, and when they turned out they looked more like a flock of sheep than a Regiment of Royal Highlanders. Every officer does as he pleases, and the N.C.O.s are commanded by their men.

Innes was in no doubt that the fault lay with 'a Commanding Officer who hardly commands common respect from the private soldiers'.

Colonel Macara appears to have been the epitome of that sort of officer which provoked Wellington to exclaim, 'By God there is nothing so stupid as a gallant officer.' He combined superlative courage with a marked incompetence in his profession; apart from the lamentable state of the Regiment in Portugal, later at the Nive he failed to cut off a French column, because he had marched the Battalion into a clump of thorn bushes; at Toulouse he put the men through an unnecessary parade ground drill under intense short-range fire; and at Quatre Bras he left them in open formation when charged by cavalry. Despite it all, in battle they obeyed him implicitly and with zest, and if the Regiment reached its nadir under his command, it also attained its zenith at Toulouse and Quatre Bras while he was Colonel. Perhaps he possessed qualities which escaped the adjutant and other observers, but on the evidence the Regiment's later success owed more to a sense of tradition which soon began to re-appear, to the work of competent soldiers such as Innes, R. S. M. Clark and Sergeant Anton, and finally to the self-confidence of victory.

In the spring of 1813, Wellington's army, which had now been in the field for four years, was at last properly equipped with a siege train, with hospitals, and, of most immediate interest to the soldiers, with tents. At the end of May they left their winter quarters, and marched in two columns. The smaller column moved eastward to mask the direction of the main force which was due north. This time there was to be no advance on Madrid and no siege of Burgos, instead the whole French position was to be turned on its right flank. They abandoned the roads, and marched through fields and country which the French considered impassable. They crossed the Esla, but, unlike Moore, from west to east, and when the two columns had reunited at Toro, the whole army turned north again. Now Wellington could switch his supply point from Lisbon to Santander. The French had early lost contact with them but, as shadowy reports came in of 100,000 men on their flank, they were forced to withdraw their troops from Burgos to the Ebro, and from the Ebro to Vittoria. In that town, King Joseph had collected all the spoils which the French had taken in Spain, the paintings, women and jewels, provoking one of their officers to comment, 'Nous étions un bordel ambulant.'

The 42nd had marched with the main force. It had been transferred from the 1st Division, the 'Gentlemen's Sons', to form a Highland Brigade in Pakenham's 6th Division, the 'Marching Division'. In the four weeks which brought them to Vittoria, they earned their name. The anonymous private explained how exhausting it was to march through ripening corn, and later, how much more exhausting it was to scramble along mountain trails. But, when the other divisions fell upon the French at Vittoria, the 6th drew the unlucky lot of guarding Wellington's rear against the unseen menace of Clausel's army. The 42nd could echo Pakenham's words, 'I did my duty, but lost my laurel.' While the victors indulged their genius for riotous conduct among the painted mistresses and masterpieces which the French had left behind, the Regiment waited a few miles back at Medina de Pomar. Having missed the glory and pleasure, they could also claim to miss the consequence, which was Wellington's sizzling report, composed after witnessing the orgy: 'It is quite impossible for me or any other man to command a British army under the existing system. We have in the service the scum of the earth.'

While the main force pursued the French north towards the Pyrenees, the 6th Division was sent eastward down the banks of the Ebro in pursuit of Clausel and 14,000 Frenchmen. After weary marching and counter-marching in vain attempts to trap the enemy, the Division returned to the army, taking up a position in the centre of the line between San Sebastian and Pamplona, the last two fortresses of consequence still held by the French in Spain. Here they could act as a reserve to foil any attempt to relieve either of the besieged towns. Their chance to perform that role came on the 26th July, when Soult counter-attacked through the Pyrenees towards Pamplona, which was guarded by only two divisions. For two-and-a-half days, the Division marched through the valleys and ravines towards Sorauren where Cole's Division waited to block Soult's path. Throughout the morning of the 28th, a day of stifling heat, they must have heard the noise of the battle ahead of them as Soult repeatedly attacked the ridge on which Cole's men were situated. About noon Soult detached a powerful force to bypass the ridge and break through to Pamplona, but as the French marched out of Sorauren, Pakenham's exhausted 6th Division was snaking down a converging valley, with the 42nd and its anonymous private in the lead. 'At this moment we turned round a hill, and in two minutes we were in sight of a strong corps of the enemy, 6,000 men marching directly for Pamplona. We were only about 200 yards from them, and in an instant their whole line stopped. It was the most beautiful sight I ever saw.' The timing could hardly have been better. As the 42nd advanced the French turned and retreated briskly into Sorauren. The divisional Light Companies made a raid on the village, but by then the French had recovered, and the raiders drew off. Total exhaustion enveloped both armies as the day ended, and while Cole's Division rested on the ridge which they had bravely held, the 6th took post on a hill overlooking the valley down which it had come.

For thirty-six hours no one stirred, then Soult tried to slip out of the Sorauren bottleneck, and the battle erupted again. His movement on the road below the 6th Division was spotted, and following an artillery bombardment, Stirling's brigade, with the 42nd, charged down the hill. The dispirited Frenchmen tried to escape into the mountains, but Soult's army was almost surrounded, and in the terrible rout less than half his 30,000 men escaped. The success of these two battles, commemorated in the honour 'Pyrenees', allowed the investment of Pamplona to proceed at leisure.

Indeed after the furious pace of the previous months, lassitude seemed to overtake the British. Wellington's immobility was due to the negotiations for peace between France, and Prussia and Austria. If those countries made peace, Napoleon could turn all his strength against Spain, and until the outcome was known, Wellington preferred to hold a defensive position. The 42nd was sent forward to guard the vital Maya Pass through which Soult had broken in July, and it remained there for two months.

During that time, it received a draft from the 2nd Battalion which came in under the command of Sergeant James Anton. Anton's *Recollections of a Military Life* is based on a diary which he wrote in verse, but then tore up after reading some lines of Wordsworth. Reading the odd purple passage which survived, one can hardly help feeling that, painful as it must have been, the decision was the right one, but mixed among his lofty reflections on the mortality of man and the love of a good woman, are the observations of an unsentimental eye, and they make his book a prime source of information for the period.

It is clear that the dark days of Portugal had been left far behind by the time he arrived. Although not deeply impressed by the discipline he found, Anton thought its cause was the large influx of recruits who could not be given any training because of the foul weather and mountainous country. Otherwise any lapses stemmed from drunkenness, 'a vice of so long-standing that it had been passed over by the best commanders'. For Macara he had faint praise; the men he found outstanding were Lieutenant Innes, 'strict and correct', and Sergeant-Major Clark, who inspired a fine flight: 'Fortunate is the regiment with a good sergeant-major. He is like the pure mountain stream which from inaccessible sources derives its never-failing supply, and sweeps off everything impure from its channels.'

Anton's wife had come out with him, and he was less inspired by the conditions in which they both had to live. They shared a tent with between a dozen and seventeen soldiers. Each slept with

> his knapsack below his head, clothes and accoutrements on his body; one half of the blankets under, and the other spread over the whole so that we all lay in one bed. The whole of the men were affected by an eruption on their skin similar to the itch, and their clothing was in a filthy state owing to its seldom being shifted, and always kept on during the night.

s soon as possible, he and his wife moved out and built themselves a flimsy hut of
branches, and it is worth noting that Anton considered 'we might have left it to its own
keeping from morning to night without an article being abstracted; thieving was unknown
the Regiment.'

The women of the 42nd deserve attention for the considerable part they played in the
egiment's life. For every 100 men, six wives were authorised to follow the Regiment.
They received half rations, half a pound of beef and biscuits, and their children one-third
tions. It was better than remaining at home where they received nothing, and might not
e their husbands for a decade, thus there were always far more than the official number of
ives, ready to share the harshness of a soldier's life. Some thrived on it.

There was Mrs MacKenzie, who

> began her career of celebrity in the accommodating disposition of an easy virtue at the
> age of fourteen in 1745. That year found her in Flanders, caressing and caressed.
> After a campaign or two, Scotland saw her again, but, wearied of rural retirement, she
> then married and made her husband enlist in the Royal Highlanders in 1756. With
> him she navigated the Atlantic, and sallied forth on American ground in quest of
> adventures, equally prepared to meet friends or encounter enemies in the fields of
> Venus or Mars as the occasion offered. After a variety of vicissitudes in Europe,
> America and the West Indies, her barque is now moored in the village of Tomintoul.
> She added 24 children to the aggregate of birth, besides some homunculi that
> stopped short in their passage. Wonderful, however, as it may appear, she is as fit for
> her usual active life as ever, and except for two or three grey hairs vegetating from a
> mole upon one of her cheeks, she still retains all the apparent freshness and vigour of
> youth. [Reverend John Grant of Tomintoul, quoted in *Highlanders and their Regi-
> ments*, by J. Brander.]

nother who took to the life was the virago of St Vincent, whom David Stewart described.

> When the enemy had been beaten from the third redoubt, I found myself tapped on
> the shoulder, and turning round, I saw my Amazonian friend with her skirts tucked
> up to her knees. 'Well done my Highland lads' she cried. 'See how the Brigands
> scamper like so many deer.' On inquiry, I discovered she had been in the hottest fire,
> cheering and animating the men, and when the action was over, she was active as any
> of the surgeons in assisting the wounded.

The other side of the coin was described by Anton after the battle of Toulouse.

> Here fell Cunninghame, a corporal in the grenadier company; he was a married man,
> and was interred before his wife entered the dear-bought field. She flew to the place
> where the wreck of the Regiment lay. 'Tell me' she asked, 'where is Cunninghame
> laid that I may see him and lay him in his grave with my own hand.' Twenty men
> started up to accompany her to the spot, for they respected the man and esteemed the
> woman. They lifted the corpse; the wounds were in his breast; she washed them, and
> pressing his cold lips to hers wept over him, then wrapped the body in a blanket, and
> the soldiers consigned it to the grave.

They were nurses long before Florence Nightingale made it a respectable profession

for women. They washed and mended their husband's clothes, and brought them fo[
when they were away from camp. Above all they provided a source of humanity in th
often bleak and unforgiving life.

It was an inevitable consequence of their long stay at the Maya Pass, that the soldie
began to fraternise with the opposite numbers in the French regiment. Sentries used
pass drink to each other in the cold nights, and several were discovered drunk or aslee
which provoked the anonymous private to a rare mood of censoriousness, perhaps becau
he had just regained his corporal's stripes. He recommended sleepy sentries to pri
themselves with pins, or wash their eyes with urine to stay awake. But the problems of t
N.C.O.s were solved on the 19th October when the battle of Leipzig broke the armisti
between the French and Prussians. Almost immediately, Wellington's troops were on t
move.

At the beginning of November they came out of the Pyrenees into France, and on t
10th they attacked the huge twenty-mile-long position which Soult defended beyo
the Nivelle River.

Wellington made feints on both the right and left to draw off Soult's reserves, but t
main attack came in the centre. The 6th Division provided part of the central force, a
they crossed the Nivelle almost without opposition, only when they climbed the hills
the far side did they come under heavy fire. Opposite the 42nd, the enemy had retired t
fortified post, but the speed of the Highlanders carried them into the redoubt on the he
of the French, and they took possession of it with little difficulty. The same succe
attended the entire attack, and the only moment of doubt came when the Regiment look
back across the river to see a sizeable French force under General Foy marching stealth
on their camp. His hopes of easy success were frustrated by the wounded, the hospi
orderlies and, no doubt, the wives, who grabbed weapons and began firing. Faced with t
resistance, and realising that the position behind him had collapsed, Foy withdrew.

Their first victory in France affected Wellington's army in much the same way
their success at Vittoria. They celebrated with a night of plunder and looting, which th
looked upon as one of the perquisites of the trade. The authorities described the search
spoil as 'marauding', or, if accompanied by violence, 'rapine', but the soldiers preferred
call it 'reconnoitring'. However it was named, Wellington was determined to halt it, for
was essential to his plans that the civil population should regard him, not as an invader, b
as the restorer of the legitimate monarchy. His measures were draconian. At every hour
the night and day, each company called its roll to see that no man was missing, and anyo
detected reconnoitring received five hundred lashes.

In its early years, flogging had been unnecessary in the Regiment, and even und
Macara it was uncommon. He was not a harsh man; Anton records an incident at this tim
when Macara found his men tearing down vine-supporters for firewood. He ordered t
wood to be returned, and some men did so, while others just dropped it on the groun
Private Henderson, the gomeril or clumsy oaf, tried to run away, tripped over his woo
and fell over; 'the Colonel seized him by the kilt, the pins of which yielded to the tug, a
left his naked posterior to some merited punishment.' Anton suggested that a cou
martial and the lash might have been in order. He justified its use by saying: 'Phila
thropists who decry the lash ought to consider in what manner the good men are to
protected; if no coercive measures are to be resorted to, to prevent the ruthless ruffia

om insulting the orderly-disposed, the good must be left to the mercy of the worthless.' On the other hand, not only was it a brutalising weapon, its very effectiveness may be doubted. Private Tom Morris of the 73rd pointed out that 'it invariably makes a tolerably good man bad, and a bad man infinitely worse. Once flog a man and you degrade him for ever in his own mind; and thus take from his every possible incentive to good conduct.'

To this perceptive comment, there was perhaps one exception – Private Adams. He went to Spain in 1809 with the 2nd Battalion, and at the time was quite illiterate, but for two years he gave up his rum ration to a soldier who taught him how to write and read. Despite his education he was caught marauding by the Spanish, who disarmed him and decided to hang him from a convenient tree growing by a well. The rope was round his neck, and they were preparing to haul away, when the leader of the party came up to Adams and spat in his face. Adams at once booted him so hard that he fell down the well. This put the rest of the party in a dilemma, since the only rope which might be used to pull him out was round Adams' neck. Reluctantly, it may be guessed, they unnoosed him and rescued their leader, at which moment the Provost-Marshal appeared and promptly arrested Adams for not carrying his musket. He was summarily court-martialled, and received five hundred lashes. Bursting with indignation Adams complained to Lord Blantyre about the injustice of his punishment, and his Colonel, that understanding man, agreed with him, and gave him credit of the lashes against his next crime. Sadly it was soon used up, and in fact Adams must have been a remarkably inefficient marauder, for in France he was caught yet again, this time by the French. He escaped hanging on this occasion by promising to fight the Prussians, but in 1814 slipped back into the Regiment claiming to have been a prisoner of war, which entitled him to a handsome sum in back pay. When the devil looks after his own he does them proud, for in an idle moment during the Regiment's stay in Ireland in the 1820s, Adams began grumbling about the miseries of army life to a suspected Irish terrorist. The latter was sufficiently encouraged to confess that he too hated authority, so much so that he had in fact just murdered a magistrate. The confession was passed on, Adams was promoted and immediately became zeal personified. When he finally retired after twenty years service, he did so with a first-class character and a sergeant's pension. If Adams is an exception to Morris' rule, he is also remarkably convincing proof of it.

Nevertheless, Wellington's measures against marauding had their desired effect, and soon the French farmers were bringing in their livestock to sell to the regimental butchers, and fresh bread could be bought in the villages. To give further encouragement to covert or timid monarchists, he offered them another victory over the Marshal, and one which drew him out of the Lower Pyrenees.

On the 9th December, 1813, the 6th Division crossed the Nive, and began to clear some lightly held defences. Towards evening the 42nd reached the core of the position, a commandingly situated farmhouse, whose buildings and environs were strongly held by the enemy. To eject them from such a position was a job for the Light Company, the men who were particularly trained to fire quickly and move in dispersed order. It cost nearly half the company's number before the farmhouse was taken, but by nightfall the 6th Division was securely established across the Nive. In Bayonne, Soult sent his armies first against the divisions which had not crossed the river, but on the 13th he switched his attack to the 2nd Division which was on the same bank as the 6th. Pakenham's troops were hurried up in support, but heavy rain had made a morass of the river valley, and by the time they arrived, the 2nd Division had held off the attack. The only opportunity for action was offered to Macara, who was ordered to intercept an enemy column advancing for a final assault against the 92nd. According to Anton, 'the Colonel led us into such a brake of furze, thorn and brambles that it would have been impossible to take our bare thighed Regiment through. The General, observing our painful but ineffectual struggling withdrew us from that spot, and pointed to another which would have been more practicable at the start.' By then the French had gone by, and with mixed feelings the men watched them being hurled back by the 92nd.

Vile weather brought an end to the Nive battle, and both armies went into winter quarters. The atrocious winter turned the land into a quagmire. Lieutenant McNiven who had just joined the Regiment, walked across an old battlefield, and saw a nightmare scene as the rain washed the soil away so that 'arms and legs protruded from the ground' or left 'faces looking through the surface while the bodies remained covered'. Everything turned to the colour of mud, and when men went out on picquet duty they sank up to the waist in the mire. Their clothes were falling to pieces, and strange mixtures of uniform appeared, as men converted tattered kilts into trousers, or wore both trousers and kilt simultaneously to guard against the cold.

Soult's army had been split in two by the Nive battle, and about a third of it was trapped in Bayonne. To draw the rest of it away from the city, Wellington marched eastward, threatening to outflank the French left wing. Soult retired on Orthez, where he took up an almost Wellingtonian position along the crest of a steep ridge shaped like a cat's back, and running from east to west. Wellington planned his main assault for the western end of the ridge, while in the centre of it a strong show of force was offered as a red herring.

The army marched at daybreak to a pontoon bridge which crossed the river in front of the French position, and as the Regiment waited for its turn at the bridge, McNiven was struck by the size of Wellington's forces. 'I could see column after column emerging from the mist, with dense masses of cavalry crowning the distant eminences.' Once across, the 6th Division marched parallel to the ridge, which rose steeply on their left. Their role was to support the diversionary attack in the centre, but the division detailed to lead the attack was behind them, so at mid-morning the 6th halted by the road to let them pass. It was a windless day, and the resting soldiers could see the artillery smoke rising in perpendicular columns above the battle on the western slope of the ridge. The assault there had in fact come to a stop, and the 42nd soon saw the familiar figure of Wellington come riding up from that direction. The orders he now gave to the 6th Division changed the shape of the battle, for its central attack became the focal point.

The Division was directed on to a lane which climbed diagonally up the hill. The 42nd was the leading battalion, and their Light Company was sent ahead as a screen. They moved through the allotments on either side of the lane, and as they disappeared into a wood beyond, the Grenadier Company took post on the bank above the narrow road. Warning shouts were heard from the wood, and two more companies were sent up as reinforcements, then moments later a party of the Light Company

came running out of the wood pell-mell with the cry 'Cavalry, cavalry', while almost at the same instant a squadron of mounted Chasseurs came dashing at full gallop down the narrow road, little anticipating the grenadiers of the Highlanders occupied the spot they did. They received a most deadly volley, and when the smoke cleared away men and horses were seen to lie dead and dying in one common mass.

It was an extraordinary place to use cavalry, and the French must have imagined that they were faced by no more than skirmishers rather than a well-prepared battalion. The 2nd climbed upwards through the wood, and among the trees they met and drove back the French in a series of duelling exchanges. When they reached the top of the hill, resistance began to die away for the back of the French position was broken but, apparently tireless, the Highlanders began to run eastward along the ridge in pursuit of their demoralised enemy. Some distance on they came to the village of Sallespisse, where Foy's troops were defiantly holding out. The Regiment was ordered to evict them, and the inexhaustible men began to cheer when Lieutenant Innes gave them the command to advance at the charge. Even that stern and upright man would have relished the manner in which he was obeyed, for the charge went in so fast that the French were tumbled out of a position which they might have been able to hold until nightfall. But Innes did not live to see them go, for a French bullet hit him in the chest and he died near the village.

The rout of the French at Orthez completed the Regiment's restoration. Their good opinion of themselves survived the rain, the long pursuit across the south of France, the rotting of their clothes, and the disintegration of their shoes. 'We were hardier and stronger every day,' wrote Anton. 'The more we suffered, the more confidence we felt in our strength. The man in patched clothes and untanned hide about his feet felt a pride in despising any newcomer with dangling plumes, crimped frills, white gloves and handsome shoes.' And back in the ranks, the anonymous private crowed, 'The most self-conceited regiment in the army – a regiment that thought and said there was no regiment under the crown like them.' Who could quarrel with that?

By the end of March, 1814, Soult had led his army into Toulouse, and was busy trying to make it proof against assault. At the same time rumours began to filter south that Napoleon had abdicated, and on the 10th April, more definite information came that Blücher and the Allies were in Paris. The news came too late, for on that day, Easter Sunday, Wellington launched his army against the formidable defences of Toulouse.

From a castle to the west of the town, the 42nd had been watching the fortifications go up. A canal and the river Garonne protected Toulouse on three sides, but what occupied the Regiment's attention was 'behind the town, to the east, a long range of high ground, two or three miles in length, called Mont Gave, upon which we could clearly see the piled arms of the enemy glittering in the morning sun, while the soldiers and working people were busy throwing up works, as we afterwards found to our cost, of a very impregnable nature.' [Diary of Lieutenant McNiven; unpublished.]

Uninviting though it was, Mont Gave presented the only feasible way into Toulouse, and early in April the army circled round the city and encamped a few miles north of it. As at Orthez, the 6th Division were to march alongside the ridge, before cutting in to climb onto its crest. Their attack, about two-thirds of the way down the ridge, was to coincide with an assault by the Spanish on a fortification called the Great Redoubt, at the north or nearest end of Mont Gave.

The Regiment was roused at midnight, and marched off in silence under a clear,

starlit sky. They halted while Colonel Macara was given his instructions, and when the
restarted, the left wing was leading – a detail which produced a malign result later in th
battle. Their path lay along an embankment between the river Ers on their left, and som
marshland on their right. Beyond the marshes, Mont Gave rose bright in the earl
morning sun. The 79th (Camerons) led the brigade along the embankment at a fast tro
while the enemy artillery tried to get the range, but most of their shots were 'overs' which
sent up tall jets of water as they landed in the river. 'We ran along till we came to a plac
where we could leap down and form on the swampy ground. We had scarcely formed whe
a strong column of the enemy with drums beating descended the hill.' ('As if they had bee
going to scare crows from the cornfield,' wrote the private in his account.) The immedia
threat of attack left the 42nd no time to reform, and when they advanced the left wing st.
led. Sergeant Anton continued: 'We were sinking to the ancles and deeper with every ste
The Light Companies of the division were by this time in front, and without hesitatic
dashed forward. We followed fast, and the opposing force reascended the hill.' On th
rising ground they had better footing, and 'we now ascended in double quick time, and th
whole division crowned the southen summit of the heights. Here we were exposed to
destructive fire of shot, shell, grape and musketry.'

This fire came from their right where a long line of fortifications, connected b
trenches, stretched northwards along the spine of Mont Gave to the Great Redoub
Turning to face the fire, the Division advanced a small distance to take cover in a sunke
road which cut across the ridge. In front of them were two notable positions, the near
called the Mas des Augustes, and beyond it the Colombette Redoubt; further still was th
Great Redoubt, which should by this time have been in the hands of the Spanish, but the
gallant attacks had been beaten off, and there was now a lull at the north end of the ridg

Early in the afternoon the Light Companies and a Rifle Corps were sent out in fron
but these skirmishers met such a furious barrage that they returned hastily to th
protection of the road. The enemy began to move towards the Division, and the Gener
ordered the 42nd and 79th Regiments to advance against them by wings, that is, in tw
lines with, by custom, the right or senior wing leading. Unfortunately the Regiment's le
wing was in front, as it had been throughout the day. Anton described what happened.

> The left wing could have sprung up the bank in line and dashed forward on th
> enemy at once. Instead of this, the colonel faced the right wing to its right, counter
> marched in rear of the left, and when it had cleared the left flank it was made to file u
> the bank, and as soon as it had made its appearance, shot, shell and musketry poure
> in. In this exposed position we had to counter-march again to bring our front to th
> enemy.

They were the target of almost every weapon on the ridge, and as they performed the dril
their impatience grew to such a pitch that when at last the order came to charge, the
erupted forward with a shout which Anton thought must have frightened the enemy mo
than any bullet or bayonet. They raced across ploughed land to the Mas des Auguste
There could scarcely have been 150 men left in the wing when they burst into the redoub
It was held by two battalions who unhesitatingly turned and fled from the wrath at hand
Then the line of trenches and breastworks took their attention, and they drove forward
clearing the defenders out of one after the other. A tremendous fire was directed at ther

ɔm the Colombette Redoubt, a fortified cottage in a garden; they returned the fire, then ɔrmed through the surrounding hedges, and threw themselves into the cottage. There nally they succumbed to reality and halted.

Their position, like their performance, was quite impossible. They had advanced far nead of the 79th and their own left wing, and were quite unsupported. An artillery ɔmbardment began from near the Great Redoubt; the enemy brought up three fresh attalions on their flank, and their 'muskets were getting useless by the frequent discharge French muskets lay scattered about, but they were equally unserviceable for the same ason.' Wisely they were ordered to retire which they did, said Anton, 'like a crowd of ɔys pursuing the bounding ball to the distant limit'. The Portuguese relieved the left ing and the 79th in the Mas des Augustes, and the Regiment reformed in the road, aving the French defences in chaos. The reserves were committed, enabling the Great edoubt to be taken, and by nightfall the British held Mont Gave, and with it the key to oulouse.

There were 62 survivors of the right wing, and of the Regiment as a whole, 436 were lled or wounded from the 565 who had begun the day; among the dead was that 'pure ream' Sergeant-Major Clark, who, disdaining to stoop his great height in the road, was ruck in the head by a bullet. Lieutenant McNiven was hit in the side by a musket ball, ɪd described what happened to the many wounded.

He was carried first to a field hospital, where the wound was briefly examined, then ɪndaged up and his bearer directed to the farm-house where the Highland Brigade ɔspital was situated. There he was left on a midden pit. While he lay there, 'Dr Swinton ɪacLeod, the Regimental Surgeon, came to inspect my wound, and finding his probe ɔme upon the ball, introduced his forceps, but come the ball would not.' McNiven inted with pain, and was carried into the house and laid on the floor. There he watched e wounded of the 42nd coming in 'in such numbers and in so mutilated a condition, I ɪgan to think none would be left to tell the tale.' After two days on the farm-house floor, ɪey were moved to hospitals and houses in Toulouse, where they were nursed with traordinary kindness. By then they knew that their final, costly victory, which had 'iven Soult from the city, had been won after peace had been signed.

# CHAPTER 7

# Quatre Bras and Waterloo

Although subsequent events were to show that war was in abeyance rather than ended, t
government wasted no time in reducing the army to its peacetime level. The 2nd Battali
was disbanded, and old soldiers and limited service men like the anonymous private we
discharged. Within a year, Anton reckoned that, even including returned prisoners of w
no more than 50 per cent of the Regiment had served in battle. Those intervening mont
were spent in Ireland, drinking, swapping tall stories with the Irish, and wheedli
accumulations of back-pay from the pay-sergeants. In peacetime these grey eminenc
ruled the inner workings of the Regiment, and their malign influence became all-pervasi
in the long peace after Waterloo. But even in 1814, Anton, a sergeant who had not be
paid for 11 months, could not get his wages until he complained to an officer who sto
over the pay-sergeant while the money was counted out. Those who did get paid tended
celebrate it all away in drink. At their annual Alexandria Ball, the sergeants, 'the select
the ranks for intelligence, temperance and orderly behaviour', let their hair down un
dawn, then staggered back to the barracks, where, to show the staring *canaille* ho
intelligent, temperate, orderly men held their liquor, they danced a reeling reel on t
parade ground.

On the 15th June, 1815 the sergeants danced another, less extravagant reel for t
guests at the Duchess of Richmond's Ball, and when dawn came after that party, they an
the Regiment were marching out of Brussels to the tune of 'Highland Laddie'. Even at th
hour, there were people on the streets to see their departure, and fear for the safety of tho
'charming men with petticoats who, when billeted on the inhabitants, helped to make t
soup, and rock the cradle for the half-frightened mistress of the family'. Indeed, from t
moment they landed in Belgium, their behaviour seems to have won golden opinions fro
everyone, with the notable exception of their colonel. At Ghent the men had been issu
with double-thickness blankets, and it occurred to the sharper-practised of them that
might escape notice if one thickness were detached and sold in lieu of the pay they had n
received. A stringent kit inspection revealed the loss, and the single blanketeers we
flogged. The punishment aroused unusual bitterness, for Macara was not usually so hars
although his rising prospects may have changed his attitude. After Toulouse he had foug
a characteristic, head-on and successful battle to be made a K.C.B. This was not a comm
honour for a colonel, and it held out the promise that he might achieve general rank.

However, there was little on the 16th June to suggest that as Sir Robert he was an
luckier than as Lieutenant-Colonel Macara. From Brussels the Regiment marched to t
assembly point, where 'our brigade, consisting of the 1st, 42nd, 44th and 92nd regimen
stood in column, Sir Denis Pack at its head, waiting impatiently for the 42nd, t

commanding officer of which was chidden severely for being so dilatory.' [Anton, *Retrospect of a Military Life*.] There was some need for haste, for this was the day of real crisis in the Waterloo campaign. Wellington had two, almost contradictory objectives; the first to protect Brussels from westerly attack through Mons, the second to support Blücher's Prussians at Ligny, thirty miles to the south. It was Napoleon's intention to defeat the two armies in detail, thus, while false reports suggested he might advance through Mons, he advanced at speed through Charleroi. There the road forked right to Ligny, some eight miles away, and left to Quatre Bras, Waterloo and Brussels. While Grouchy with 80,000 men marched against Blücher, Ney took 20,000 troops to capture the vital crossroads at Quatre Bras, from which position they could dominate the day, poised either to attack Brussels, or to come in behind the Prussians and complete the destruction of their army.

When true reports of Napoleon's movements came on the night of the 15th June, Wellington exclaimed 'He's humbugged me, by God,' and the success of the humbuggery can be measured by the disposition of his forces – 30,000 guarding the road to Mons, 20,000 in reserve, and only 7,000 guarding the cross-roads. Throughout the 16th the reserve came hurrying down from Brussels, among them Picton's Division with the 42nd in Sir Denis Pack's brigade. It was a swift moving Division, composed largely of riflemen and a Highland brigade which was accustomed to advance almost at a trot under 60 lb packs. Their speed allowed them to play the crucial role in the day, for they arrived at Quatre Bras just as the main obstacle to Ney's capture of the cross-roads, the hill and farm of Quatre Bras, fell into his hands.

The 42nd was posted first, close to the cross-roads, and on their left was General Halkett's brigade containing the 2nd Battalion of the 73rd; thus at Quatre Bras, as later at Waterloo, the two tributaries of The Black Watch were united. With the *savoir-faire* of Peninsular veterans, the 42nd lay down for a light sleep before battle, 'when General Pack came galloping up and chid the Colonel for not having the bayonets fixed. This roused our attention, and the bayonets were instantly on the pieces.' In front of the Regiment was a field of rye growing up to six-feet high; beyond it were open pastures, and to the left the forest of Bossu. At 4.0 p.m., as Ney sent forward his own formidable attack, the 42nd was literally coming through the rye.

'"Forward" was the word of command,' wrote Anton, 'and forward we hastened though we saw no enemy in front. The stalks of rye hindered our advance; the tops were up to our bonnets. By the time we reached a field of clover we were much straggled, however, we united in line as fast as our speedy advance would permit.' Ahead of them, Belgian skirmishers were being thrown back by the French light infantry. The situation was much the same in Bossu Forest, where the Duke of Brunswick's cavalry, followed by the 73rd, advanced parallel to the 42nd. 'The Belgic skirmishers retired through our ranks, and in an instant we were on their victorious pursuers. Our sudden appearance seemed to paralyse their advance. The singular appearance of our dress, combined with our sudden debut tended to stagger their resolution; we were on them, our pieces were loaded and our bayonets glittered.' They drove on fast in the usual manner, but behind his *voltigeours*, Ney had positioned his cavalry – lancers, then heavy *cuirassiers*.

Near Bossu Forest, the lancers broke the Belgians and the Brunswicker cavalry; the 73rd retired into the wood, but both sets of horsemen came galloping across the field.

Macara halted the 42nd in line, thinking they were all Allied cavalry, but Sergeant McEwan, who had been a prisoner of the French, recognised their lancers. Macara refused to accept the identification, but several men fired at them anyway, and the lancers wheeled round towards the Regiment, as a Brunswicker horseman galloped past shouting 'Franchee, Franchee.' A square was the only formation in which to face cavalry, and to form square from line, the centre ranks stood firm, the companies either side of centre fell back to form right and left faces, while the two flank companies ran in to form the rear. The lancers' charge, coming from the rear, arrived before the flank companies could form up, and the horsemen thundered into the square through the open face. In the confused carnage and close-quarter fighting, the command was held by four different officers in as many minutes; Macara was killed, Dick severely wounded, Major Davidson mortally wounded, and Major Campbell survived. The lance had longer reach than the bayonet, and the horse was heavier than the man, but the three sides of the square held firm. Turned towards the centre, the Highlanders inexorably pressed in on the lancers, and the battles in the enclosed space took on the heroic quality of the sagas. There was Captain Menzies, six-and-a-half feet tall, who received no less than seventeen wounds in the maul 'and fourteen of them mortal', he used to declare. There was a favourite story of the Victorians about the lancer faced by a gigantic Highland sergeant wielding an appropriately sized sword. 'Quarter, quarter,' pleaded the lancer. 'Inteet, she's not going to put you in quarters at all,' replied the sergeant reassuringly. 'Chust the two halves.' More authentic was the untold courage with which the Regiment as a whole not only withstood the charge, but, in a rare military feat, eventually closed its square on the horsemen inside, forcing them to surrender or be killed.

Ney's light cavalry had shot their bolt, but as the 42nd began to form line again to continue its advance, Kellermann's heavy cavalry, the *cuirassiers*, were launched in a last bid for victory. 'The fate of France is in your hands,' Ney told them, and under the impetus of their attack success at first seemed possible, for two regiments scattered before them. In the 73rd Private Morris had advanced with a company of skirmishers under the command of a sixty-year-old Captain Robinson whose wits tended to wander so that his mind went blank when the French cavalry came trotting forward. His company waited out in the open while the cavalry came closer and Captain Robinson fumbled for the right words to order the men back to join the 73rd's square. At the last moment the adjutant rode up and gave the command, and they rushed back in time to repel the charge. Baulked there, the same squadron of *cuirassiers* turned against the 42nd.

'Our last file had got into square when the cuirassiers dashed full on two of its faces; their heavy horses and steel armour seemed sufficient to bury us had they been pushed forward onto our bayonets.' There was a momentary hesitation – General Pack had taken refuge in their square, and Major Campbell waited for him to give the order – then the General raised his hat, and with the cavalry closing rapidly, a lethal volley was fired from close range: 'riders cased in heavy armour came tumbling from their horses, which reared, plunged and fell on the dismounted riders, steel helmets and cuirasses rang against unsheathed sabres as they fell on the ground.' In their long jackboots and steel breastplates, the horsemen lay almost helpless, reminding Wellington, who was in the 92nd's square nearby, of 'so many turned turtles'. The firing became general, more horsemen fell, and those still able to do so rode back to the French lines.

More than any other battle since Alexandria, Quatre Bras shows the 42nd at its best; the extraordinary resistance of the uncompleted square to the lancers' charge, the disciplined fire which broke the *cuirassiers,* and that they had accomplished these feats at the crucial stage in the battle when Ney was on the brink of victory, justified Wellington in selecting the Regiment as one of only four for special mention in his despatch from Quatre Bras.

The 42nd maintained their position, one so far advanced that they were fired on from flank and rear, until evening, and then, reduced by 280 casualties, they withdrew from the field as the remainder of the reserves arrived to relieve them. Six miles away the Prussians were retreating from Ligny, and they were able to continue their withdrawal without interference, for the next day, the 17th June, Napoleon switched the direction of his advance from Ligny to Quatre Bras. That position, however, was no longer occupied, for the Allies had fallen back on their commander's chosen position at Mont St Jean, a few miles south of Waterloo.

The 42nd, the main stream of The Black Watch, was not directly involved in the fighting at Waterloo until late in the battle, but that short-lived tributary, the 2nd Battalion of the 73rd, ended its brief history by playing a vital part in Wellington's victory.

The 73rd had begun its life as the 2nd Battalion of the 42nd, but was established as a separate corps in 1785 and, in 1809, raised its own 2nd Battalion. While stationed in London, the 2nd Battalion enlisted a gossipy Cockney, Tom Morris, who combined the love of a good story with his passionate admiration of Napoleon to write a critical but entertaining account of the Regiment. In 1813, the Battalion sailed in a British force to the Baltic to aid the Alliance against Napoleon. The British were not intended for battle, but only to release Swedish troops from guarding Pomerania. However, General Gibbs soon took the 73rd stravaiging across Europe in search of some fighting. They covered thirty miles a day through a devastated country inhabited only by the old and children, where fields were unharvested and no animals remained. 'During our forced marches through Germany,' wrote Morris, 'the most serviceable man we had was our old Scotch bagpiper, Hugh MacKay, who, when the men were fatigued, on receiving a hint from the Colonel would fall back to the rear, and striking up some lively tune on his pipes, and pushing forward at a brisk pace, would soon have the whole regiment about him like a cluster of bees.' Alone among the 73rd, MacKay still wore the Black Watch kilt, for the Regiment by that time had taken to breeches, in common with other Highland corps.

At Gorhde, they eventually stumbled on a battle, most opportunely as Count Walmoden was attacking Davoust's Frenchmen who threatened to break past the Allied line. The French were posted on two hills, from which they had already repulsed attacks by the Prussian cavalry. Walmoden now approached Colonel George Harris of the 73rd. 'Addressing our Commanding Officer, he said "Colonel I want that hill taken," pointing to the one with the two pieces of cannon and about a thousand men on it. "Will you charge them, Colonel?" "Yes sir".' And thus simply, if Morris is to be believed, the Battalion was launched on its first battle. Walmoden offered a Hanoverian regiment in support, but Colonel Harris declined the offer; and indeed it was unnecessary for when the 73rd charged up the slope, the sight of the Regimental Colours and the line of British redcoats caused the French to lose heart, and they fled almost before the 73rd reached them. The collapse of the centre broke open the position, and both hills were taken without further difficulty.

Morris was quite definite about the effect of the red coats on French morale, and cited another example later in the year, when the Regiment joined Sir Thomas Graham's expeditionary force in Flanders. In freezing weather, the men, wearing dark greatcoats, attacked the French outside Antwerp, and at first the fighting was most severe, but when Graham ordered them to remove their greatcoats to reveal their identity, the French again retired. The shadow of the Peninsula must have loomed very large across France, but despite its influence, the Flemish campaign achieved only partial success. During the advance on Antwerp the country was flooded and frozen, and in one action the 73rd fought across an icebound lake which eventually broke beneath the weight of French troops struggling to escape. In a snowstorm the Battalion captured a village on the very outskirts of Antwerp, but then the heavy guns in the city began to shell them, and poor Graham, starved of ammunition for his own guns, had to withdraw his forces. The great fortress of Bergen op Zoom was stormed, but before the larger part of the army could join them the assaulters were culpably taken by surprise and thrown out.

Like Abercromby, Sir Thomas Graham took to soldiering late in life, and for a strange reason; his wife died in Italy, and as her body was being brought home across France, the French burst the coffin open to examine its contents. The outraged Graham raised his own regiment, the 90th Perthshire Light Infantry, to inflict some retaliation. In the Peninsula he became a general, one of the few Wellington trusted to operate independently, and from Barossa in the south to Vittoria in the north, he exacted a notable revenge for his dead wife. If Flanders failed to give further satisfaction, the French were not left for long in possession of their fortresses, for in May, 1814 Napoleon abdicated, and the garrisons surrendered.

When peace came Morris used the phrase 'Peace is war, and war is peace', to decribe the changed relationship between officers and men. In place of the intimate routine of war, there were endless parades, inspections and punishments, 'the average punishment for slight offences was 300 lashes,' he wrote. What rankled with him was the absence of compensatory rewards for good behaviour; N.C.O.s could be broken at a word from an officer, and commissions from the ranks were rare. The outburst of affection with which the French soldiers greeted Napoleon on his return from Elba was due, Morris thought, to the Emperor's habit of promoting soldiers on merit, and Morris' admiration for the man and his system was not qualified, even by memories of Quatre Bras and Waterloo.

The Allies had fallen back on Waterloo on the evening of the 17th June through a heavy thunderstorm which continued to drench both armies through the night. When the rain ceased at dawn, the men were stiff with cold or shivering uncontrollably, although Morris himself 'having shaved and put on a clean shirt, felt tolerably comfortable'. To his right he could see an infantry square, composed of the 33rd and 69th regiments, and beyond it Hougomont Farm, occupied by the Guards. The 73rd itself was in square with the 30th, while some distance to their left lay Pack's brigade, with the 42nd, posted behind La Haye Sainte.

For most of the morning, the Regiment slept beneath the thunderous duel of more than three hundred cannon, but the Light Company was sent out just before mid-day to repel French sharp-shooters. When Morris awoke, he was detailed to draw the company rations, and, like a good forager, collected the gin ration for the full complement, although many had fallen at Quatre Bras. After everyone was served, Morris proposed to share what was left over with his sergeant, a fellow-Londoner, but he was told to keep it for after the battle; 'there is no shot made yet for you or me,' said the sergeant, thus proving that even Cockneys have second sight.

A verse in the 73rd's song describes their exploits at Waterloo:

> A troop of the French cavalry came bravely charging down,
>> We were ordered to form solid square, and quickly it was done,
> But when their Colonel came in sight our numbers for to see,
>> He quickly cried, 'Retraite mes braves, for them's the 7 and 3.

The account, which follows, more than justifies these lines.

There were three ranks in the front face of their square, the first two kneeling, and the rear standing. Early in the afternoon they received the first charge of *cuirassiers*. They held their fire until the horsemen were ten paces away, then the rear rank fired. As the horses wheeled and plunged, the two front ranks each fired in turn, and there was no need for the fourth volley, which the rear rank now had ready. When the next charge came, Wellington rode into their square, and Morris was much distracted, with the Iron Duke behind, the steel-helmeted *cuirassiers* in front, and the soldier on his right muttering a malapropism, 'Tom, Tom, here comes the calvary.' That charge too was repulsed, but then, ominously, they saw artillery being wheeled into position. They could see the guns being loaded with grape shot, the charge rammed home, and the touch-light applied. The grapeshot tore

> complete lanes through us; and then the horsemen came up to dash in at the openings. But before they reached us, we had closed our files, throwing our dead outside, and taking our wounded inside the square, when they were again forced to retire. They did not, however, go further than the pieces of cannon – waiting there to try the effect of some more grapeshot. We saw the match applied, and again it came thick as hail upon us.

Men were falling by dozens with each shot, yet with the *cuirassiers* close at hand, they could not move, and when a large shell landed just in front of the square, they had to watch its fuse burning down, 'wondering how many of us it would destroy. When it burst about seventeen men were killed or wounded by it.'

'The Duke of Wellington riding by, addressed our general with "Well Halkett, how do you get on?" "My lord, we are damnably cut up; can you not relieve us for a little while?" "Impossible," said the Duke. "Very well, my lord, we'll stand till the last man falls".' By that time the crisis of the battle had been reached. The 73rd's ammunition was spent, and they could only watch as the French cavalry walked their horses up to the bayonet-points, but although the *cuirassiers* cut and thrust at the men behind, they still could not break through.

At last Wellington felt confident enough to release his own cavalry. From behind the 73rd, the Life Guards came trotting out, and the battered infantry watched their charge remove the menace of cannon and *cuirassiers*. Further to the left, the tide of French attack mounted past La Haye Sainte, until the very ridge of Mont St Jean seemed in danger. At the critical moment, the Highland Brigade was ordered forward. They were pushing

PLATE 9    *'If it be windy!' Paris, 1815.*

painfully through a hedge of holly, when the thudding of hooves was heard behind. With a roar of 'Scotland for ever', the Scots Greys came thundering through and, as they passed, the Highlanders plucked at their stirrup leathers to be carried into battle by those massive horses. The irresistible surge swept the French infantry off the ridge, past La Haye Sainte and into the valley, and the position was never again threatened. Late in the day, the Imperial Guard was thrown in, but even they broke on those immovable squares, and when evening and the Prussians came, the 73rd stood within fifty yards of the place it had occupied at morning.

For the victors of Waterloo the reward was Paris. The city was thronged with visitors, ministers, chancellors, generals and royalty, before whom the Allied armies paraded in a display of colour more varied than a herbaceous border. From The Black Watch tartan to the white tunics of the Austrians, the uniforms spanned the spectrum, and of reds there was every shade to which the dye on a British infantryman's coat could fade. Off-duty soldiers went when they could to gaze at the treasures that Napoleon had looted, and on duty the 73rd supervised the removal from Paris of the four most famous pieces, the bronze horses stolen from San Marco in Venice. But the kilted 42nd were objects of display themselves. Tremulously the Parisian ladies admired their thighs and 'as they eyed the short kilts through their lorgnettes, confided their fears to each other in whispers, "My dear, if it be windy!"' Tsar Alexander III was bolder. Inspecting six men from the kilted regiments, his curiosity about the famous mystery could not be restrained, and one of the sergeants wrote indignantly, that the Tsar 'pinched my skin, thinking that I wore something under my kilt, and had the curiosity to lift my kilt to my navel that he might not be deceived.'

In December, 1815 the 42nd returned to Britain. They marched north through a crescendo of rapturous greeting. When they halted, the men were fêted for the heroes they were, and at each new halt the gifts were greater and the drinks deeper, until they arrived in Edinburgh 'to the most distinguished reception a regiment had ever had. Two nights free to the Theatre, two to the Olympic Circus, two to the panoramic view of Waterloo, and an entertainment at the Assembly Rooms.' On that seventh night the occasion was Lucullan. They were feasted on roast beef and plum pudding, and their glasses were kept filled with enough wine and whisky to sate the thirsts of even those mighty cupmen. It ended with a speech from Sir Walter Scott comparing them to mythical and classical heroes beyond their ken, and then the soldiers heaved themselves to their feet, for the return through the cold winter evening to Edinburgh Castle. 'We marched as if a whirlwind had been blowing amongst us, and sweeping us out of our ranks,' wrote Sergeant Anton. 'At North Bridge our heads were knocking against the balustrade . . . . by the time our front files reached the Castle, the rear were groping their way down the High Street. No lives were lost, though many a bonnet and kilt changed owners.'

There was nothing moderate about those veterans of the 42nd, if they were excessive in their carousing, they were equally excessive in their courage and that in the end was what counted. In the summing up, all their crimes, their drinking, brawling and marauding, counted for nothing beside their impeccable behaviour in battle, and it was clearly with that in mind that the Duke of Wellington said late in life, 'I could have done anything with that army. It was in such perfect order.'

CHAPTER 8

# The Reformers

'Long wars make good soldiers,' commented Sergeant Anton, and by the end of the Peninsular War, it was clear that the 42nd were extremely good soldiers; the long pursuit at Orthez, the manoeuvre and charge at Toulouse, and closing of the square at Quatre Bras stand out as examples of extraordinary endurance and discipline and in Wellington's army there were no more valuable qualities than these.

Accordingly, in the long years of peace which followed, the Regiment's reputation sailed high, and the interest in things Highland, which Walter Scott and Queen Victoria promoted in their different ways, carried its good name higher still, so that when war came in 1854, an heroic performance was expected of them. In the theatrical setting of the Alma, that expectation was amply satisfied, which immediately begs a question of Sergeant Anton: how could a long peace make soldiers as good as his Peninsular veterans?

It is more remarkable than it might seem, that the 42nd should have maintained its standards over forty years of peace. A general's mind may be confidently relied upon to retain the impressions of a campaign for forty years or more, but a regiment must renew itself continually. Reckoning fifteen years as the life of a soldier, it was the third generation since Waterloo that faced the Crimean test; if they passed it more successfully than others, then their preparation deserves some credit. In fact, the history of the 42nd in these years illustrates exactly how it was possible to produce a good regiment in a thoroughly bad army.

Reminiscing in 1871, General Sir Duncan Cameron, who led the Regiment at the Alma, gave as his opinion that most of the credit was due to Sir Charles Gordon, who commanded from 1828 to 1835, and to John Wheatley, adjutant from 1832 to 1838. Theirs was a time of reform, and to understand its significance, it is necessary to look at the immediate post-Waterloo generation.

Wheatley enlisted in 1817, and in an account published many years later, he described the Regiment as 'a badly regulated one at the time, and for many years after.' He had particularly in mind the destructive power of the pay-sergeants which was allowed to flourish untrammelled by the interference of officers. Sooner or later everyone came under their influence, but for most it started when they bought their kit as recruits. Theoretically the bounty covered the cost, but in practice, as the uniform became more extravagant, the price of kit rose to almost £7 – rather more than the bounty itself – and the recruit had no choice but to buy his clothes on credit. On a weekly wage of 7/- a week, the new soldier could be in debt for over £6, and his creditor was the man who paid over his wages, the pay-sergeant of his company.

However, this was only the recruit's way into the vicious circle; a soldier might join at any time in a variety of ways. From his 7/- wage, 6d was deducted for washing his clothes, and 3/- as a contribution to the breakfast mess (instituted in 1819) for which 'each room laid in a supply of beef, oatmeal and potatoes for the week'. The only other meal of the day was dinner, and for that the government provided a pound of 'poor, half-fed beef', including the bone, fat and gristle. Its cooking was primitive, for each soldier simply tied a rag round his portion to identify it, and dropped it in a cauldron of boiling water. As Fortescue remarked in his history of the army, the government seemed to expect a soldier to live on boiled beef and broth throughout his career. These two meals were hardly sufficient to satisfy a soldier's appetite, and in consequence 'the greater proportion of young soldiers spent their weekly surplus' after deductions for washing and mess 'before the second day had passed on bread and butter, and many of the older ones on drink, for verily we were a drouthy set.' If the prospect of five days' unassuaged hunger or thirst seemed overpowering, the pay-sergeant offered a solution. The soldier could purchase a shirt for 7/6d (twice the normal price), and the pay-sergeant would buy it back from him for 2/6d cash. One man had no less than twenty-two shirts charged against him in eleven months.

An accident could put a man in the pay-Shylock's clutches. From 1816 to 1820, the bonnet was sixteen-inches high, open at the side and without a chinstrap. This 'craw's wing' seemed almost designed to be lifted off and sent bowling away by a gust of wind, and with it went three weeks' wages. The shoes, nicknamed 'toecases' because they were so thin and slender, quickly disintegrated or simply fell off, and on rainy days when mounting guard at Dublin Castle in 1819, men would commonly finish the march to the castle shoeless. Yet the footwear was expected to last for two years, and replacements cost 2/- a pair.

It was easy to be in debt, but paying back was painful. 'So many men were perpetually in debt to the pay-sergeants that all extra payments were absorbed in the liquidation of the debt.' In 1819 Ireland was gripped by famine, and the price of potatoes soared so high that an extra 3d a day was paid to the men to cover the cost. If that went instead to pay off debts, the man ate less, and if the debt were very pressing, the pay-sergeant could allow the man to leave the mess, and make over his 3/- a week breakfast money. Wheatley described the result. 'The wretched man lived on 2d a day, for which he supplied himself with sour milk and potatoes. When nearly out of debt, many of them drifted into it again. And continued in the same way until they became poor, emaciated creatures, unfit for service, and discharged without a pension.' It was literally a rake's progress.

Wheatley went on: 'It may be doubted that such doings could be carried on, and reasonably be asked, "What were the officers about?"' While the Regiment was in Ireland, officers rarely appeared in barracks, and indeed Sergeant Wheatley's detachment was stationed at Omagh for six months, during which time 'no officers ever appeared on parade, nor visited a barrack room'.

There were several reasons for the officers' aloofness. Outside Dublin most of the barracks had been built for cavalry acting to enforce the law. As a result, they were small, designed to hold a squadron at most, and, like police-stations, they were scattered across the country. The Regiment, therefore, was always split up. In 1819 the officers had instituted their own mess, and they tended thereafter to stay together in the town where

the headquarters was situated, rather than to live separately in villages with their companies. Another malign result stemmed from Wellington's encouragement of riding amongst
his officers. Since the kilt led to chafed thighs, officers in the 42nd habitually wore an
almost Ruritanian costume of sky-blue trousers laced with gold or 'white Cashmere
pantaloons with short Hessian, tasseled boots', the whole topped by the craw's wing or
later the feather bonnet. These clothes did not distinguish officers so much as set them
apart from their men, and they became so reluctant to risk their fineries in bad weather that
Wheatley recalled one period of three weeks when all parades were called off because of
rain. What Lord Blantyre might have said may be imagined; in the 79th Colonel Cameron
fulminated in writing against officers, who 'being accustomed to wear breeches [are]
consequently averse to that free congenial, circulation of pure wholesome air (as an
exhilarating native bracer) which has hitherto so befitted the Highlander for activity.' On
the rare occasions when officers had to wear the kilt, they complained so bitterly that the
men quite naturally began to resent having to wear such an inferior garment themselves.
Not until Duncan Cameron became Colonel and put the officers back in the kilt did that
particular grievance disappear.

However, the strongest excuse for an officer's lack of interest in his men lay in the
contemporary attitude to his job. A commission was property, worth between £1,500 (for
an ensigncy) and £7,000 (for a colonelcy), for which an officer received a wage roughly
equal to the return he might have expected if he had invested the money in land. The cost
of messing and uniforms made it difficult to pretend that it was a good investment, but on
the other hand there was also a gambling element. A convenient death by war or illness
might promote an officer to a more valuable property without his having to pay for it, and
if, more rarely still, he attained the colonelcy of a regiment, he became an entrepreneur
with a monopoly for clothing his men, from which he could make £1,000 a year.

Since promotion did not depend on merit, there was no incentive for an officer to do
his job properly, but Wheatley described one who did, and it suggests some of the
opportunities which were missed. 'Captain Alexander Fraser looked upon his company as
a family, ready with advice on their private concerns, as well as on matters military. He was
the banker for his men before savings banks were known, and was the cause of much
benefit, especially to the married men.'

It would be inaccurate, however, to leave an impression of the 42nd at this time as a
corps of starvelings indifferently commanded by peacocks. 'While all this was going on,'
wrote Wheatley, 'the Regiment was remarkable for its appearance and field discipline.'
The reports of general inspections are quite unstinted in their praise, and although the
standards of inspections were less rigorous than later, there were clearly other elements to
the Regiment which have not so far been considered. The most obvious was Dr Dick's
gallant son who had, on Macara's death at Quatre Bras, become the commanding officer.
Throughout his career, he set and obtained the highest standards on parade and in the
field, and some years after he left the Regiment he was promoted Major-General, became
Colonel of the 73rd, and died a hero's death in 1846 in India. His strictness was legendary,
on a par with that martinet, Duncan Cameron, and though he might not have shown
much interest in the men's welfare, their self-confidence clearly flourished under his
command.

In Dublin the 42nd was quartered with the 93rd (Sutherland), 'the soberest and best

PLATE 10 *Major-General Sir Robert Dick* KCB. *Commanded the 42nd from 1815 to 1828, became Colonel of the 73rd and died a hero's death in India in 1846.*

conducted corps in the Army' in Wheatley's opinion, although the rest of the Regiment considered them milksops because they had not served in the Peninsula. One night Wheatley overheard a revealing, libellous and extravagant rebuke from a 93rd officer to one of his men. 'Dougal MacIntosh, you're a disgrace,' said the officer. 'You're as drunken as a Royal man [Royal Scots], as saucy as a 7th man [Fusiliers], as proud as a 42nd man, and as dirty as a 91st man [Argylls].' If its outstanding characteristic was pride, the 42nd was not in such bad shape.

Unfortunately, to allow his men to express their good opinion of themselves, Colonel Dick indulged his perfectly deplorable taste for designing flashy uniforms. Apart from the white cashmere pantaloons, which must have had his sanction, the sixteen-inch craw's wing and the buckled toecase were his innovations. As an economy, he replaced the four-yard plaid with one of four feet ('that pinafore' said Anton contemptuously), and he battled to add wings to the uniform. The long-suffering Colonel of the Regiment, the Marquis of Huntly, was not enthusiastic. 'You should think only of the wings of love,' he said, but the wings of dress made the men's shoulders look broader, and Dick insisted. They were finally added, after his departure, in 1830. The men were only too glad to pay for these gaudies. Feather bonnets replaced the craw's wing at a cost of 30/- to them, the sergeants provided the silver lace for their coats, and other extravagances multiplied.

> White leather, pipeclayed gloves were also part of the soldier's uniform, and 'gloves off' became a regular word of command before the manual and platoon exercises. In short, what with shoes, buckles, frills, a stock up to the ears, about six yards of garters on each leg, muskets with clear locks – burnished in many cases – and beeswaxed stocks and barrels, they were a most singularly equipped set of soldiers.

Oddly enough, Dick was extremely lax about the one item of dress which seems important today, the Red Hackle. The Regiment's exclusive right to the 'Red Vulture Feather' had been made clear by the Adjutant-General in 1822, yet three years later when Sir George Murray, the new Colonel of the Regiment, appeared on parade wearing a red hackle himself, the Regiment still wore a variety of colours – 'Grenadiers white, Light Company green, the Band white about one fifth red, Drummers yellow with about one fifth red. Sir George was under the impression that the red feather was a particular mark of distinction granted to the Regiment, and desired in future "that the red feather should be worn by everyone in the Regiment."' His wish was met, and since then the Red Hackle has been worn on whatever headgear the Regiment has found itself wearing – feather bonnets, Wolseley helmets, glengarries, and Tam O' Shanters – and it has taken on the same significance as the tartan as the outward and visible sign of the Regiment's identity.

In its pride and its finery, in its cramped, unhealthy barracks, and in its disciplined, drunken, hungry men, the 42nd was an outstanding example of the post-Waterloo army, but while the rest of the army stood still for the next thirty years with disastrous consequences, the Regiment was about to be transformed.

In 1825, the Regiment left Ireland for Gibraltar. Little had changed since it was last on the Rock, although the New Mole was at last completed. Otherwise, Gibraltar itself remained a little village nestling in farmland beneath the Rock. Soldiers were still confined to its two-and-a-half square miles, for fear that, if they were allowed to cross the border to visit Spain, they might desert, and that little patch of land could be their home for more than a decade. The annual death-rate continued to run at about 28 per thousand men, and the only recreation continued to be drinking. The food, however, had deteriorated. The government beef ration for dinner was salted six days a week, and fresh on only one. Wheatley noticed, to his dismay that, in 1827, the salt meat was being taken from barrels stamped 1812 and 1814; it was known as 'the mahogany', while the fresh was 'so blubbery that it would hardly lye on the hand-barrow carrying it to the Cook-house'.

Three years after it arrived, an epidemic decimated the garrison, 422 men dying in the six regiments there, of which the 42nd's loss was 54. It raged for seven months; at first men volunteered to work in the hospitals, but they died as quickly as the patients – one of the last to volunteer from the 42nd did so with the brave words, 'I want to know the grand secret,' and his wish was granted within three days. The only antidote suggested was calomel, a solution of mercury which acted as an emetic, and which Anton considered to be as deadly as the disease. The confined and cramped garrison made it easy for infection to spread, but the appalling diet, the boredom and consequent heavy drinking, undoubtedly weakened the men so that they had little strength to fight off sickness.

This was the situation into which Sir Charles Gordon swept as a reformer. He succeeded Dick as Colonel in 1828, and came out to Gibraltar a year later. His first action was as brave and as unpopular an action as a new commanding officer could take – he cancelled the top bibulous event of the year, the sergeants' Waterloo Ball. Drunkenness was abhorrent to Gordon, and he came from a regiment where it was still rare, the 93rd Sutherland Highlanders, the youngest and most fiercely Highland of the kilted regiments. The officers preserved a clannish sense of responsibility for their men, and the men were sober, upright and religious. Posted to South Africa, they had put aside part of their wages to pay the stipend of a Presbyterian minister for the Regiment while they were out there, and with the encouragement of their officers they saved money to send home, over £500 being remitted. These were the customs which Gordon intended to introduce.

Drinking was the first problem. It was encouraged partly by the example of the sergeants, and partly by tradition – 'a growing lad, if detected eating at an unusual time, was very apt to be hailed with a volley of, why did he not spend his pay like a soldier, that is to say in drink' – but above all else, men drank because they were bored. There simply was nothing else to do when parades were finished. The merit of Gordon's reforms was that they attempted to deal with the causes of drinking; thus he not only cancelled the sergeants' jamboree and curtailed the hours of the Regimental 'wet' canteen which normally sold spirits through the day, he also started a Regimental library, tried to get permission for off-duty men to visit Spain, and persuaded the War Office to introduce a rota system among the Mediterranean stations so that the garrison in Gibraltar was relieved after three or four years rather than being cooped up for ten or twelve.

The library was opened in 1830, and proved at once how much it was needed. Within a few hours, there were 224 subscribers, who each paid six days' wages to join. By the time it was broken up in 1854, it consisted of 3,000 volumes. Quite apart from the pleasure the library gave, it saved lives by giving the men some other recreation than drinking, and for the next quarter of a century, the number of deaths in the Regiment from disease was less than a quarter of what would normally have been expected. As a measure of Gordon's far-sightedness, it was not until the 1860s that a garrison library was introduced in Gibraltar, but when it did come, the annual death-rate dropped by 50 per cent.

But the path of a reformer is filled with pitfalls. Everyone warned Gordon that, if men were allowed to cross the frontier to visit Spain, they would certainly desert. The Colonel insisted that the risk be taken, and men duly deserted, including three from the 42nd, two of whom returned, however, by way of France and England. On the other hand, the rota system among the Mediterranean garrisons was introduced, and the 42nd was one of the first to benefit, when it sailed for Malta in June, 1832.

On the island Wheatley was commissioned and later made adjutant. For fifteen years he had seen the corruption of the pay-sergeants, and now he had his chance. In 1833 the system was exposed, and the money-lending operation on which they thrived was stamped out, and once stamped out, both married and single men were encouraged to save money and send their savings home. Before that time, 'single men did not remit money, and any who did were looked upon with something approaching contempt'. Although the 93rd had encouraged soldiers to send money home, it was so uncommon that even twenty-one years later the Secretary for War could declare quite unequivocally, 'The soldier is not a remitting animal.'

Admirable as these reforms were, there was no guarantee that they would persist so long as the officers remained uninterested in the welfare of their men, and so the alteration of officers' attitudes to their job must be accounted the most significant of all the reforms which Gordon and Wheatley introduced. In 1834 subalterns of the 42nd were required to answer a questionnaire designed to test how much they knew about the men in their company. The very first question, as one might expect, was 'Are you satisfied with the conduct of the Pay Sergeant of the Company?', and later 'Which men are habitually in debt?' The subaltern was also expected to know who the best duty-sergeant was, whether the lance-corporals could take orders, the state of the men's muskets and marksmanship, how many married men there were in the company, about the conduct of their wives, the price of food, of equipment, and who was out of mess. It would be impossible to answer all those questions unless the officer took a close interest in his men, and had some concern for their welfare.

For the 42nd, 1834 marked both the beginning of the modern conception of an officer's duties, and a return to the idea of them which had been held in the earliest days of the Regiment. Unfortunately, the Regiment's example was not followed by the rest of the army and, in the winter of 1854/5, London was filled with officers from other regiments who, because they were bored or cold, had abandoned their men in the Crimea. It could hardly have been coincidence that three times as many of their men died from disease as in the 42nd; indeed it would be more accurate to say that many of their men simply died from neglect.

One question the subalterns were asked must be considered by itself: 'How many men are at school?' The answer for the Light Company was six, the same as the number of illiterates. The school was probably another of Gordon's innovations, although there had been a schoolmaster-sergeant in the Regiment as early as 1803. It seems likely, however, that his job was only to teach English to monoglot Gaelic-speakers, and the post does not seem to have existed in Colonel Dick's time. To put this innovation in context, it may be noted that Florence Nightingale's suggestion of a school for soldiers in the Crimea provoked the reply, 'You will only spoil the brutes.'

The Regiment went to Corfu in 1834, and the following year Sir Charles Gordon died in a Swiss sanatorium. But the line of succession by which his ideas flowed is clear. Wheatley remained as adjutant until 1838, when he was succeeded by Duncan Cameron, the very man who led the Regiment at the Alma, and commanded it during the bitter winter it spent in the valley of Balaclava. Twenty-six years later when, as General Sir Duncan, he paid tribute to the work of Charles Gordon and John Wheatley, he added of the latter that 'he had put a stamp on the regiment which it still preserved'. To that compliment, Wheatley, looking back over the half-century which had taken him from private to lieutenant-colonel, replied, 'I was once, and once only, a great man, and that was when I was adjutant in the 42nd.'

Twenty years after it had left Edinburgh, the Regiment returned there in October, 1836. The popularity of the army had faded since their last triumphal appearance in the city. Reduced expenditure was demolishing its supply system, the Royal Waggon Train; medical services had been cut to a fragment, and the number of troops was reduced at every opportunity. Three-quarters of the army was employed abroad, and since the home troops included the Guards, who did not travel, and a disproportionate number of cavalry to assist the yeomanry in quelling civil disturbance, an infantry regiment rarely stayed home for long. Two years after they arrived, the 42nd set out again on the same route as before, to Ireland for three years, and then to the Mediterranean.

They took with them a new recruit in the person of John Drysdale. Like Wheatley, he was to have a moment of glory as adjutant, but a moment also of personal disaster. His diary reveals a very Victorian traveller, fascinated to the point of pedantry by foreign climes, peoples and customs – one intriguing piece of information he recorded was that in Corfu the Gaelic speakers in the Regiment could understand the speech of the Albanian policemen on the island – but it also, unconsciously, reveals an extraordinary change in the character of the sergeants, the heart of the Regiment. Wheatley described an N.C.O. at Waterloo: 'John Forbes was an extraordinary specimen of ignorance, scarcely spoke English, and a wonder to many as an N.C.O. Still at this time there were many sergeants who could not read or write, gallant soldiers and highly respected by officers and men.' He cited, as examples, Sergeant George MacDonald, who had been chosen to appear before the Tsar, and Sergeant William Grant, who was known to his men, simply and respectfully as 'The Gallant'.

Compare that description with one of Sergeant Drysdale and two colour sergeants who, after the Regiment arrived in Malta in 1842, took their Bibles to St Paul's Bay to read the last chapter of the Acts of the Apostles *in situ*; and to judge by the letters of two other sergeants, it would seem that the Victorian habit of reading works of devotion had become quite common among the N.C.O.s.

While they were in Malta, they were joined by the Reserve Battalion, which was raised in 1842. Its birth had not been a particularly easy one. It was formed largely from 'Scotch volunteers' from English regiments, and, after much prodding and menacing by the Commander-in-Chief, a quota of sixty-five men was drawn from each of the three Highland regiments stationed in Britain, the 79th, 92nd and 93rd. Either several regiments took the opportunity of ridding themselves of their black sheep, or the tug of regimental loyalty was exceptionally strong, for eventually the 42nd received the following rocket:

> The attention of the military authorities has been attracted to the alarming extent to which Desertion has recently taken place in the Reserve Battalion. [It has] gone on increasing until the unprecedented number of 34 men have gone off within a single month. If immediate steps are not taken to check desertion, the Commander-in-Chief will be compelled to fill up by recruiting throughout the Empire.

Since the Empire by now spanned the globe, the threat was dire enough to have its effect, and normal recruiting methods soon made up for those lost. The two Battalions together numbered some 1,200 men.

Only eight years after he had enlisted, and while the Regiment was still at Malta, Drysdale was made sergeant-major. In 1847 both Battalions sailed to Bermuda, and soon after their arrival, he was commissioned an ensign. His company's duties were largely ceremonial, interspersed with periods guarding the naval dockyard and convict hulks on Ireland Island.

Life in an isolated and confined garrison was so claustrophobic that tempers quickly became charged. During the 1820s, when the Regiment had been in Gibraltar, the adjutant had challenged the assistant surgeon to a duel after a quarrel at whist, and both men had to be sent home. Later, while Gordon was on leave, the Major in command became unbalanced, and subjected the Regiment to a reign of terror in which most of the N.C.O.s were court-martialed, the Drum-Major was broken to private, and the Regimental Sergeant Major was threatened with imprisonment. The Regimental tailor was so driven to distraction that he tried to shoot the Major but, being the tailor, he missed at point-blank range to the disappointment of the entire Regiment.

In Bermuda there was more space, but six hundred miles of ocean separated them from the nearest land, and the monotony of their life can be gathered from a day repeated a thousand times in Drysdale's diary. 'Guard relief 8 am. Parade 9.30. Orderly Room 10. Defaulters 12.0. Parade 5.0 pm. Guard mounting 10.0 pm. Temperature 75.' Occasionally there were echoes of the outside world. 'July 21st 1848 News of disturbances in Paris, 25,000 people killed. Orderly Room 11 am etc.' '13 November 1848. Settled that the Evening Mail, Edinburgh Advertiser, Quarterly Review, Edinburgh Review and Blackwood's Magazine be ordered for the mess.' (A judicious mixture of Whig and Tory publications.)

In December, 1848 Drysdale was appointed adjutant; it had been a rapid, flawless advance, and perhaps he allowed his pride to show a little. He always handled men superbly on parade, but apparently he was a little too free with advice for brother-officers who were less able. He was not popular, and one officer in particular, Captain Rollo, who later succeeded Cameron as Colonel of the Regiment, spoke to him sharply on several occasions. Pitifully few officers came to visit him and his wife. Then, in February, 1849, appears an entry, *'Placed under arrest'*. His crime was to have authorised the release of three corporals whom Rollo had confined to the guardroom. Drysdale's punishment was to be removed from the adjutancy. There were two reasons for such a harsh decision. Colonel Duncan Cameron never tolerated the slightest infringement of authority, whether it was exercised by himself, a captain or a corporal. When a court-martial sentenced a

PLATE 11    *Sir John MacDonald* GCB, *Colonel of the Regiment, 1844*–50.

private to ten days' hard labour for accusing a corporal of having his handkerchief, the members of the court received a stinging rebuke from Cameron for their undue leniency. The second reason was Drysdale's unpopularity, which became intolerable in an isolated garrison. From Wheatley, he learned 'that I had presumed to joke, that I was too free in passing an opinion on drill, etc.' He allowed himself one line of self-pity: 'Poor Drysdale, he rose from the Ranks', then threw himself back into his work.

There must have been a widespread sense that he had been unfairly treated, for his diary is soon filled with visits and invitations from brother-officers, including several from Captain Rollo. Before the Regiment left Bermuda, Colonel Cameron unbent sufficiently to tell Drysdale that he was 'a zealous officer who performed his duties in exemplary manner, but he wanted judgement'. That quality apparently developed in Nova Scotia two years later, for there he was reappointed adjutant.

In April, 1850 the Reserve Battalion was amalgamated with the 1st, and the occasion offers a particularly acute example of the gambling element in promotion. The year before, Major Dunsmure had offered to buy Colonel MacDougall's commission. Initially his offer had been refused, but he steadily increased his bid until at £7,000 – £2,500 above par – it was accepted. Now, as Colonel Dunsmure, he was placed on half-pay due to the amalgamation, and his property became worthless. Others suffered, too: sergeants being reduced to corporal, and corporals to private. Three companies were detached to form a depot in Scotland, and the rest of the Regiment sailed for Nova Scotia in 1851, leaving behind in Bermuda one memorial to their stay which still exists, the Black Watch well, dug during a long drought.

For a Highland regiment, Nova Scotia was an extremely congenial posting, so much so that in 1853, when the 42nd was ordered home, over 100 men volunteered to transfer to the relieving regiment or to the Canadian Militia. About the same number, who had served their time, were discharged after the return to England and, to take their place, almost 200 English and Irish were hurriedly recruited, for by then there were signs of imminent war.

CHAPTER 9

# The Crimean War

Throughout the nineteenth century it was British policy to protect the Ottoman Empire, both as a counterweight to Russia, and to safeguard the overland route to India. When Russian troops crossed the Bulgarian border to invade the territory of the Sublime Porte, war was inevitable, and when the Tsar's Black Sea fleet destroyed a Turkish squadron, retaliation was bound to be directed at the Russian port of Sebastopol.

At the outbreak of war in 1854, the Regiment was 944 strong, and contained an equal number of freshly joined recruits, and, thanks to its good health, of 12- and 15-year veterans. 'They were very tall and strong,' wrote an officer who had just joined from an English county regiment; Scottish recruits were, in any case, larger than English ones at this time, but the better feeding since the abuse by the pay-sergeants had ended must also have contributed. However, only 13 per cent of the Regiment now came from Highland areas, and many of those Highlanders were recruited in the streets of Glasgow. Potato blight, the end of the kelp boom, and the introduction of sheep had all contributed to the fall in the Highland population, and, as a result, it was about now that the soldiers began to call themselves 'Jocks', a Lowland name, rather than 'Rories', the old Highland nickname. A large proportion were handloom weavers from the south-west, who had been put out of work by steam-powered looms; the education and initiative of these men made them outstandingly valuable, both to the Chartists or early Socialists, and to the Army. Overall, the Regiment enlisted a high ratio of craftsmen and artisans, and while over 60 per cent of the army's recruits in the 1840s were uneducated labourers, they accounted for only 37 per cent of the 42nd's recruits.

Their Colonel was Duncan Cameron, now in his eleventh year of command, and to Sir Arthur Halkett, a new officer, 'Colonel Cameron, with his white hair and stern cast of counternance, seemed the very beau ideal of a commanding officer.' The appearance was not deceptive.

With the declaration of war, the Highland Brigade, consisting of the 42nd, 79th (Camerons) and 93rd (Sutherland), under the command of Sir Colin Campbell, was placed in the 1st Division with the Brigade of Guards. They sailed first to Scutari on the Turkish coast, and then across the Black Sea to Varna in Bulgaria, where their presence was intended to assist in persuading the invading Russian armies to withdraw behind their own frontier. One of Campbell's staff officers soon found occasion to write bitterly, 'Never, if you can help it, be brigaded with the Guards.' By right of seniority, the Guards took precedence on the march, so that the other troops always had to follow through their dust, gathering up their baggage and sick, and their officers had seniority over line officers of similar rank. These were merely irritations, however. The real problem, especially for a healthy battalion like the 42nd, was that the Brigade of Guards was the most diseased corps in the whole unhealthy army. Their Knightsbridge barracks, inhabited only by young men in the prime of life, had a death rate five times as high as that of the surrounding borough of Kensington, which included everyone from babies to ancients. They suffered from dysentery, typhoid fever, typhus, cholera, and 25 per cent of them had venereal disease. It was like being brigaded with a medical dictionary.

The 1st Division landed at Varna in June. They marched some ten miles inland, and at once large numbers of the Guards started to fall out. In the hot weather, cholera began to spread rapidly, and Colonel Sterling, Campbell's staff officer, marked the growing difference between the two brigades. 'The Highland Brigade is considered healthy in the army, but the Guards are sickly and dispirited, and accordingly have lost three times as many men.' Their physical deterioration was so marked that they were unable to march the ten miles back to Varna carrying their packs, and mules and baggage carts had to be provided.

The manoeuvrings in Bulgaria, and the threat of intervention by Austria, had the effect of making the Russians withdraw their forces behind their own frontier but, since the declaration of war, almost every newspaper in Paris and London had been urging an assault on the Russian port of Sebastopol on the Crimean peninsula. They were now to be satisfied. In September the French and British took off their troops from Varna, sailed slowly up the coast and, in uneasy alliance, landed them again at the aptly named Calamitas Bay. (The French actually moved the buoy dividing the bay between the two forces, and left so little room for their allies that Raglan disembarked most of his force elsewhere.)

Raglan commanded 26,000 men and 66 guns, while there were 30,000 men and 70 guns under Marshal St Arnaud, the former dancing-master and billiard-marker. Because of St Arnaud's illness, Raglan was permitted to exert overall influence, subject to messages from Paris, but, having the larger force, the French demanded and received the privilege of advancing on the right of the Allied line. Their right wing, therefore, was on the sea, and the troops of the 1st Division, on the left of the British army, were the furthest inland. Ahead of them the Russians had prepared a strong defensive position on a grassy ridge behind the river Alma; its steepest point was inland, opposite the left of the British line, and it then sloped down towards the sea. A redoubt had been constructed half-way up the slope against the British centre, and guns were sited on its crest to cover the river in front.

The 42nd had landed on the 16th September, carrying the rations they would need for three days, for all the mules and baggage wagons had been left at Varna. Halkett made a list of his burden: three days' rations of salt pork and biscuits (9 lbs in all), cocoa and sugar in his haversack; shirt, hose, boots, brushes, shelljacket, towels and sponges in his knapsack; blue blanket on the back of his knapsack; greatcoat, claymore, dirk and revolver on top of his knapsack; and the Queen's Colour in his hand. The Regiment was armed with the Minié rifle which had replaced the smooth-bore Brown Bess. It was still a muzzle-loader, requiring enormous skill to load on the march, and no change had been made in tactics as a result of its increased range of 800 yards.

The armies marched from their landing-place on the 19th September, and that night bivouacked in the open; at 10 a.m. on the 20th they began their march on the Alma. Skirmishers from the Rifle Brigade advanced in front, the Light Division formed the first

PLATE IV (above) *'At Seringapatam we fought, and Tippoo Sahib we slew'. The 73rd at the storming of the fortress in 1799.*

PLATE V (below) *Lieutenant McNiven's portrait of the 6th Division crossing the Garonne before Orthez in 1814; made from a watercolour painted on the spot.*

PLATE VI  *'The Highlander's Farewell' by Thos. Duncan* R.S.A. *Between 1815 and 1865*
*the 42nd spent scarcely five years in Britain.*

line of troops, and the Highland Brigade was on the left of the second line, with the Guards on their right. Half an hour after they began their advance, the Russian guns opened fire from the Alma ridge. Carrying the Queen's Colour must have concentrated the mind wonderfully, for Halkett was afterwards able to write an extremely detailed account of the day.

> Colonel Cameron now rode up and said to me, 'Uncase the Colours.' The Queen's and Regimental Colours were unfurled, the end being held in the hand to prevent it being blown about. We now came to a long, stone wall, and on the other side was a vineyard. The grapes were just ripe, and though the fire became very heavy, the soldiers kept picking the grapes as they pushed their way along. The river Alma was below the vineyard, and the opposite bank ascended rather steeply towards the intrenched camp of the Russians. I could see our Rifle Brigade far in advance up the hill in skirmishing order, lying down and firing, and then advancing by little runs. The firing, both of muskets and artillery, was incessant, as the French were attacking vigorously on our right. The village of Alma was in flames adding volumes of white smoke. We now arrived at the river and began to cross – the water was about up to our knees. I was much encumbered with the Colour, and a soldier gave me a hand and pulled me up the bank.

Under the partial shelter of the steep slope in front, the Highland Brigade halted while Campbell conferred with the Duke of Cambridge, the divisional commander. The Brigade was on the far left of the Allied line. In front of them, and a little to the right, the Light Division's attack on the central redoubt was in difficulty, and the confusion had spread to some of the Guards in the second line.

> The Russian gunners had now got the exact range, for they had prepared by fixing posts in the ground at every 100 yards from the river, so they sent shot into us with great accuracy. Sir Colin, seeing this, hurried his Brigade into line. The Light Division we saw in front of us, also in line and advancing slowly, but losing an enormous lot of men – we could see great gaps suddenly in their ranks, which again closed in but leaving little heaps of red-coated men on the ground. The noise of the artillery with the whiz of round-shot and grape, the harsh scream of the jagged fragments of shell rushing through the air, made our inaction very tedious. We could see the guns being pointed and aimed at us. Two of them especially the men christened 'Maggie' and 'Jessie'. 'Look out for a shot from Jessie.' 'Now Maggie's coming.' So deafening was the noise, it was difficult to hear words of command, but under cover of the rising ground, Sir Colin addressed the Brigade, and as he did so in front of the 42nd, we could hear him, 'Now men' he said 'Keep steady – fire low – keep silent – and make me proud of the Highland Brigade.'
>      We were ordered to advance and began to march over little heaps of men of the Light Division and an occasional dead Russian. Very soon we saw the Light Division in front of us, forming into 'fours' and halted. The Highland Brigade was immediately formed in 'fours' also and passed through the Light Division. As we passed through the 33rd, I heard one of them say 'Ah let the Scotchmen go on, they don't know what they're going to get.' Again forming line, we advanced and found

ourselves the leading division of the army on the left flank. I had now some anxiety as
the whole Regiment 'dresses' upon the Colours in the centre of the line, and Lord
Forth, who held the Regimental Colour on my right, kept hanging back requiring me
to say, 'Come on, you're putting out the whole line.'

Their steady advance had outflanked the central redoubt, and Sterling, the staff
officer, wrote: 'Our manoeuvre was perfectly decisive; as we got on the flank of the
Russians in the central battery, I saw the Guards rush in as the Russians abandoned it.'
The Highland Brigade continued to advance in echelon; the 42nd on the right and leading,
the 93rd behind them and to the left, and the 79th on the far left in the rear. They could not
see beyond the 'false' crest ahead, but on its far side the ground dipped slightly before
rising to the true summit of the ridge.

On arriving at the crest of the undulating ground, we found ourselves confronted by
five columns of Russian infantry. At this moment the 42nd was alone, and closest to
us were two columns on the further side of the hollow; the Sousdal and Kazan
column; one battalion wore helmets, the others were in forage caps. We were now
advancing firing, and approaching nearer and nearer the great solid mass of Russian
infantry who poured in a hot fire, their front rank kneeling. The Russian columns
were beginning to waver, and we could see their officers waving their swords and
pushing the men into their places.

From the left the other Russian columns started to come down to their support.

These were now caught on their right flank by the 93rd coming up . . . The 79th
appearing, the columns faced about and began to retire. Seeing the time had come,
Sir Colin lifted his hat; in an instant each man seemed to grasp the situation, fixed
bayonets and charged after the retreating Russians; such a cheer went up from the
throats of the three Highland Regiments as never was heard. On arriving at the
summit of the ridge, the Brigade was halted and formed once more into line. We
could see the masses of Russian infantry retreating along the whole line; they several
times halted but we kept firing into them. Gradually fire began to lessen, and at last
ceased altogether, with the exception of an artillery gun now and then. The battle was
over and the enemy in full retreat.

The men collapsed on the ground with exhaustion, but when Campbell rode up, they
came to their feet 'waving their feather bonnets on the points of their bayonets. The old
chief was delighted – he said he had just been congratulated by Lord Raglan on the
behaviour of the Highland Brigade, and that he had asked from the Commander-in-Chief
just one favour, which was that, in place of his cocked hat, he might wear a Highland
bonnet.' The honour of designing the unique headgear fell to John Drysdale, who
produced for it a hackle, one third red for the 42nd, and two-thirds white for the 79th and
93rd. The final words of Campbell's report on the battle will explain his satisfaction: 'I
never saw officers and men, one and all, exhibit greater steadiness and gallantry, giving
evidence of their instruction and discipline, and of the noble spirit with which they are
animated.'

PLATE 12 *'Forward the 42nd!' by Robert Gibb* RSA. *Colonel Cameron is on the white horse, Sir Colin Campbell on the black and Captain Halkett holding the Queen's Colour.*

Halkett's day was not yet finished; he went searching across the battlefield for a friend, and, as night fell, he saw a marquee with a light inside. Through the tent flaps he could see 'a long table on trestles, covered crossways with wounded men – the Doctors were in their shirts with sleeves rolled up above their elbows. Although there was no chloroform, only a few suppressed groans could be heard, and as fast as the legs and arms could be amputated, they were placed outside the tent. There was a heap of these.' Wandering further he found another tent lit up, and the contrast was extreme for this was Lord Raglan's, and on the table inside there were 'silver candle-sticks on a white tablecloth'.

Their superb victory left the Allies within striking distance of Sebastopol, which was still unfortified and might have been taken with an immediate attack. However, its harbour had been blocked and only two days' supplies remained in the soldiers' packs. Since all the transport had been left in Varna, the most pressing need was for an anchorage from which the fleet could directly supply the army. Accordingly the Allies circled round Sebastopol to establish their bases at two natural harbours south of the city. The narrow inlet at Balaclava served the British, while the French were supplied from Kamiesh Bay several miles to the west.

When the Highland Brigade marched down into the valley of Balaclava, it seemed 'one immense garden – plums, apples, cherries in abundance'. The 93rd was left to guard the harbour, while the 42nd and 79th returned to the high ground above Sebastopol to begin digging trenches and making fascines and gabions – the ancestors of the sandbag. Cameron allowed no drink in the Regiment, and there was almost no crime. Sterling wrote of bad conduct in other regiments, 'but no such scenes can ever occur without detection and prevention in any good regiment like this 42nd.' Everyone hoped for an assault on the city; they could see its white houses and towering churches with green domes surmounted by golden crosses and, beyond the buildings, the harbour crammed with naval ships. Todleben, the engineering genius who commanded Sebastopol's defences, wrote that an attack at this time would have been successful, but while both sides were preparing their positions, the Russian army outside the city launched an attack on Balaclava. It failed to reach the harbour owing to an efficient, controlled charge by Scarlett's Heavy Brigade, and the unwavering courage of the 93rd's 'thin, red line'. If the Light Brigade had been properly commanded, the Russians might have been completely repulsed, but as it was they were left in command of part of the road by which supplies had to travel from the port to the besiegers on the hill.

The threat to his supply line persuaded Raglan to post the entire Highland Brigade in the Balaclava valley to defend the port. There the 42nd began again the process of entrenching, coupled now with fatigue parties to carry supplies up to the troops on the high ground above Sebastopol. In the absence of baggage animals, the men claimed they were turned into 'damned commissariat mules'. They were worked far harder than the besiegers, but they were spared the confused fighting at Inkerman, which they could hear but not see. The battle, on the 5th November, altered the state of the siege less than the terrible hurricane nine days later. It sank thirty-five supply ships in the harbour, blew away the men's tents, and reduced the supply system to an even more parlous state than after the Alma.

'The storm,' wrote Halkett, 'was the beginning of the miseries.' It was followed by rain and snow which swiftly melted, turning the garden of Balaclava to a mud patch 'as bare as a ballroom floor'. Food stores had gone down in the supply ships, and there were no tents or warm clothes to replace those blown away in the storm. The trees had been chopped down, so that there was no firewood to cook food or dry clothes, and in December the temperature dropped to 20°F below freezing at night. Until January food of every description was in short supply, except salt pork, and the men became so sick of the sight of it that they left their rations untouched. The unbroken diet of salted meat produced gastric ulcers, and scurvy broke out. To add to the Highland Brigade's misery, Balaclava harbour itself produced a stench which made men faint. After the battles of Balaclava and Inkerman, it had become a watery Golgotha of amputated arms and legs and an occasional corpse which bobbed up through the scum on the surface. In January, when the stores began to percolate again through the miasmic inefficiency of the supply system, the Highland Brigade went back to being 'damned commissariat mules', hauling barrels of pork, 112 lb bags of biscuit, 32 lb shot, and planks for gun platforms, through the quagmired tracks up to the besiegers on the hill.

In the light of these conditions, it is interesting to find that later in the year *The Times* attacked 'Sir Colin Campbell who has been laid up in lavender all the winter with his Highlanders'. The assumption that all was lavender in the valley was obviously the result of ignorance, but it was probably provoked by the relative success of the Highlanders, compared to the rest of the army, in surviving the rigours of that wretched winter. In the 42nd about 15 per cent of the men died of disease during the entire war, but at the other end of the scale, Florence Nightingale wrote of '73 per cent in 8 regiments in 6 months from disease alone'. By February, Raglan had only 11,000 men in front of Sebastopol;

9,000 others had died, and 13,000 were in hospital. It was the harvest, not merely of unforgivable inefficiency in supply and administration, but also of that regimental system, abandoned by the 42nd twenty years before, in which responsibility for the soldier ended at ensuring that he was smart and disciplined on parade. Unchecked drinking, poor diet, and a monotonous life in unhealthy barracks had sapped the soldiers' strength, so that cholera, scurvy and dysentery spread easily, killed easily, and sent thousands to the Barracks Hospital at Scutari, which as often as not was a death sentence in itself.

In the 42nd Cameron did not allow either mud or pestilence to alter his peacetime standards. He insisted on pipe-clayed belts, polished buttons and white gaiters on parade, even if it meant that the men carried the gaiters in their pockets on fatigues to save them from the mud. On the 23rd March, the Regiment was ordered to make a night march to attack the Russian positions beyond the Tchernaya river. A blizzard was blowing when it set off, and indeed the weather was so vile that a French regiment detailed to support them was called back, but the messenger carrying similar instructions for the 42nd unfortunately became lost in the snow. The Russians were sheltering from the storm when the Regiment arrived at dawn, but without support the surprise could not be exploited in the face of such huge numbers. It was a fruitless expedition, but a vivid demonstration of the Regiment's strength at the end of that miserable season.

With spring the baggage animals came at last, and the 42nd returned for a short period to the trenches in front of Sebastopol. The city was never more than partially invested, remaining open to the north, but Raglan now decided to cut the stream of supplies which flowed across the isthmus from the mainland on to the Crimean peninsula, by sending the British fleet into the Sea of Azov to bombard the isthmus from close range. Late in April the Highland Brigade was carried up the coast to Kertsch to clear the fortifications which guarded the strait into the sea of Azov. The little town of Kertsch seemed like another world after the mud and filth of Balaclava. It reminded Halkett of Edinburgh with its clean houses, squares and cobbled streets. The shops were open and the inhabitants appeared to be grateful when they drove off the Tartars who had been quartered there. With scarcely a struggle the strait was opened to the fleet, which wreaked enormous damage on the supply ships and convoys carrying material for Sebastopol. In the long term the drain on Russia's resources caused by the Navy's harassment of her supply line to the Crimea was such that the eventual fall of Sebastopol proved enough to bring her to make peace.

Characteristically Cameron did not allow the Regiment to relax in the warmth and quiet of Kertsch; he drilled a different company each day so that efficiency did not slip, and insisted that his men be as immaculate as though they were in Edinburgh Castle. Their anger, therefore, was justifiable, when they returned to Sebastopol in July to discover that their feather bonnets, which had been left there, had been used by the sacrilegious French to make feather beds, and were squashed flat. However, there was no end to the qualities of that excellent headgear, and with the wire frame straightened out, and the hackle cocked out, it was as good as new, though no doubt suffused with a garlic scent.

In early summer the Allies tightened their hold on the city by capturing at heavy cost the Mamelon strongpoint in its outer defences, and some quarries nearby. From there Sebastopol was continually shelled, so that Tolstoy, describing the scenes and the reactions of people inside the city, conjured up a picture which might suggest London and

PLATE 13    *Captain R. C. Cuninghame, photographed at Sebastopol by Thomas Fenton in*
*1855. Note the square spats – twenty-nine years before the broken square at Tamaii.*

Londoners during the Blitz. Outside the city, conditions more nearly resembled the First World War with trench warfare, patrols in no-man's-land, and massive artillery bombardments. The resemblance would have been closer still, if the Secretary for War had not refused, as unsportsmanlike, an enthusiastic suggestion from the Earl of Dundonald, better known as Cochrane the dauntless, whose eighty-year-old mind had just invented tear gas. On Waterloo Day, the British and French assaulted two vital strongpoints of the city's defences, the Redan and the Malakoff, but both attacks were bloodily repulsed, and this disappointment finally crushed Raglan's spirit. He fell ill and died shortly afterwards.

In September the attacks were repeated. The Highland Brigade was in reserve, despite its protests, to the Light Division. There was little doubt that they should have been given responsibility for the attack, since they were by far the healthiest of the Crimean troops, and the Light Division, which had mounted the June attack, was under strength and composed largely of untried troops. Although the French, storming forward 'like a pack of foxhounds', successfully threw themselves into the Malakoff, the British assault collapsed against the fire from the Redan. That evening, the 8th September, the Highland Brigade was moved forward to the front line for an assault the next morning, but during the night a sergeant in the 42nd became curious that there was so little noise to be heard beyond the walls. He crept forward with some men, and climbed into the Redan. It was empty. Then a series of explosions shook the city and, the next morning, the last of the Russian garrison could be seen streaming out of the city to the north.

Peace was not signed until March, 1856, but after the fall of Sebastopol, there were no more serious military operations. Campbell and his Highlanders had reason to feel disappointed that they missed the last chance of storming the city, but it did not alter the opinion held of them by those who knew them. General Pelissier, whose men took the Malakoff so bravely, said of Campbell, 'Je ne vois jamais cet homme sans avoir envie de l'embrasser,' and his Highlanders he thought the finest soldiers in the world. Colonel Sterling, an Englishman who had known nothing of Highland troops when he first went to the Crimean War, wrote to friends when he left, 'I cannot tell you how much I regret leaving these Highland soldiers; they are so entirely different and so superior to any of the other Divisions.'

Before they quitted the Crimea, Colonel Cameron was given command of a brigade in the newly formed Highland Division, and from there he went on to fight in the Maori war in New Zealand, to be Commandant of the Camberley Staff College, and to be appointed Colonel of the Regiment. A century later, one of his successors in the Colonelcy discovered that he was still well remembered by the Maoris. It was not, alas, the purposeful Colonel of the Crimea they recalled, but a snowy-haired General, who advanced his army so hesitantly that the Maoris nicknamed him 'the seagull with the broken wing'. Yet, if years and responsibility had changed the man, they could not touch the memory of what he had accomplished with the Regiment.

# CHAPTER 10

# India and the Regiment's Character

The military effects of the Crimean War were far-reaching. A programme to build healthier barracks was initiated by Sydney Herbert, under the vigorous prodding of Florence Nightingale, and the contract for regimental uniforms was bought in by the government, so that the quality was improved, and recruits were no longer required to buy the bulk of their clothing. That improvement was matched by higher wages and better food, but the longest-lasting change was in the emphasis which military commanders now gave to the matter of supplies. When Sir Colin Campbell arrived in India to take command during the Mutiny, though Delhi was in the hands of the rebels and Lucknow under siege, he spent the first six weeks in Calcutta, organising the transport and administrative services, and in the last quarter of the nineteenth century, Wolseley, the pre-eminent military figure of the period, owed his reputation in large part to logistical wizardry. The new emphasis was certainly needed, but there was a cost. Writing of his Burma campaign in the Second World War, Sir William Slim commented, in *Defeat into Victory*, 'The British Army, ever since the terrible lesson of the Crimean War, had tended to stress supply at the expense of mobility.' It is a thesis which the next half-century of the Regiment's history largely substantiates.

The Indian Mutiny is also known to the Indians as the First War of Liberation, and there is merit in both names. It began as mutiny in March, 1857, when the high caste Brahmans and Rajputs, who largely composed the Bengal Army, refused orders to load their new Enfield rifles with a cartridge greased with the defiling lard of cows and pigs. The substitution of an innocuous, vegetable lubricant, coupled with firm action, might have halted the trouble there. From the Punjab, John Lawrence sent a grim telegram, 'Clubs not spades are trumps,' and his methods maintained peace there. But most of the Bengal Army was drawn from the state of Oudh, which had been annexed just twelve months before,* and the mutiny swiftly spread into the province, where it took on the character of an independence movement, with native princes providing the leadership. Lucknow, the capital, was besieged, and, at Cawnpore, Nana Sahib massacred the garrison and their families after promising them safe-conduct. However, the armies of Madras and Bombay were not affected by mutiny, and they provided valuable reinforcement to the British troops which gathered to suppress the uprising.

When the 42nd arrived in India in November, 1857, Sir Colin Campbell was preparing to attack the rebels in Cawnpore, and half the Battalion was ordered to join him

---

* 'Peccavi, I've Sindh,' said Napier so proud,
 Dalhousie, more humble, said 'Vovi, I've Oudh.'

there. The treachery of Nana Sahib had aroused the fierce god of Victorian retribution as no other action could, and Private MacKintosh expressed a typical reaction when he wrote in his diary, 'I wanted to have some share in revenging the *horrid atrocities* committed there on our *women* and *children* by those *fiends*.' Thus spurred on, the half-battalion began an energetic week by covering seventy-eight miles in two-and-a-half days to arrive in Cawnpore on the 5th December. In the battle on the following day, they led the pursuit of the defeated sepoys for twelve miles, galloping down the road like surrogate cavalry, and capturing fifteen guns. When the chase was halted, they marched the twelve miles back to camp, and were ready the next morning to follow up a rebel contingent which had escaped in the confusion. For nineteen of the next twenty-four hours they were on the move, and eventually caught up with the rebels as they breakfasted beside the Ganges. Seventeen more guns and some hot *chupattis* were added to their haul. The best known of their trophies, however, which the Grenadier Company had discovered in a dung-cart the previous day, was Nana Sahib's gong; it eventually found its way to the officers' mess where it boomed the hours of the day, to the confusion of strangers who could not believe the 42nd ate so frequently. The gong still remains in the Regiment's possession.

The Battalion was reunited before Christmas, and in the New Year Campbell's army began to sweep through Oudh, re-establishing order, collecting revenues, and hanging rebels found with arms. After their initial burst of activity, the 42nd slowed to the measured pace demanded by an army, which on the march began to resemble a race migration; the 25,000 soldiers were accompanied by 15,000 attendants, 16,000 camels, 12,000 oxen, and sundry mules, horses and elephants. The rebels rarely waited for them, but on one occasion when they stood their ground, they provided an example of the difficulty Campbell faced in inflicting decisive defeat upon them.

In January, 1859 the sepoys gathered in some force on the far bank of the river at Futteguhr. The 53rd was ordered across the bridge to hold a small perimeter, so that the naval guns could be brought over, while the cavalry circled behind the enemy. Campbell was widely suspected of favouring his Highland troops, and when the 42nd was sent across to reinforce the 53rd, the latter charged at once rather than risk sharing the glory. Because neither the guns nor the cavalry were in position, the rebels escaped with small loss.

In his history of the 42nd, Forbes recounted how the General galloped up to the 53rd 'in high wrath, and objurgated them in terms of extreme potency', but the precise words of his extremely potent objurgation were lost to history, because the men's thunderous cheers drowned Campbell's voice, and presumably reinforced whatever prejudice he had in favour of Highland troops. The work of subjugating Oudh continued, but in the opinion of Lord Canning, the Governor-General, the province would continue to flare up while the mutineers held its capital, Lucknow. In March, therefore, Campbell assembled his 25,000 men against the 60,000 rebel soldiers holding the city.

Lucknow was an enormous sprawl of tangled streets, bounded on the eastern side by palaces, courtyards and gardens. It was from this side that the main attack was made by the infantry, while the cavalry and artillery patrolled and bombarded from the north. The 42nd was posted in the palace of the Dilkusha (the heart's desire) where they were shelled for several days by the sepoys in a large military college, called La Martinière. Then on the 9th March, Campbell launched his assault with the order, 'The 42nd will lead the attack – the men employed will use nothing but the bayonet.'

The Regiment advanced in two lines, with the 93rd on their left, across the thousand yards which seperated them from the line of defences in front of La Martinière. The first line under Colonel Priestley cleared the fortified huts and houses to the left of the building, while Colonel Alexander Cameron took the second up the parapet to the right, where one of his officers, Lieutenant Farquharson, led an attack on two guns, which put them out of action and won for the Regiment its first award of that new decoration, the Victoria Cross. W. H. Russell, *The Times* correspondent, wrote of the troops which attacked Lucknow, 'Most of the Regiments were in a highly efficient state, but the Highlanders were most conspicuous, not only for their costume, but for their steady and martial air, on parade and in the field.' They cleared men and artillery from the defences round La Martinière in a style which merited the compliment, and by nightfall they were deep inside the complex of parks and courtyards, close to the walls of the Begum's Palace and the more prosaically named Bank's House.

The next day the bungalows round the Palace were taken, and the enemy driven out of Bank's House. If the surroundings had been less palatial, it could have been called street fighting. Russell described a typical scene.

> The buildings which surround the courts are irregular – columned fronts and lofty porticoes with richly gilt roofs and domes. You hear the musketry rattling inside; the crash of glass, the shouts and yells of the combatants, and little jets of smoke curl out of the closed lattices. Lying amid the orange groves are dead and dying sepoys and the white statues are reddened with blood. Leaning against a smiling Venus is a British soldier shot through the neck, gasping and at every gasp bleeding to death.

It took another week to capture Lucknow, but after making the break-in, the 42nd was pulled back to guard the camp, and later to occupy the Begum's Palace.

With the fall of the capital, Campbell obviously expected the spirit of the revolution to die, for he was reluctant to risk his men's lives in pursuit of the fleeing enemy. But Lord Canning now issued a proclamation that the land of the rebels would be confiscated, and since all but half-a-dozen princes had at least tacitly supported the revolt, they had little to lose by continuing the fight. To snuff out this last resistance, flying columns were sent against the forts and cities of the rebellious princes, but Campbell was still utterly set against unnecessary loss of life, and he issued an order: 'The Commander-in-Chief prohibits columns from moving to the attack of forts, large or small, without at least two heavy guns.' Campbell's cautious pursuit of the enemy does not compare well with Sir Hugh Rose's simultaneous campaign in Central India, which was characterised by swift movement and daring battle against superior forces. It may be argued, however, that in the north the war had been won, even though the last battle had not yet been fought, and if Campbell had wanted justification for his order, a subordinate, General Walpole, soon provided it.

Walpole was sent north-west to clear the province of Rohilkand with two columns, one of which, commanded by Brigadier Adrian Hope, contained the 42nd. On the 11th April, the column approached Fort Ruhya, a town surrounded by mud walls, and without waiting for his artillery to come up, Walpole ordered Hope to make a frontal attack across the open plain. The Brigadier advanced with four companies of the 42nd and the 4th Punjab Rifles. They were soon the targets of fierce firing from the town, by which Hope was killed and the men pinned down in the open for six hours. At dusk Walpole ordered them to return, but Sergeant Cooper of the 42nd, in common with many of the attackers, felt certain that the order should have been to storm the fort, and he recorded in his diary that 'when the order to retire came, nothing was heard but loud and deep cursing'. The General completed his day of folly by leaving the fort unguarded, so that the enemy slipped away during the night. The Regiment did what it could to mitigate the waste; two N.C.O.s and two privates went back under heavy fire to bring in the wounded from the plain, and the award of Victoria Crosses recognised their gallantry.

By early May, the column, much reinforced, was in front of Bareilly, the capital of Rohilkand. It was a city of spreading, undisciplined suburbs, more than six miles in circumference and far too large to be surrounded. Campbell had come up to take command, and he now formed his troops into a diamond formation, with the artillery in front, three regiments of infantry in the second line, and the rear brought up by one infantry regiment and men of the Royal Engineers. Cavalry and skirmishers from the 4th Punjab Rifles covered the front and flanks. There is some interest in comparing this formation with Wolseley's Imperial Square, in which the Regiment was later used, where each face was composed of a battalion with the artillery in the corners. Both of them were designed to cope with a foe technically inferior, but far superior in numbers, and in both cases, the necessity of bringing the guns to close range while protecting them on all sides, gave the formation the clumsiness and invulnerability of a tortoise.

At Bareilly the 42nd was on the left flank, and they had just moved up alongside the artillery in two lines, right wing leading, when a heavy fire was opened on them. Suddenly the skirmishers in front ran back through the Regiment's ranks hotly pursued by Mohammedan cavalry, called Ghazis. Sergeant Cooper described the attack:

> Uttering loud cries 'Bismillah, Allah, deen, deen', about 150 of these fanatics, sword in hand with small circular bucklers on the left arm, and green cummerbund on, rushed out after the Sikhs and dashed at the left of the right wing. With bodies bent and heads low, waving their tulwars [swords] with a circular motion, they came on with astonishing rapidity. At first we took them for Sikhs, whose passage had already disordered our ranks. Fortunately Sir Colin, close at hand, cried out, 'Close your ranks, bayonet them as they come.' Some of them got in rear of the right wing. Three dashed at Colonel [Alexander] Cameron, pulled him off his horse, and would have hacked him in pieces, but for Colour Sergeant Gardiner, who, stepping out of the ranks, drove his bayonet through two of them, and the third was killed by Private Gavin.

There was fierce bayonet and sword fighting, and the Ghazis came within ten yards of the guns before the last of them was killed.

While the battle was in progress, the second Rohilkand column entered on the far side of the town, providing an anvil to the hammer of the main force, and the next day Bareilly was in British hands. Although the hot season had arrived, and indeed eight men of the Regiment died of heatstroke during the battle, patrols were immediately sent out to cordon off the rebel strongholds. Each wing of the Regiment spent a month on patrol, followed by a month in Bareilly, and this pattern was largely maintained during the two years the 42nd spent there.

PLATE 14   *Colour–Sergeant William Gardiner* VC. *The 'bearded look' began in the Crimea, but the successes of the clean-shaven Prussians in the 1860s eventually made it unpopular.*

Towards the end of 1859 three companies were sent to guard the river border between Rohilkand and Oudh. Steep bluffs rose up from the river, but they were broken by occasional gaps, and one such opening, Maylem Ghat, was guarded by Captain Lawson commanding Number 6 Company and some Indian levies. On the 15th January, 1860, 2,000 rebels crossed the river into the deep jungle in Maylem Ghat. An ensign with half the Company was sent out as a picquet, but they lost touch with the others, and Lawson had only thirty-seven men and the not too reliable levies to face the attack. When it came in, Lawson was wounded, and later died, the N.C.O.s were all killed, but Privates Cook and Miller 'went to the front and took a prominent part in directing the Company, and displayed a Courage, Coolness and Discipline which was the admiration of all who witnessed it.' Such is the Victoria Cross citation, and of the eight awarded to the Regiment during the Mutiny, none was better earned. They held off the attack until evening, when reinforcements arrived to drive the rebels back across the river. The pipe tune 'Lawson's Men' commemorates this action, and the survivors were paraded before Sir Hugh Rose, who had succeeded Campbell as Commander-in-Chief, when he presented new Colours to the Regiment.

In the now customary fashion, the 42nd provided itself with recreation to fight the demon drink and break the boredom of barrack life. In hot weather the troops were confined to barracks for eighteen hours out of the twenty-four, so the problem was particularly acute. The library was begun again, and amateur theatricals and concerts were organised. Private MacKintosh found two concerts especially memorable, 'A Nicht wi' Burns' by Mr Black, and Signor Pompie 'who played several soloes on the Hobo, and sang several songs, but we did not know one word he was saying.'

In March, 1861, however, the Regiment moved to Agra, where everyone was suitably impressed by the Red Fort and the Taj Mahal, and where the town sewage flowed unnoticed into their water supply. At the end of the hot season, when the water in the tanks was low, cholera struck the Regiment. It was endemic in the Ganges valley, and periodically swept across Asia and into Europe, the previous occurrence coinciding with the Crimean War. The connection between sewage and the disease was at least partly understood in the 1860s, for that was when the present sanitation system in British towns was installed, thus ridding the country of cholera. Its treatment, however, remained a mystery. Continuous diarrhoea and vomiting drained the body of fluids, and as dehydration began, severe cramps convulsed the legs and stomach. 'I have seen both the Doctor [McMann] and the Colonel [Priestley] with their coats off rubbing those in agony with the cramps,' wrote MacKintosh. Massage probably eased the pain, but Dr McMann, making his rounds with bottles of whisky to pour down the men's throats, may unwittingly have found the right solution, which was to replace the lost fluid. Despite his ministrations, 46 men died in a month, but at its worst almost 500 men were in hospital or convalescing. When it was over, Dr Murray, the Surgeon General, presented a set of pipes to the Regiment to commemorate 'the calm Heroism of the 42nd', and it was indeed a notable form of courage to remain calm in the midst of plague, nor was it the last time they were tested.

In 1867, when the Regiment was in Peshawar, MacKintosh wrote in his diary, 'May 20th. The cholera broke out in the station, we were the first Regiment attacked. The first man that took it was one of my Company; another and another were seized shortly

afterwards, taken to hospital and died in a few hours. By next morning we had lost 7 men and 2 children. God grant that this may not be such a scourge as we had at Agra.' The prayer was not answered, and in twelve days, 66 men, 2 women and 4 children died, and when the Regiment was moved to the hill station at Cherat, dysentery raised the toll to over 100. On their departure from India at the end of that year, a General Order praising their conduct in the country, rightly emphasised that 'trials, which would have demoralised a less-disciplined regiment, were undergone without a murmur'.

The dominating spirit of those years was Colonel Priestley. 'Let our Colonel be the Devil on parade, he was a good man to those in hospital,' wrote MacKintosh. Devil on parade he may have been, but he achieved the heavenly result of producing a regiment so perfect that an inspecting Brigadier burst into tears, and in his report wrote that 'a more orderly and respectfully well-behaved body of men cannot be found in any army in the world.' Repeatedly their drill and intelligence in skirmishing were commended, and their marksmanship, under the guidance of John Drysdale, reached a higher level than any regiment had ever attained in India. It was the apotheosis of his career. When he died in

PLATE 15  *The 42nd in camp at Dartmoor in 1871, displaying the varieties of uniforms worn at the time.*

1865, MacKintosh wrote, 'He was a great favourite in the Regiment. He spoke so kindly to the men, and the Regiment moved better with him than with anyone else.' It is good to know that the handicaps of Bermuda were finally recognised as qualities.

In his obituary of Priestley, who died on the Regiment's return to Scotland in 1868, MacKintosh was less kind. 'A harsh, stern old man' was his epitaph, but that was at least partly due to their differing views on drink. Priestley hated drunkenness, whereas MacKintosh liked to get 'royal' from time to time, a point of view which generally landed him in the guard-room. By Indian standards, however, he was almost a teetotaler. A Royal Commission in 1861 reported that in an Indian station described as 'temperate' in its drinking, one-third of the hospital cases were suffering from delirium tremens or alcoholism. Such excessive drunkenness never overtook the 42nd, and the credit for that must be ascribed to Priestley. In the 1880s Lord Roberts was acclaimed for introducing coffee-houses to combat the paralysing drunkenness in the Indian Army, but the inspection reports show that Priestley had provided one for the 42nd twenty years before, as well as gardens, workshops and a gymnasium.

If the Regiment was still in the forefront of progress in looking after its men, it could, on its return to Britain, at last see that the Army was moving in the same direction, particularly in the programme of barracks reform instituted after the Crimean War. New, large buildings were put up, so that regiments were not dispersed, and in the old barracks, gas-lighting replaced tallow dips, windows which could be opened were put in and heating installed, the cooking cauldrons were supplanted by ovens where the food could be baked or roasted, and in place of the single wooden tub, which served as wash-pot by day and chamber-pot by night, running water was installed.

While the army was reforming itself, the country remained mired in the almost Crimean miseries of the Industrial Revolution. With two-thirds of all families in Scotland living in one or two rooms disease was rampant. In the 1860s typhus was endemic in Glasgow, and in another Regimental recruiting area, Dunfermline, *The Scotsman* esti-mated that 60 per cent of the working-class suffered from the disease. The factory conditions of the time are now notorious, but the Army saw their destructive effects at first hand; one-third of all recruits had to be turned down because of physical deformity or ill-health, and the minimum height standard gradually had to be reduced from 5 ft 6 in. in 1845 to 5 ft 2 in. in 1897.

By recruiting from every corner of Scotland, the Regiment faithfully reflected the economic changes in the country\*. Textile workers gradually diminished in number as the industry lost its pre-eminent importance after 1850, but the flourishing iron and steel works provided a stream of former moulders and puddlers. An unusually high proportion of craftsmen and skilled workers was still recruited, and from the mid-century there was a steadily growing number of refugees from shops and offices.

There were naturally many recruits to the Regiment who did not fall into these categories; the tailors who left their basement sweat-shops where they worked on assembly-lines over the newly invented sewing-machines; the hinds, loons, carles – otherwise farmworkers – who preferred to fee with the Queen, who paid weekly, rather than with the best farmer, who only paid half-yearly; the wandering pipers, of whom most deserted, several were discharged as bad characters, and one, William Ross, became piper to Queen Victoria; the Fife and Lanark miners who had worked in seams as low as twenty inches, and slept six or seven to a room; the Edinburgh coach-builders, whose crane-necked carriages were prized in Paris and St Petersburg; the butchers, bakers and candlemakers, the rubbers, dressers, skinners and fleshers. And was James Fraser, as he claimed, really a 'Card Sharper' by trade?

Whatever they had been before, they became soldiers in the 42nd Royal Highland Regiment (The Black Watch). The old name was added in 1861, and twenty years later, when the 42nd and 73rd were united, the official title became quite simply The Black Watch.

---

\* Appendix page 225.

# CHAPTER II

# The History of the 73rd

By its victories over the French in 1870-1 the Prussian army became a model to be followed, especially its trained reserve which enabled a small peace-time force to be rapidly and efficiently enlarged in time of war. Such a reserve, however, could only be formed under a system of short-service enlistment. In Britain, enlistment for life (in practice about fifteen years) produced an army of 200,000; to maintain that strength after the introduction of short service – six years with the Colours, and six in the Reserve (later seven and five respectively) – it was necessary for recruiting to be almost doubled. This, in its turn, required a system which would stimulate the flow of volunteers, and yet permit the army to keep its forces abroad for long periods.

As completed in 1881, the Cardwell-Childers system linked the 42nd with its former 2nd Battalion, the 73rd, and they became the 1st and 2nd Battalions of The Black Watch, with a recruiting area of Fife, Forfar and Perthshire. The two Regular battalions formed part of an administrative brigade, with its Perth depot serving the Militia in the recruiting area, who became known as the 3rd Battalion, and the Volunteers of Dundee, Forfar, Perthshire and Fifeshire. These latter had been raised in 1859 during a rumour of war with France, and in 1908, by Haldane's reforms, they became the 4th, 5th, 6th and 7th Territorial Battalions, The Black Watch.

The local connections stimulated recruiting, both from the area, and from the Militia and Volunteers, and since one of the Regular Battalions was, theoretically, always at home, the other could be kept abroad for many years, with men transferring between the two when necessary. It was a neat solution, which required one bitterly unpopular measure. In order that the officers of linked battalions could be placed on a single list for promotion, the purchase of commissions was abolished in 1871.

It was appropriate that the 73rd should rejoin the 42nd when the purchase of commissions was abolished, for it was over the vexed question of these properties that they had originally parted. The 2nd Battalion of the 42nd was raised in 1780 while the 1st was fighting in North America, and the only connection between the two was that the officers and men of the old battalion's depot companies formed the core of the new battalion. To these officers came the windfall of immediate promotion, without purchase; thus Major Norman MacLeod, who had less than five years service, found himself in command of the 2nd Battalion, having overtaken Major Charles Graham, in America with the 1st, who had twenty years service and 'had purchased every Commission but his Ensigncy'. The rub came when Graham achieved command of the 1st Battalion, and realised that if the Regiment were reduced at the end of the war, he, as the junior lieutenant-colonel would be the one put on half-pay. In 1785, he sent a Memorandum to the Horse Guards to protest at the injustice which he and other officers in the 1st Battalion would suffer from 'depriving them of their properties in their commissions, and, what is nearer the heart of a soldier, blasting all his hopes of promotion'. Instead, Graham suggested, the 2nd Battalion alone should be reduced.

By then the 2nd Battalion had won undying glory in Mysore and Mangalore, and its officers, no doubt a little hurt, at once sent a Counter-Memorial claiming that it would be equally unjust to them to ignore the regulation that both battalions in a corps suffered equally when it was reduced. A Board of General Officers considered the hypothetical question, and decided in favour of the 2nd Battalion, but a year later they cut the Gordian Knot by establishing the junior Battalion as a separate corps, the 73rd Regiment of Foot.

The 2nd Battalion had arrived in India in March, 1782, after a year-long voyage in which 121 men died of scurvy, and the troopship *Myrtle*, with Captain Dalyell's company on board, was lost. Having become separated from the fleet in a storm, the *Myrtle*'s captain confessed that he had no charts, but Dalyell, a resourceful officer, navigated it to St Helena, picked up some maps, then brought the ship on to Madras. However, there were little more than 500 men in the Battalion, when, for the first time, they met the flamboyant figure of Tippoo Sahib. A large Mysorean army, with French officers and soldiers among them, assaulted the town of Paniani, which Colonel MacLeod held, but, sickly and out of condition though they were, the 2nd Battalion charged repeatedly until they broke the enemy outside the walls of the town. The following day, they prepared to resume the battle, but patrols discovered that the host had disappeared from its camp; news had come in the night of the death of Tippoo's father, Hyder Ali, and the son had gone to claim his inheritance.

The heart of Hyder Ali's fabulous store of wealth was the treasure town of Bednore, hidden up in the mountains about forty miles from the sea. General Matthews, the nearest British commander, was preparing a well-thought out expedition to the town, when the Bombay Council ordered him to march immediately from the coast straight into the mountains to take Bednore. Irritated beyond measure by the interference of cross civilians, Matthews obeyed, but only to show the Council how impossible their in-structions were. Without ammunition or transport, Matthews marched his army through a harassing fire of rockets and musketry to the foot of the hills, where the road was blocked by two lines of fortifications defended by 3,000 men, and, behind them, a fort. Disclaiming all responsibility for the absurd operation, Matthews directed the 2nd Battalion against the defences. MacLeod led his Highlanders with a rush at the first breastwork, bayoneted four hundred of the enemy, drove the rest back to an abatis, cleared them from that position, and only came to a halt outside the walls of the fort. The next morning, the fort's garrison was found to have fled, and following the pattern of the previous day, the 42nd stormed on through a continuous chain of defences along the road, so that Bednore despaired, and surrendered while they were still some distance off. It was a glorious example of the art of the impossible, but even in the moment of hubris, nemesis was visible, for with the surrender of Bednore came that of Mangalore, a town on the coast which was now garrisoned by the 2nd Battalion and two sepoy regiments. They were under the command of Major Campbell, since Colonel MacLeod at once took ship to Bombay to persuade the Council to remove Matthews because of his incompetence. Tippoo forestalled him.

With an army of 100,000 men, including a French battalion and officers, Tippoo advanced on Bednore, recaptured it, imprisoned Matthews and his army, then descended locust-like on Mangalore. His cannon quickly reduced the walls of the town to rubble, but every attempt to storm past the ruins was resolutely driven back. It is impossible to do justice to Campbell and his garrison during their siege. It lasted for eight months, the last six of which the Bombay Council spent in a futile effort to conclude a peace with Tippoo, while the sepoys and Highlanders inside Mangalore were reduced to eating rats and their own shoe-leather. Colonel MacLeod, returning with supplies and reinforcements, was forbidden to land them by the Council, for fear of offending Tippoo. By the 20th January, 1784, starvation had reduced the garrison by half, and the remainder could scarcely stand, yet even with their opponents in that condition, the besiegers preferred not to risk another assault, but to allow the garrison to march out with colours flying. In the history of sieges, the defence of Mangalore must rank as one of the most gallant.

Many of the 2nd Battalion had been recruited from the MacLeods of Skye, and in the course of the siege, their Colonel issued a splendid challenge to Tippoo, which showed how close he remained to the clan spirit. Suspecting that Tippoo had accused him of uttering an untruth or 'making a mensonge', MacLeod declared, 'This is an irreparable affront. If you have courage enough to meet me, take a hundred of your bravest men and meet me on the seashore. I will fight you, and a hundred men of mine will fight yours.' The challenge, alas, was not taken up. The adjutant, Lieutenant Oswald, a former goldsmith and practising Hindu, was still more temperamental. He became so capricious that he had to be removed from the adjutancy, upon which he offered his services to the French. His was obviously a chameleon character, for, as he had become a Hindu in India, so in France he became a republican and revolutionary, eventually being killed while commanding a French regiment in La Vendée.

In April, 1785, during the peace that followed Mangalore, the Battalion was established as the 73rd, and a year later received a new Ensign in the person of Arthur Wellesley. It may be conjectured whether he ever wore the kilt during his eighteen months with the Regiment, but he certainly did not arrive in India until 1796, by which time he was in command of the 33rd. By coincidence, his old Regiment came under his direction, in the preliminaries to the storming of Seringapatam in 1799, when it formed part of the force which made a crucial bridgehead on to the island where the city stood. For the capture of the fort itself, however, the 73rd charged under the command of the redoubtable Sir David Baird, who had been a manacled prisoner within its walls. In the attack, Tippoo Sahib was killed, thus ending a long and chequered career, and giving the 73rd its revenge for Mangalore. The Regiment sang its own praise in a fine, immodest piece of verse:

> Great Mars, the God of War, did never see such men before,
>> Nor Alexander fight like us at Mangalore;
> At Seringapatam we fought, and Tippoo Sahib we slew.
>> 'Twas there we showed the black dog what the 73rd could do.

In the decade that separated Mangalore and Seringapatam, the Regiment had taken part in the capture of Pondicherry, and, in what Fortesque described as the most obscure campaign he had ever researched, it helped to mop up the Dutch colonies in Ceylon.

Their annexation, trivial as it may have appeared, stored up trouble for the future.

The 73rd returned to Britain in 1806, when it raised a 2nd Battalion whose flamboyant history has already been told. Recruiting in Scotland had become so difficult that the Horse Guards directed the 73rd, in common with most of the other Highland regiments, to forego the kilt so that Englishmen might not be discouraged from joining. The breeches seem to have done the trick for the 73rd was almost at full strength when it sailed for Australia in 1809.

The consequences for Australian history were immense, for Lachlan Macquarie, Commanding Officer of the 73rd, may be said to be the founder of modern Australia. He was given his chance by Governor William Bligh, whose bountiful folly had stirred up the second mutiny of his career, requiring Macquarie to supersede him as governor. Detachments of the 73rd, the first Regular troops in the country, were scattered through New South Wales and Van Diemen's Land to restore order, and hunt down bush-rangers, a task in which they were notably successful. They formed the nucleus of a mounted police force, whose indefatigable energy and skill won Fortesque's admiration; 'no body of men,' he said, 'reflected greater honour on the British Army.'

On his own responsibility, Macquarie initiated a vast programme of road-building, as a means of drawing the country together, and, of still greater importance, he began to emancipate convicts who had served their time so that they could return to the life of a normal citizen. The officers of the 73rd were less broad-minded, refusing to associate with former convicts, although they themselves were no sea-green incorruptibles. Macquarie had to remove Lieutenant Murray from his post when it was found that he had transferred labour gangs from building roads to building Murray's mansion. Major Gordon, who possibly was engaged in similar malpractice, suffered a more humiliating fate. An Irish pirate named McHugo sailed into the port where Gordon had his headquarters, and peremptorily accused him of crimes against the government. Astonished, presumably, at being found out, Gordon allowed the pirate to hale him before a mock court, try him, find him guilty, and sentence him to be shot. At the eleventh hour, as he lay awaiting his fate, a young subaltern arrived, and briskly threw McHugo out, threatening to blow his ship out of the water if he ever returned. Then he released his senior officer, rebuked him, and arranged for his court-martial for pusillanimity.

After four years of this life, the 73rd left, reluctantly it would seem, for many men bought themselves out and settled down in Australia. The remainder sailed to Ceylon, whose inhabitants had begun hacking the limbs off British subjects. Although Kandy was taken in 1815, unrest in that mountainous country did not cease with the capture of its capital. Among several gallant exploits, the cool action of Lance-Corporal McLaughlin's patrol, ambushed in a jungle valley, seems especially notable. Leaving part of his section to cover the bodies of two men who had fallen, McLaughlin fought his way out to get reinforcements, which he then led back in time to rout the ambushers. The rebellion reached a new height of frenzy, when someone purloined the Buddha's tooth from its niche in a temple in Kandy, but fortunately a subaltern of the 73rd arrested the thief and returned the molar to its cavity. Thereafter peace returned to the island.

In the century that elapsed between the sailing of the 2nd Battalion to India, and the eventual amalgamation of the 73rd with the 42nd in 1881, scarcely a dozen years of the Regiment's life were passed in Britain. On two occasions, in the 1820s and 1840s, both

PLATE 16  *The uniform of the 73rd after the adoption of trousers in place of the kilt.*

PLATE 17  *Colonel Lachlan Macquarie. Commanding Officer of the 73rd, and later Governor of New South Wales. Oil painting, 'The Father of Australia', by John Opie* RA.

decades of poverty and social unrest, the 73rd was employed on police duties in the Midlands, but otherwise they experienced the Victorian army's familiar mixture of harsh conditions in exotic places.

The Regimental song recorded their departure from England in 1827.

> Then next for Gibraltar, we got our second route,
>> We scarce had landed there three weeks, when a fever it broke out,
> Which laid some of our comrades low – but God defends the corps,
>> For where our Regiment lost fifteen, some regiments lost four score.

Divine protection did not apparently extend to the 42nd, which lost fifty-four men in the epidemic, but on the other hand, Sir Charles Gordon's Mediterranean rota system did not benefit the 73rd. Eleven years passed before they were sent to Canada to repel American invaders trying to take advantage of trouble between the Upper and Lower Colonies. The subsequent brief spell in Britain was followed by a bizarre intervention in South American politics, where they endured the second marathon siege of their history by defending Montevideo for seven months. There was a strong suggestion of comic opera to this siege, for the dictator Rosas could easily have entered the city, but refused to do so, while the greatest irritation to the 73rd was provided by a party of Italian pirates under Garibaldi. The Regiment had been en route to South Africa, before the diversion, and in 1846 it eventually continued its journey there. Over the next six years, it fought variously against Basutos, Boers, Hottentots, Xhosas, and Zulus, in what were known as the Kaffir Wars, but were more accurately punitive raids to protect the farms and cattle of the colonists.

'The ridiculous coatee' was the aspersion Fortesque cast at the red serge jackets worn by infantry at the time. They were conspicuous, hot and, in South Africa, invariably caught on the hooked thorns of 'the wait-a-bit' tree as the wearer brushed past. However, the 73rd soon came under the command of a peppery, bespectacled Colonel named Eyre, who, apart from his reprehensible opinion of the pipes – 'a useless relic of a barbarous age' – was an admirable commander. He dressed the 73rd in grey, canvas jackets, and used the Regiment like light infantry, covering enormous distances at such exceptional speed that they became known as the Cape Greyhounds. Eyre pursued the cattle-raiders right into their mountain bases, and in one action, reminiscent of Buchan's *Prester John*, the 73rd was conducted down a secret staircase in a cliff-face by a woman prisoner to an enormous cavern, called Macomo's Den. When the soldiers dashed in, they found over a hundred women and children cowering inside.

Eyre's hard driving inevitably caused casualties, and in 1852 a large draft for the 73rd came out on the troopship *Birkenhead*. At 2 a.m., the ship struck rocks in Simon's Bay, and many of the troops, caught in the rush of water below decks, were drowned. The remainder were ordered on deck, where parties were sent to man the pumps and lower the boats. 'Everyone did as he was directed,' wrote a survivor. 'All received their orders and carried them out as if the men were embarking, instead of going to the bottom; there was only this difference – that I never saw an embarkation conducted with so little noise and confusion.' The captain attempted to steam off the rocks, but the strain broke the ship's back, and the women and children were immediately conducted into the boats which were then pushed away from the settling ship. Then the senior officer told the men – they were little more then freshly-joined recruits – that if they tried to swim for the boats, they

PLATE 18    *The wreck of the* Birkenhead, *1852, in Simon's Bay, South Africa.*

would swamp them; he therefore asked them to remain where they were. Four hundred and thirty-eight men '. . . Biding God's pleasure and their chief's command, Went down erect, defiant to their grave, Beneath the sea.'

Having the largest contingent on board, the 73rd bore the heaviest toll with fifty-six of its men drowned, but the manner of their death resounded through Europe. The aged Duke of Wellington made his last appearance in public to praise their discipline, and, representing another era, the Kaiser ordered an account of their heroism to be read to his troops on parade. Even in the twentieth century, the tradition that women and children leave first in a shipwreck, is that established by the troops on the *Birkenhead*.

The path of the 73rd again crossed that of the 42nd in 1858, when they were both in India, but thereafter the Regiment was confined to the Oriental outposts of the Empire, only once returning home in the 1860s from an odyssey of twenty-three years which took them to Hong Kong and Ceylon, and back to India. It was there they received the news that they were to be amalgamated with their former Regiment, and, symbolically enough, as the Colours were paraded for the last time, the Roman numerals 'LXXIII', at the head of the standard, fell to the ground.

# CHAPTER 12

# The Years under Wolseley

The amalgamation of regiments was no less agonising then, than it was eighty years later, when the Cardwell-Childers system was replaced by the Sandys-Healey model. Much of the credit for the successful union of the 42nd and 73rd, must go to Colonel John MacLeod, last Commanding Officer of the 42nd and first of The Black Watch. His term of command lasted a decade, but he was the last colonel to have such a span of power, for his successors were limited to four years. Even he, however, could do nothing to ease the pangs caused by the loss of the regimental numbers. Captain Cockburn, who left the Regiment in 1870 and survived until 1924, was so devoted to 42 that, his obituary recalled, 'he always took off his hat when he passed the number in the street, or if hatless, made a deep salaam.' But just as 'The Black Watch' had never entirely disappeared, so 'The Forty Twa' continues to flourish as an unofficial title.

In 1873 the new system was tested while it was still only half-complete. At the time the Regiment's linked battalion was The Cameron Highlanders, and 126 of them were transferred to bring The Black Watch up to strength when it sailed to join Wolseley on the Gold Coast in November. Although the Ashanti campaign established Wolseley's military reputation, it was no more than a punitive expedition, which, it would not be too much to say, the Regiment rescued from the brink of failure.

The Ashanti were the dominant tribe in the Gold Coast interior, and under their king, Kofi Karikari, they had established a form of feudal suzerainty over their neighbours by force of arms, and in so doing they had intimidated some coastal tribes, who were nominally under the protection of the British. Wolseley was sent out to raise a Gold Coast army, but when his training failed to convert the coastal tribes into reliable soldiers, three British battalions were sent out at the end of 1873.

The administrative problems were immense. West Africa was 'the white man's grave, that dreaded bourne whence few return'. 'The bush is so dense,' wrote H. M. Stanley, who reported the campaign in flowery prose, 'that one wonders how naked people can have the temerity to risk their bodies in what must necessarily punish their unprotected cuticles.' The supplies for almost 3,000 men had to be transported through 130 miles of jungle, suitable weapons, clothes and tactics had to be produced, and the expedition had to be concluded by February, when the rains began making rivers impassable.

Wolseley and his 'ring' – a staff which included nine future generals and a field marshal – were masters of logistics: the weapons, short Enfield rifles converted to breech-loading; the clothes, Wolseley cork helmets, and grey Norfolk jackets and breeches; and the tactics, 'like fighting in twilight', were all designed for the bush. Seventy miles of jungle roads were constructed by cutting down trees, bridging 276 rivers, and laying corduroy and logs over the marshes. Along the road thousands of porters carried 400 tons of biscuits, rice and bully beef in tins, and a million rounds of ammunition.

Kofi had retreated precipitately during the preparations, fever rather than fear being the cause, and from his capital of Kumasi, sent placatory messages to the coast. On the 2nd January, Wolseley sent back an impossible demand for hostages and gold, failing which he would attack Kumasi; on the same day the great Kuma tree in the capital's market-place, heavy with symbolism and termites, slowly toppled over and crashed to the ground.

Two days later the army advanced and, on the 30th January, some sixty miles from Kumasi, it deployed into battle formation. In a booklet on bush warfare, Wolseley stressed the difficulty of communication and support, but he now adopted a square-shaped formation singularly unsuitable for thick jungle. A battalion made up each face, The Black Watch, 'my best battalion' according to Wolseley, taking the leading face. On the 2nd February they encountered the Ashanti at Amoafu, where the road descended into a swampy, heavily overgrown defile and then climbed up to a plateau. The enemy were posted in the valley and on the hills overlooking it.

The three leading companies entered the valley at 8 a.m. Fifteen minutes later, Stanley, back with Wolseley's headquarters, heard the Enfield rifles' 'cracking, ripping sound varied by the louder intonations of the Ashantis' overloaded muskets.' Over the next two hours, Brigadier Allison, commanding the advance, sent all but one of the remaining companies up in support. 'As company after company descended with their pipes playing into the ravine, they were almost immediately lost sight of in the bush,' Allison reported. 'Where a company was sent to support another, it saw nothing but bush in front, and speedily came under fire from the enemy. In these circumstances the men wanted to open fire, which would have taken their own men whom they were sent to support, directly in the rear.' In these conditions subalterns and N.C.O.s had to exercise individual fire control which they did so effectively that the Regiment was afterwards commended for the small amount of ammunition used.

Neither wing of the square was in a position to support them, and when Allison sent word that he might need reinforcements, Wolseley had only one company that he could have spared from guarding supplies. But gradually the Ashanti were driven to the slope beyond the valley's swampy floor, and the guns under Captain Rait could be brought forward. They fired several rounds up the hill, and the Regiment drove the Ashanti to the crest of the hill. Another salvo, another charge, and this time the soldiers were on the high ground, and the front was broken. Through sporadic firing from the bush, they moved swiftly on to take the enemy camp with a final rush.

Almost 25 per cent of the men had been hit by slugs, but owing to the ineffectiveness of Ashanti muskets only eleven of them died. As this first block on the road to Kumasi was broken, raiders cut the army's line of supply behind them, but Wolseley had no time to deal with this threat. The first rain had begun to fall, and he had to gamble that his present supplies would suffice for the advance to Kumasi. On the 4th February, his troops crossed the Ordah river, which was already rising, but on the other side the 60th Rifles, the leading battalion, came to a halt in the face of continuous ambushes.

Wolseley ordered up The Black Watch. Colonel MacLeod reported: 'I advanced rapidly, 50 paces at a time, passing the skirmishing companies [on either side of the road] through each other. The enemy met us persistently, and at first men fell, but pressing steadily on his flanks with my skirmishers, and storming his ambuscades on the road, he gave way before us.' Allison took up the account: 'Without stop or stay, the 42nd rushed on cheering, their pipes playing, ambuscade after ambuscade was successfully carried, village after village won, until the Ashantis broke and fled in wildest disorder.' The Regiment entered Kumasi peacefully to be greeted by many of their enemies still carrying muskets, but of Kofi there was no sign and, when Wolseley arrived later, the Ashanti disappeared, leaving an empty capital to the victors. For two days they waited for Kofi to surrender, and while they waited, they toured his palace and famous death-pit, where, in an acre-sized hollow, a mound of skeletons was covered with layers of bodies in successive stages of decomposition, 'the whole mass living and writhing with the worms that live on corruption'. Thunderstorms broke over the town, flooding the square, and Wolseley could wait no longer. The palace was blown up, the town burned, and through torrential downpours, the expedition raced back to the coast.

The psychological impact of the triumph was out of all proportion to its importance. When the Regiment returned, they received a rapturous reception, and were greeted with garlands and a flood of McGonegalloid poetry of which one verse may illustrate the others.

> Yes home again, my gallant boys –
> I'm but a Scottish lassie,
> But ah that I had been with you
> The day you burned Coomassie!

Parliament was grateful that honour had been maintained and military reform justified at a cost of less then £800,000, and the Queen decorated Lance-Sergeant Samuel McGaw with the Victoria Cross for his gallantry at Amoafu, giving rise to more verse, but a good song.

> The Ashantees, when they saw the shanks of Jock McGaw,
>     They turned aboot an' ran awa'.
> The rain may rain, an' the snaw may snaw,
>     The wind may blaw, an' the cock may craw,
> But ye canna frichten Jock McGaw,
>     He's the stoutest man in the Forty Twa.

The adulation tended to obscure how close the expedition had come to failure, and Wolseley had ample justification for the praise which he later poured upon the Regiment in his autobiography.

The year after Kumasi, Disraeli rescued the Khedive of Egypt from bankruptcy by purchasing his shares in the Suez Canal, and Gladstone grumbled presciently, 'Our first site in Egypt, be it by larceny or emption, will be the almost certain egg of a North African Empire.' The Imperial egg was laid in 1882. The growing involvement of France and Britain in Egypt's economic affairs provoked, in that country, a wave of nationalism, which erupted into violence, and fifty Europeans were killed in Alexandria. In July the Mediterranean squadron under Admiral Seymour bombarded the town, and the Liberal Government, with Gladstone dissenting, decided to invade. Even before the decision had been reached, Wolseley had arranged to purchase tents, American mules, railway lines and rolling stock. Intelligence work on the Egyptian position at Tel-el-Kebir was complete, and his plan of attack was drafted out before the first troops sailed. It is not surprising that Wolseley thought this his 'best managed campaign'.

The Black Watch departed in August, and in the first harvest of the short-service enlistment, they had been brought up to strength by calling up the First Class Reserve – those who had left the year before. In Alexandria they joined the Gordons, Highland Light Infantry and Camerons in a Highland Brigade under General Allison. Wolseley planned to attack Tel-el-Kebir from Ismailia on the Suez Canal rather than advance from Alexandria, but it was essential that the Canal should not be blocked, and so the Highland Brigade manoeuvred vigorously around Alexandria to distract the Egyptians' attention. When the Canal had been seized by the British, the Brigade was shipped to Ismailia, where it found that the speed of the operation had outwitted both the Egyptians and the supplies. Until the mules and the railway arrived in September, there were endless fatigue parties to unload and transport stores and ammunition.

The Tel-el-Kebir position was strong, and the Egyptians, commanded by Arabi Pasha, numbered about 20,000 men, armed with modern rifles and 60 Krupp guns, but Wolseley's prime cause for concern was that they might retreat before he could give battle. To secure his water supplies he was forced to capture the lock on the Sweetwater Canal at Qassassin, and on the 8th September his troops, repelling an attack, pursued the enemy to within four miles of their camp. For the next three days Wolseley reconnoitred the intervening desert while his army of 11,000 infantry, 7,000 cavalry and 60 guns moved up.

On the 11th September, Private Gordon in The Black Watch wrote, 'We are to march at night, and at daybreak storm the enemy's trenches at the point of the bayonet. We are not to fire.' They marched at 1.30 a.m. in two divisions, with the Highland Brigade leading the left division, and Graham's Brigade leading the right. Lieut. Rawson R.N. navigated a course by the stars for the Highland Brigade, and the march proceeded in silence through the dark. At 3 a.m. they halted, but the flanks did not receive the orders at once, thus their formation was crescent-shaped when they stopped, and on restarting the two wings almost met in the middle. However, the Highlanders made rather better progress than Graham's Brigade on the right, which dropped about 900 yards behind. Just before five o'clock, the Egyptian sentries saw them and opened fire at about 500 yards' range. The order was given to fix bayonets as they advanced, and Gordon wrote 'we noted the enemy's aim was high, for as our rear ranks sloped arms, the bullets rattled on the bayonets like hail on a tin roof'. Now the pipes began to play, and the Highlanders covered the last yards at a rush so that their line of double companies arrived as a line four deep.

They were faced with a high embankment behind a dry moat, eight feet wide, and opposite the Highland Light Infantry on the left, and The Black Watch on the right, there were heavy Krupp guns behind parapets on the embankment. The soldiers swarmed up the bank, and the most severe fighting occurred round the guns. In the centre of the Brigade, the Gordons and Camerons advanced into the second line of defences, but were driven back. For almost fifteen minutes the Highland regiments were unsupported in their furious battle, but when Graham's Brigade at last began to come up on the right, the Highland Brigade broke through the second line and into the camp behind. The Egyptians fled towards Cairo, but few survived for Wolseley's cavalry lay between them and the city. By 6 a.m. the battle was over, and Egypt passed into British control.

From the high excitement of battle, The Black Watch descended to depths of boredom, guarding a railway station, where they were forgotten for nine days, during which they contrived to live off their wits and forty-eight hours' rations. Recalling the experience, Gordon found Kipling appropriate.

> Wot makes the soldiers's 'eart to penk, wot makes 'im to perspire?
> It isn't standing up to charge nor lyin' down to fire,
> But it's everlastin' waitin' on an everlastin' road
> For the commissariat camel and his commissariat load.

They were eventually remembered and relieved, and for almost two years they remained part of the British garrison in Egypt.

Gladstone's Imperial egg proved to contain a chicken, for Egypt exercised suzerainty over the Sudan. Her most recent governor had been Charles Gordon, but after his departure in 1879, rebellion broke out under the leadership of the Mahdi, claimant to Mohammed's religious inheritance, and in December, 1883, he defeated an army under Hicks Pasha. The Liberal Government was determined to limit 'empire' to Egypt, and rather than respond to the provocation, it decided to abandon the Sudan, recalling Gordon to organise the evacuation of Egyptian settlers and officials from the country. As the breakdown of order accelerated, another leader, Osman Digna arose in East Sudan, and quickly defeated two forces of para-military police. At this the government reacted, and General Graham was dispatched with a division to restore order east of the Nile. Like Wolseley and Kitchener, Graham was a Royal Engineer; all three shared a talent for organisation, but only Wolseley seemed capable of finesse.

Graham elongated the square used in the Ashanti campaign, by placing two battalions on each flank, with one each at front and rear. Inside were staff and transport, with Gatling machine-guns at the corners. On the 29th February, 1884, this mobile fortress slowly approached the wells at El Teb, near the Eritrean frontier, where the Sudanese army was encamped. Digna's victories over European-armed forces had supplied his men with rifles, machine-guns and enormous self-confidence. They opened fire as Graham's square came in sight, and continued firing as it passed majestically down their left flank and halted about 800 yards in their rear. From that position Graham started to return the fire and, after half-an-hour's bombardment, ordered the square to face about and march on the Sudanese. The Black Watch, which had been the rear face, now found itself in front.

Despite the modern weapons which they had captured, most of the Sudanese were armed with only spears and double-edged swords. Their guns and riflemen were placed in the outer trenches, but their firing was not well-aimed, for The Black Watch reached them almost unscathed and were soon fighting hand-to-hand. They had no sooner taken these outer works, than the British cavalry, which had been wheeling round outside the square, charged on the main, unbroken force of Sudanese, and were cut down. In view of Graham's later comments, it should be noted that the infantry were now considerably disordered, and that when they reformed into line, they continued their advance with deliberation. 'Great black masses of Sudanese rose from their shelters in one wild rush for the square,' Gordon wrote. 'We stood ready with our Martini's, and at the right moment opened fire; the great masses flattened like waving grain in a hailstorm, the few that reached the square met our bayonets.' With superb courage, the Sudanese collected themselves and charged twice more, but against rifles and composed discipline it was hopeless and, at 2.30, after four hours of fighting, the wells were captured.

In his diary Wolseley would write scathingly of Graham's abilities as a commander, and particularly of the heavy losses he incurred fighting a primitive enemy. It is not clear whether he was responsible for ordering the cavalry to charge at El Teb, but he was certainly the cause of The Black Watch's heavy casualties at the battle of Tamaii a fortnight later. Before that battle Graham told The Black Watch, to its blank astonishment, that he had not been satisfied with its performance at El Teb; 'he expected us to charge the enemy's position and fight hand to hand, instead of meeting the enemy's advance by rifle-fire,' wrote Gordon. To give them a chance of regaining their reputation, as Graham put it, he promised to put them in the front line again.

The Sudanese had cut the route between the port of Suakin and Berber on the Nile, which was also the shortest road to Charles Gordon in Khartoum, and Graham now marched against their army at Tamaii, close to Suakin. For the battle he divided his force into two squares, presumably to achieve more mobility, and placed himself and The Black Watch in the second square. Colonel Green, normally as imaginative in vocabulary as he was short in temper, confined himself to describing the Regiment's mood as 'sticky', which hardly did justice to the furious, insulted pride in the ranks. They moved off in front of the first square, and soon approached a gully, in front of which some of the Sudanese were formed up. The Black Watch was in a right-angled formation, providing half the front face of the square, and half of its left face, and when they were a short distance from the gully, Graham ordered them to charge. In that curious formation they drove the Sudanese back, but were at once surrounded as the main force of the enemy came out from the shelter of the gully. The remainder of the square, opened up by the charge, was similarly invaded.

Facing front and rear, and left and right, the Regiment began to force its way back to the square. The fighting was frenzied with spears and swords against bayonets and claymores; rifles could not be used because of the British beyond the enemy, and anyone who fell was stabbed through repeatedly by the Sudanese, who themselves were bayoneted as they stabbed. Captain Scott-Stevenson, swinging his claymore furiously, 'clove a piece of a man's head as one does an egg for breakfast', and Private Edwards, in an action for which he was awarded the Victoria Cross, destroyed in hand-to-hand fighting a group of Sudanese trying to take a Gatling machine-gun. As the Regiment retired, the first square came up, and under their protection, the second square re-formed, and then with rifle and machine-gun fire they drove off the Sudanese.

Kipling again:

> Then here's *to* you Fuzzy-Wuzzy, an' the missus an' the kid,
>  Our orders were to break you, an' of course we went and did.
> We sloshed with Martini's, an' 'twasn't hardly fair,
>  But for all the odds agin you, Fuzzy-Wuz, you broke the square.*

* The broken square remained a standing jibe for many years. It was rumoured that the reason for the square cut of Black Watch spats was to remind the Regiment of its disgrace, and a fight could be started in any pub in a garrison town where a Black Watch battalion was stationed simply by calling for 'A pint of Broken Square'. At that, belts would be flailed, eyes blackened and knuckles bloodied.

A poem to Graham might have been less picturesque, but he certainly deserved some of the credit.

Graham's force was recalled to Egypt in April, leaving the unsubdued Sudanese to continue their investment of Berber. When it fell in May, not only was Gordon trapped in Khartoum, but the relief expedition which set off in September had to follow the longer Nile route instead of the shorter Suakin-Berber road. Wolseley, the expedition's commander, greeted the Regiment with an assurance that it would mostly be hard work, 'but if fighting should become inevitable, I know I shall only have to call on The Black Watch'. A navy of whalers was provided to carry the force up the Nile, with Canadian boatmen acting as pilots, but the Nile was so low that the soldiers were forced to frequent portage, entailing the repeated unloading and transporting of the four tons of equipment carried in each 900 lb boat. At the start of the Sudanese campaign, the Regimental Gordon made a perceptive comparison that naval efficiency tended to be superior to military, due to the close intimacy of officers and men, whereas 'soldiers only now and then meet their officers man to man'. On the Nile, however, he noted that 'the officers threw themselves into the struggle, working side by side with the men', so that only minutes separated them from the prize for the fastest passage to Korti. There the force divided: a desert column making a desperate dash for Khartoum, while the river column, with The Black Watch, followed the Nile. On the 10th February, 1885, the Regiment fought its third and last battle against the Sudanese, when the enemy was encountered on the high bluff of Kirbekan overlooking the Nile. The Black Watch made a determined bayonet charge up the rocky slope to dislodge the enemy from their prepared defences, and indeed the Sudanese suffered badly by adopting more static tactics, for the cavalry raided their rear, and when the remainder barricaded themselves in a farmhouse, the South Staffordshires stormed it. The victory was marred by the death of General Earle in the last minutes, but worse was to follow, for four days later news came that all their efforts were fruitless, and Gordon was dead. Sadly the column returned to Egypt.

The Sudanese campaign continued intermittently until 1899, but the Regiment took no further part. After a tour of duty in the Mediterranean, it was split between Cape Town and Mauritius. To describe the horror of being posted to the island, Charles Gordon told of an apocryphal conversation, in which the Duke of Cambridge, the Commander-in-Chief, ordered his Adjutant-General to send some incompetent to Hell. 'We have no station there, your Grace,' replied the Adjutant-General. 'Very well, send him to Mauritius,' said the Duke. By contrast, Cape Town was regarded as next to Paradise as a posting, so there were some interesting comparisons to be made in 1896, when the Battalion was reunited in India.

In the last years of the 1880s, two technical developments transformed the power of the rifle. The French introduced a smokeless cartridge, so that for the first time a concealed marksman might remain invisible, and repeating rifles became widely available. It was unfortunate that British commanders, faced by primitively armed enemies, continued to find that close formation drill answered most of their tactical problems.

Plate VII (above)    *The Highland Brigade (42nd, 79th and 93rd Regiments) to embark for India in 1857.*

Plate VIII (below)    *In the moat before the Egyptian position at Tel-el-Kebir 1882.*

PLATE IX  *The broken square at Tamaii in 1884. The York and Lancaster Regiment, who formed part of the square, and General Graham, on the white horse, are also portrayed.*

PLATE X  *Major-General Andrew Wauchope* C.B., C.M.G. *of the Regiment, killed while commanding the Highland Brigade at Magersfontein 1899.*

# CHAPTER 13

# The Boer War and its Aftermath

Throughout the summer of 1899, there was a mounting conviction that war with the Transvaal must come, the only doubt being whether the Orange Free State would join in. Students at the Staff College prepared schemes for the possible British response; Captain Archibald Cameron of the 2nd Battalion, The Black Watch, proposed a concentration of forces in the north of the Cape Province, followed by a general advance up the main railway through the middle of the Orange Free State to Bloemfontein, and then, still keeping to the railway, on to Pretoria, centre and capital of the Transvaal. It was essentially the same plan as that which Wolseley suggested to Sir Redvers Buller, commander of the force sent to South Africa.

Although the British had been planning for war during that summer, it had been the main preoccupation of the Boers for a decade. Each state was a republic under British suzerainty, a condition of relative independence which they had won by their victory over the British at Majuba Hill in 1884. In the next decade the limitations of their independence were exposed by foreigners, attracted to the mines at Kimberley, who appealed directly to the British government when they were denied citizens' rights. It had long been the opinion of Kruger, President of the Transvaal, that another Majuba Hill would not only win the Boers full control over their own affairs, but might also incite the Dutch in Cape Province to rebel, thus driving the British out of Southern Africa altogether.

War was declared on the 11th October, and within a fortnight the Boers had invaded Natal, invested Kimberley, Mafeking and Ladysmith, and were threatening to over-run Cape Province. Faced with so many dangers, Buller jettisoned Wolseley's plan, and unwisely, as both Cameron and history decided, split up his forces. Taking a division with him to Natal, he left General Gatacre to defend the eastern approaches to Cape Province, General French to hold the centre round Naauwspoort, and General Methuen to advance in the west to the relief of Kimberley.

The Highland Brigade was part of Methuen's force, but he had marched before any but the Argylls had arrived. The 2nd Battalion of The Black Watch had been sent out from Britain to join the Brigade, dressed in an unaccustomed uniform of khaki tunics, and aprons to cover the kilt, and it eventually caught up with Methuen at Modder River, after he had won three expensive actions against the Boers. Cameron wrote a grim description of his force.

> I do not consider the morale of this camp good. Everyone has entirely lost confidence in Methuen. He just banged his head against Belmont and Grasfran without any previous artillery preparation, and Modder River was disgraceful. All the officers

who were in the battle openly say they have had enough fighting to last them the rest of their lives. So, in the next battle, there is no doubt that we three fresh battalions [Black Watch, Seaforths, and Gordons] will be put in the front line.

North of them they could see the beam of the Kimberley searchlight in the night sky, and all that lay between them and the city was a line of low hills, fifty-five metres high, and Cronje's Boers. The hills might have been by-passed to the west but, when patrols showed that the Boers were fortifying the position, Methuen must have decided that there was a chance of annihilating an enemy who had ridden away from earlier defeats. He had been present at Tel-el-Kebir, and he now planned a similar night march and dawn attack. At Majuba Hill, the Boers had successfully stormed a hill-top camp by making use of the dead ground on the lower slopes, and it was reasonable to assume that the same shelter could be found at the bottom of the Magersfontein hills, where his troops might deploy before making a bayonet charge on the trenches on the crest. Unfortunately, during the two weeks that Methuen delayed at the Modder River, the same thought occurred to the Boer tactician, de la Rey, who persuaded Cronje to entrench at the bottom of the hills. Perhaps to avoid alarming the Boers, Methuen made no reconnaissance in force, and discovered neither the trenches, nor the one weakness of the Magersfontein position, a gap in the centre of the hills, which was lightly held by a small force of Scandinavian volunteers.

On the 10th December Methuen divided his force into three: the Highland Brigade was to attack the central *kopje* or hill, just west of the gap; the Guards Brigade was to hold the attention of the Boers on the *kopjes* to the east of the gap; and the third part was detailed to create a diversion to the west of the range. A brief bombardment helped to alert the enemy but caused them no casualties and, in the afternoon, General Andrew Wauchope, who had served in the Regiment in the Gold Coast and the Sudan, led the Highland Brigade to within three miles of the Magersfontein hills, where it then bivouacked. As Cameron had forecast, The Black Watch was leading with the Seaforths immediately behind, then came the Argylls, very leery of Methuen's tactics by this time, and finally the Highland Light Infantry. The Gordons, not being in the Brigade, were in reserve.

Captain Stewart, commanding 'B' Company wrote in his diary:

Marched at 12.30 a.m. Monday 11th, still raining and pretty well soaked. We kept our places by the guide of each company holding a bit of string with knots every 10 yards. No lights or noise. We stumbled over rocks and dykes, and I fancy the regiments behind were in a most fearful muddle as some of the Seaforth got mixed in my company. General Andy marched at the head of the column. We kept tacking about in the most extraordinary way until we came to a line of bushes with only one place through. Eyken and I got our companies ['A' and 'B'] through, but there was much delay, and we were told to drop the rope and go on. We were wheeled round half-left, and already [3 a.m.] it was getting rather light. Up to this it had been pitch black, but it had now stopped raining. We halted about 3.20 and must have been visible to anyone on the kopjes – halted in brigade mass of quarter companies i.e. the closest formation possible, about 800 yards from the kopjes.

After some more confusion, two companies were ordered to advance. 'At 3.35 "A" company went forward and had gone 150 yards, and I had got my company extended, when the Boers opened such a fire.'

Not until that moment did Wauchope realise that the defenders were at the foot of the hill rather than at its peak. His Brigade was further west than it should have been, and the half-wheel left had taken the two leading companies between two projecting spurs so that they were fired on from three sides, while the Scandinavian outpost could enfilade the others from the right.

Wauchope ordered Colonel Coode to extend the Battalion to the right to come opposite the gap in the hills. Shortly afterwards both officers were killed. Nevertheless, the Scandinavian outpost was taken, and one company penetrated the gap and started up the eastern side of the *kopje*. They came under heavy fire, but held their position until 4.30 a.m., when the British artillery began dropping shells on them. Later, a mixed company of Seaforths and Black Watch pushed further through the gap, and circled round to the north-east of the hill; they had penetrated deep into the defences when a roving party of Boers appeared by chance on their flank, and frustrated the last hope of redeeming the situation.

On the southern side of the *kopje*, men of the front three companies were scattered in an area within 300 yards of the trenches; some had reached the wire in front of them, but none could move. The rest of the Battalion was mixed up with the Seaforths to their right and rear, but elsewhere there was complete confusion with troops undeployed, and some, experienced in Methuen's methods, engaged in smart withdrawal. At 9 a.m., with his forward troops pinned down, the General advanced the Gordons in frontal attack across the open veld, so that they, too, shared the same fate.

Heavy casualties came from raking fire by the Boers on the *kopjes* to the right, and the Guards, who had lost a battalion during the night march, could not check it. At midday the Seaforths drew back their flank to meet the fire, the Gordons followed suit, and in the rear of the Brigade it was thought that a general withdrawal had been ordered. There was no one to take control, because the senior surviving officer did not learn of Wauchope's death until mid-afternoon. As men rose from the ground, the worst casualties of the day occurred, and a widespread retreat took place.

In the front, Stewart described the progress of the day: 'About 10 a.m. I could find only 3 sound men within 30 yards either side. We all hugged mother earth pretty close after we had finished our rounds. I was so sleepy, I went to sleep about 3 in the afternoon' (as did everyone else)

> and woke to find the Boers standing up outside their trench. I shouted to a poor boy who had 3 rounds left to fire; though I think he hit his man, it drew their fire again. Our ammunition ran out altogether about 6 p.m. The Boers saw we were comparatively harmless, and two of them came down with water-bottles. I yelled at them to go away, but couldn't stop them, so they just gave the wounded water and took stock of us. . . .

The news of their defeat came as a profound shock to Scotland. For almost a century the Highland Regiments had hardly known anything but victory; now, in the space of twelve hours, they had suffered over 900 casualties – most of whom had been hit several times – from an enemy they had hardly seen. The very quality of war seemed to have changed. Yet it was in this adversity that the underlying strength of the regiments was revealed. From Scotland came a swell of sympathy and support which flooded the Volunteers and the Militia with recruits, and helped to restore morale with a stream of messages and gifts. All the Regiment's reserves were called up, and eventually they were followed by 162 Militia and two Volunteer companies. For those who stayed at home, the best way of showing their support was to send presents, and these arrived in such profusion that the officer in charge of the mails in South Africa complained that he had delivered more packages to the Highland Brigade than the rest of the army put together.

Magersfontein was only one of the three disasters in that black week of December – the others were at Stormberg and Colenso – and the reaction of the government was unequivocal. Wolseley undertook to provide a second army corps which brought the number of troops to 440,000, and Roberts was given overall command, with Kitchener as his second. Their arrival at the beginning of the new century gave decisiveness to the campaign. On the 4th February Methuen moved west to Koodoesberg in an action which pulled the Boers out of position, and allowed General French and the cavalry to break through to Kimberley. The Koodoesberg action cost the life of, among others in the Battalion, Lieutenant Tait, the Amateur Golf Champion, but its result was to surround Cronje's forces, forcing him to a desperate attempt to break out eastward. The cavalry headed him off at Paardeberg on the north bank of the Modder River and, as infantry came up from south and west, some 3,000 Boers were trapped. They might have been starved out of their strong position but, on the 18th February, Kitchener, in Roberts' absence ordered an immediate attack from the south.

The Black Watch had arrived at midnight on the 17th, after covering eighty miles in the previous five days, but at dawn the next day they advanced across open veldt in the front line of the Highland Brigade. As usual the Boers were well-concealed in trenches and under cover of the river bank from which they opened a heavy fire, but showing that they had learned from experience, the Highlanders extended their line, returning the fire independently. General Colville described it as 'a very fine feat by the Highlanders, and one of which they will always have reason to be proud. I never hope to see or read anything grander than the advance of that thin line across a coverless plain under a hail of lead from their invisible enemies.'

They had more than a mile to cover, and only on the left were men able to reach the river. There Captain Stewart risked crossing the flooded Modder and managed to drive in the Boer outposts on the further bank. His initiative could have been exploited with reinforcement, but General Smith-Dorrien, on the same side of the river, complained that he was 'in a complete fog and knew nothing of the situation'. An attack on the army's rear by Boers outside the ring brought the battle to an end, but Cronje was now tightly corked. Deserters began to slip away and, nine days later, Stewart wrote in his diary, 'Such an anniversary for Majuba, Cronje and 2,400 Boers prisoners. Not a fine lot physically on the whole; most aged from 25 to 45, but grey-beards and boys too. Heavy stupid faces, but obstinate and not unprepossing. The ground is littered with clothing, pots and pans, dead horses and oxen (oh the stench was something appalling), millions of rounds of ammunition, and rifles.' The litter of war in this case was the Boers' personal property, and so heavy a loss brought them to their knees. Kruger himself and Steyn of the Orange Free State now joined the burghers to keep up their morale, and both might have been taken a week later at Poplar Grove but for the cavalry's failure to move more energetically. Nevertheless, on the 15th March, the Battalion entered Bloemfontein, two days behind Roberts.

Rejoining as adjutant, after being wounded at Magersfontein, Cameron found the Battalion 'extremely fit . . . bearded like the pard', but only 480 strong. It now received a draft of almost the same size and it seems clear that so large an intake left it unbalanced for some time after. Under the Cardwell system, early drafts were expected to be trained men from the linked battalion at home, but since both Black Watch battalions were abroad, these reservists, volunteers and militia had been hurried straight out, inadequately trained and physically unprepared.

Cameron's particular *bêtes noires* were the Section D men, who had already left the reserve. 'Britain's last hope' they liked to call themselves, but their adjutant reckoned they had 'the cunning of old soldiers and the independence of civilians'. It may have been with their particular qualities in mind that the Regiment, in 1901, chose as its tune for Defaulters' Parade 'A man's a man for a' that'. The officers who came out then did not inspire Cameron to much greater enthusiasm: 'We have a larger collection of large, stout officers with big, red faces and very loud, hearty laughs than any regiment I ever saw – mixed with them the smallest, most effeminate-looking schoolboys I ever saw.'

However, the next phase of the war soon shook everyone into shape. When Roberts entered Pretoria, the capital of Transvaal, on the 5th June, it seemed certain that the war would shortly end. The Boers surrendered in droves, Kruger was a fugitive, and nothing could halt Roberts' army. But The Black Watch, detailed for the pacification of the Orange Free State, already knew the frustration of guerrilla warfare. As Stewart suggested, 'It seems so futile, infantry marching after a mounted enemy.' Kitchener confirmed that 'the Boers are not like the Sudanese who stood up to a fair fight. They are always running away on their little ponies.' (*Kitchener,* by Philip Magnus). And Cameron summed up, 'We picture ourselves for years trekking round the Free State, till we become a phantom brigade, nothing to be seen, but at night the wailing of pipes and loud curses will be heard, to the terror of the inhabitants.' By August they had covered 1,000 miles on foot, and they had another 2,000 miles ahead of them.

In May the Highland Brigade marched 100 miles in six days to reach the town of Heilbron; it was a superb feat of stamina, which also provided a miniature of the frustrations the Regiment had to undergo. It was sniped at daily, almost every likely *kopje* concealed an ambush, and Boer artillery shelled them from long-range. Only eighty cavalry were attached to the Brigade, and in their attempts to scout ahead and protect the three-mile-long flanks of the convoy, they foundered their horses. Infantry patrols then had to perform cavalry duties, fanning out across the veldt to flush out snipers. Two battalions were required to attack ambushers, often no more than 100 in number, one battalion assaulting, while the other tried to cut off the horsemen as they escaped. Finally the naval guns, each drawn by thirty-two oxen, had to be protected as they ponderously moved into position to reply to the Boer artillery. There had never been a war where the infantry's dependence on cavalry and artillery was more cruelly exposed. When it reached Heilbron the Brigade suffered the further humiliation of being besieed there by 150 mounted Boers, who made movement outside the town impossible. Relief was difficult for Christian de Wet's talent for ambush made it necessary to protect convoys with an entire brigade. It was not until the Lovat Scouts learned how to stay on a horse, and thus make their poaching skills mobile, that the Highland Brigade had mounted troops to match the Boers.

However, the marching feet caught up with the galloping hooves on several occasions, most notably at Retief's Nek in July, 1900. The Nek was a passage through the hills protecting a natural fortress, where Prinsloo and 4,000 Boers were surrounded. It was reached on a night of blinding gales of snow and sleet, and the following day the Brigade attacked the line of hills, which overlooked the road into the plain beyond. The Battalion took the first peak of a saddle-back without casualties, but were shelled there during the day until their own artillery came up. Then, with covering fire from the guns, they charged through the dusk on to the further crest, where they had the rare satisfaction of firing on the Boers at close range. Theirs was the only successful attack of the day, but the hill's capture enabled the Nek to be taken the following afternoon; Prinsloo's Boers were now caught between three different brigades, and after some sharp fighting they surrendered. It had become obvious, however, that such successes occurred too rarely, and in October, the policy of chasing the commandos was abandoned for one of cordoning them off. The Battalion joined a cordon near Ladybrand, travelling part of the way there by train. 'It seemed terribly quick,' Stewart observed. '14 miles per hour, a day's march.' The cordons, however, were penetrated with some ease, and Kitchener gradually substituted block-houses and wire for troops. The Battalion spent a year in the vicinity of Ladybrand, and then, after two months in Natal, moved to Harrismith in what was now the Orange Colony. (There had been a competition to choose a new name for the Orange Free State after it was crushed, but Stewart's suggestion of Marmalade was not acceptable.)

At Harrismith the 2nd Battalion was joined by the 1st, which had come out from India in December, 1901. Their union was brief, for Kitchener now introduced the last refinement to his strategy, that of operating flying columns of cavalry and infantry inside the grid of blockhouse lines. In early 1902 companies of each Battalion were allocated to different columns, while others remained to garrison the town. But even with this final restriction on the enemy's mobility, which Cameron thought 'at last brought the infantry into its own', the foot-soldier's role remained tedious.

A young subaltern called Wavell, who came out with a draft for the 2nd Battalion at this time, found it 'not very exciting work, but it taught a young officer his job on active service, how to handle and look after himself and his men.' Coming from the most distinguished soldier the Regiment has yet nurtured, such an opinion carries weight, and the careers of three other officers equally suggest that the lessons of the Boer War were not wasted on them. Captain Stewart, the diarist, commanded the 1st Battalion in the Great War with great skill before being killed as a Brigadier-General. Captain Cameron, the adjutant, reached General rank, and became Colonel of the Regiment, and his successor in the Colonelcy was Arthur Wauchope, the General's cousin and A.D.C., who, despite the recurrent pain of wounds received at Magersfontein, became an outstanding battle commander in the Great War.

Tedious though they were, the operations of the flying columns proved extremely effective, and so many Boers were captured that, on the 31st May, 1902, their leaders accepted defeat and laid down their arms. There had never been more than 65,000 Boers arrayed against the 440,000 men mobilised by the British Empire, and it was clear that there were lessons to be learned at a far higher level than that of the regimental officer. Indeed, the performance of those officers was the only satisfactory aspect of the war that a government enquiry could find.

With most of the reforms instituted by the Esher Committee, such as the creation of the General Staff, the Regiment was not concerned, but the matter of reserves affected it directly. To make the reserve forces of the Militia and Volunteers more effective, and to avoid the sort of difficulties the 2nd Battalion experienced in South Africa, it was recommended that their training should be brought closer to that of the Regular Army, and, in 1908, Haldane, as Secretary of War, achieved that result by creating from the disparate reserve forces a Territorial Force, to which the Regular Army seconded officers and N.C.O.s to act as instructors. The Territorial Battalions of The Black Watch thus came into being only a matter of six years before the war in which they were to win such fame.

In these last years before the holocaust, there is an almost apocalyptic sense of preparation. Haldane in London, Kitchener in India, polishing and refurbishing; even in Ireland, Colonel Rose had the 1st Battalion on a regimen of physical training and early morning runs. However, commanding the 2nd Battalion in India, there was a quite unrepentant sinner, Colonel Maxwell. To improve the training of regiments in India, Kitchener introduced a competition to find the most efficient battalion in field exercises. After three years of the real thing, Maxwell refused to take it seriously, and the 2nd Battalion performed deplorably. On one occasion, racing back to camp after cutting short a wretched display in the Kitchener Cup, it was comprehensively ambushed by the Gordons, but the Commanding Officer preserved his urbanity, and when his Transport Officer hurried up for orders, Maxwell said, 'My dear Wavell, I really don't know, what do you think your mules would like? I've noticed a particularly intelligent grey one. I suggest you refer it to him, if you can't find the adjutant.'

However, long before war broke out, the influence of Major Wauchope made itself felt, and, as a trainer of soldiers he was second to none. By 1914 the 2nd Battalion was at a high state of readiness, although it may be noted as a military curiosity, that the last action taken by the officers before leaving for France was to sharpen their swords.

In the final preparations, some administrative changes must be noted. When the 1st Battalion returned to Aldershot in February, 1914, the old formation of eight companies was replaced by a four-company system. The changeover took place under the command of Colonel Grant-Duff, a brilliant officer who was largely responsible for drawing-up *The War Book*, the procedures to be followed by government departments on the outbreak of war. The Committee of Imperial Defence, to which he had been Assistant Military Secretary, had planned that in the event of war the Regular Army would at once be reinforced by a succession of new units from the Territorial Army, 'each of which would have slipped into the place of the one in front as it moved away', in Haldane's own words.

When war did come, the four Territorial Battalions of The Black Watch, recently returned from camp, were mobilised within days at their depots, and within weeks each was building a second battalion. But Kitchener, on succeeding Haldane in August, 1914, imposed a second system, by which his New Army, recruited in the regimental areas, was trained in Regular Army barracks and drill grounds. Thus the 8th and 9th Battalions were formed at Aldershot, where they were followed by the 10th. This unnecessary duplication caused confusion and delay. The Territorial Battalions, though reasonably kitted and armed, were denuded of their instructors. The New Army Battalions, filled their complements within a month of Kitchener's order, but not until February, 1915 was the first one properly equipped. Instructors were spread so thinly that the 8th Battalion had only three Regular officers, and one of those had to be lent to the 9th which had none, and yet they were the senior battalions in, respectively, the 9th (Scottish) and 15th (Scottish) Divisions, the first to be formed in each wave of the New Army.

It is necessary to emphasize these difficulties, not only to explain the long delay before the bulk of the New and Territorial Armies arrived in France, but because the unsatisfactory training renders more extraordinary the spirit and cohesion of these civilian soldiers under the most extreme stresses of the Western Front.

# CHAPTER 14

# The Outbreak of the Great War

Long before the assassination at Sarajevo, Europe was divided into two armed camps – the central powers of Germany and Austria-Hungary against France and Russia, with Britain tied to France by proximity and the *Entente Cordiale,* and Russia tied by racial solidarity to her fellow Slavs in the countries bordering the Austro-Hungarian Empire. When the schoolboy Gavrilo Princip murdered Franz Ferdinand, Archduke of Austria, and his wife on the 28th June, 1914, the spate of events, of threat, mobilisation and ultimatum, gradually, but inexorably, drew on these ties so that all Europe was dragged by the Balkan outrage into a war which none had overtly sought. This much is true, but it cannot be denied that, after the assassination, Germany, which was by far the best prepared for war of all the European nations, actually precipitated the conflict by violating Belgian neutrality and invading France in pursuance of a strategic policy devised eight or nine years before. For her military planners, the murder at Sarajevo was a most opportune excuse. Britain, which had guaranteed Belgian neutrality, acknowledged her obligation and, on the 4th August, declared war on Germany. Alone among the contending nations, she had the satisfaction of announcing idealism as the root of policy, and she became engaged in the holocaust that followed, with the avowed intention of defending small nations.

On the 4th August, the 1st Battalion, The Black Watch, landed in France with the 1st Division of the British Expeditionary Force, 'the best trained and best equipped army that had ever left these shores'. In accordance with the demands of Plan XVII, the Force was sent on to Maubeuge in Belgium to check the swing of the German right, while the French hammered at their left and centre, in a policy of *l'attaque à outrance,* which cost 300,000 casualties in the first month of the war. 'If ever a plan deserved to succeed it was the Schlieffen Plan; if ever one deserved to fail, it was Plan XVII,' wrote Wavell (*Allenby,* by A. P. Wavell). The one had failed, and the other was coming close to success. On the 24th August, the day after the Battalion took up its position on the Mons-Beaumont road to the left of Lanrezac's Fifth Army, thirty-four German divisions began to close in on the ten French and four British divisions; conforming with Lanrezac's withdrawal the British began a retreat which continued until the 5th September. Just over a century before, The Black Watch had been part of a distinctly frayed army retreating from Burgos, the last general withdrawal in which they had participated. Whatever changes had occurred since then, prolonged retirement before a superior enemy remained the most shaking test of morale. At Headquarters, it collapsed so entirely that a French liaison officer believed that 'the British Army no longer exists', but the moment to turn and attack showed it to be rather more than merely existant.

The roundhouse swing at Paris demanded by von Schlieffen's plan fell short and descended east of the city, and a gap opened between von Kluck's army at the end of the line and Bulow's on the inside of von Kluck. Into this opening, Gallieni advanced the Paris garrison while the British moved up on their left. On the 8th September, the 1st Battalion, as brigade advance guard, encountered a Jäger battalion on a wooded ridge east of Sablonnières. While two companies engaged the enemy among the trees, a third outflanked them along a road south of the ridge, and the machine-gun section (i.e. two machine-guns) and two companies of Camerons circled round to their rear position in Sablonnières, where they enfiladed the village itself. Under accumulating pressure, the Germans attempted to pull back from the ridge, but now the reserve company reinforced the general attack which entirely destroyed the enemy corps in the village. It was the Battalion's first major action, and the freedom of movement, and initiative at company level, spoke well of their training and resilient spirit after the long retreat from Mons.

The Germans withdrew their forces beyond the river Aisne to high ground along which ran the old Roman road called Le Chemin des Dames. More slowly than in its first days, the pursuit continued and on the 14th September the 1st Battalion took part in a divisional assault on this new position. In mist, they came up the slope, but instead of a retreating enemy, they found well-prepared defences. Two companies fought their way on to the road, but the others became separated and were driven off the summit. In an attempt to save the ground gained, Colonel Grant-Duff led a counter-attack which was beaten off, and he himself was killed. There were no reserves, and at dark the two leading companies were pulled back to straighten the line. During that night of pouring rain, the first spadefuls were dug of a trench system which swiftly spread as both armies began their race to the sea to find an open flank.

Late in October, the B.E.F. was brought north to make a thrust towards Bruges. Cutting deep beyond the main strength of the most northern German army, they created a large salient round Ypres, but were held short of the high ground at Passchendaele. As Gallieni pointed out, the Allies were always twenty-four hours and an army corps too late, for, to the east, Antwerp had fallen, releasing the army of first-line troops which Moltke had surprisingly detailed for its investment. Never again did the British face fresh troops of such high morale and training. They attacked in overwhelming numbers, sometimes through the early morning mist, sometimes in daylight, confidently singing 'Die Wacht am Rhein'. For eighteen days of almost continuous fighting, the Battalion, as part of a thin line of defenders, bitterly resisted the crushing pressure which slowly squeezed the salient. Trained to fire fifteen rounds rapid in a minute, and grimly confident in their craft, they opposed so fiercely that, to the dazed Germans, it seemed as if 'every bush, hedge and fragment of wall' contained 'a machine-gun rattling out its bullets'. On a significant date, the 11th November, a heavy attack overwhelmed the Battalion's corner of Polygon Wood, but a company strongpoint held out, and while the commanding officer defended his headquarters with a revolver, Captain Victor Fortune, the only officer unwounded, led a company counter-attack back to the strongpoint which halted the threatened break-through. It was the last attempt made on a position which, from then on, the maps referred to as Black Watch Corner. Two days later the Battalion was relieved, when reinforcements from the Indian Army, and the first Territorials, including the 5th Battalion, took over the line.

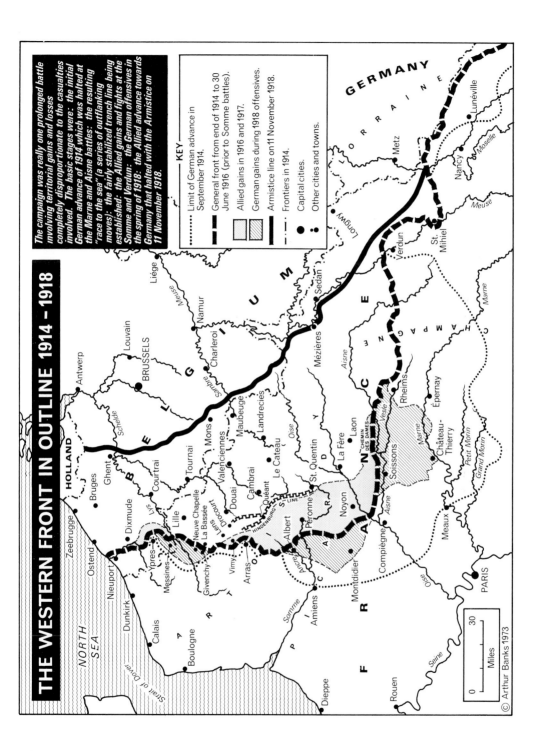

*The First World War: The Western Front in Outline, 1914–1918. Courtesy Heinemann Educational Books Ltd.*

The salient had been held, but it was the graveyard of the old army. Few of the original Battalion were left, and although several drafts had arrived earlier, over 300 men were now required to bring it up to strength. Among the officers, only Captain Fortune remained unwounded, and he was to fight through the entire war unscathed. Although Germany had failed to gain the swift victory she wanted, her territorial gains dictated that the future course of the war would be directed towards evicting her from the captured ground. But now, with the use of barbed wire and sandbags, the lines of trenches were rapidly converted into siege defences.

The British sector of the front was never more than 125 miles long, and at this stage it measured only 21 miles out of 466 for the whole front, but it possessed particular dangers which the French escaped. Strategically, the north was the more important, covering the mines and heavy industry behind the line. Yet the defenders had no room to retreat, because only fifty miles separated their supply-ports from the front, and most of that front lay in low ground where deep trenching was often difficult. A cursory glance at the map showed its major weakness.

The Ypres salient was overlooked from east and south by Passchendaele Ridge, Gheluvelt Plateau, and Messines Ridge; at that point the front dipped to the muddy floor of the Lys Valley near Armentières, where both trenches were on a level. From the Lys Valley, the line veered south-west, running for twenty miles across flat country to the German-held Aubers Ridge, then it turned south entering the soggy, ill-drained land around Festubert, Givenchy and Loos, where defensive works sat on top of the ground like grouse butts. But only a few miles further on, the front crossed the same chalk stratum which emerges from the Channel as white cliffs, and the Germans tunnel-combed it with burrows so deep that an officer brought his wife, child and nanny to live with him in troglodytic safety. Here the line remained stable until 1918. Going further south, the Germans held Vimy Ridge, and only at Arras did the British hold the higher ground. The geography alone demanded an offence from the army.

The scale of that offence on the Western Front was monstrous, out of all proportion to what had come before. Neither soldier nor general could in any way have been prepared for what was to become the pattern of their days. Slowly and late the craft of generalship developed, but from the very start, the soldier practised his skill in conditions which would have broken the mind and will of an individual if he were not supported. The ground, weapons and men themselves varied wildly, but in their high spirits, responsiveness to sight and sound, and confidence in their own ability, there is an unmistakable common stamp on the Battalions of The Black Watch. From everyone the trenches exacted an enduring courage, but The Black Watch paid its dues with generous spirit, as though confident that there was more where that came from, banked up in its history and its pride.

In almost every other way the Germans were better prepared for this military development, and possessed trenching tools, machine-guns and bombs in profusion. By contrast, when the 2nd Battalion arrived from India in October, they were forced to make their own bombs by stuffing tobacco tins with gun-cotton. The bomber would then debonairly touch off the fuse with his cigarette, and bowl the fizzing petard over the parapet before he was himself made victim. Unavoidably, premature explosions took a steady toll and, even away from the front line, loading and testing the devices made the bombing officer's life exceptionally hazardous.

One such was Lieutenant Haldane, who much later became internationally re-nowned as a geneticist; though wider, that later fame could hardly have been more vivid than the local glory he won in 1915 as the Bombing Officer of the 1st Black Watch. It was not undeserved. Apart from the uncertain bombs, the responsibility of operating the first trench mortars fell to him – a thankless task, since the weapon frequently exploded and invariably drew enemy fire. They were so unpopular that, to the physical bravery of handling them, must have been added a certain moral courage in siting them, and, on one occasion, when Haldane positioned a mortar too close to another battalion, he was unceremoniously pushed into a ditch to prevent him firing it. In the absence of machine-guns, bombs were obviously particularly important as weapons for assault and defence. Bombing platoons were formed, and wounded officers were repatriated north to Ross-shire, where the 3rd Battalion trained recruits for The Black Watch in the art.

Each winter of the war brought its own miseries, but that first season had its particular nightmare in the shortage of equipment and expertise. Duckboards were not obtainable to the 4th Battalion – the first Territorials to come out – who were in the line opposite Neuve Chapelle. The paths became running streams with deep pools. There were insufficient spades for digging proper dugouts, and the latrines became flooded. Further south at Givenchy, the 2nd Battalion endured the same conditions but, coming from the scorching plains of India, they must have felt the cold rain even more acutely. They were still wearing Highland shoes when they arrived, and the glutinous mud sucked them off the sentries' feet. Of all the deficiencies, that of munitions was the most seriously felt. On the one hand, poorly-made bombs and mortars rendered trench-life unsafe; on the other, a scarcity of shells, especially high explosive, left attacking troops to face uncut wire, and an unsubdued enemy.

The first attempt to break through the siege-line was made at Neuve Chapelle in March, 1915. There was a 35-minute bombardment beforehand but, as the attack progressed, shells began to run short, and the guns died away. At the end of the day, Aubers Ridge, which was the objective, remained uncaptured. Both the 2nd and 4th Battalions had been in support, and had suffered casualties in the battle, but, a month later, they were brought back for the second attempt on Aubers Ridge.

It had been assumed that success at Neuve Chapelle had only been missed because of the insufficiency of shells, and the battle of Aubers Ridge, therefore, was preceded by a much longer bombardment. To a newcomer, the noise was like an overlapping series of thunderclaps, penetrated by the train-roar of large shells passing overhead, and the whistling scream of smaller projectiles. The mind was stunned, but in the place of mental activity arose a curious emotional exaltation. Over the German lines towered a cloud of grey smoke and dust, streaked by columns of black smoke.

An early assault failed, and in the afternoon the 1st Black Watch (i.e. 1st Battalion, The Black Watch) were moved up to the front trenches in the afternoon. Their attack was watched by a brigade staff officer.

Suddenly at 3.59 p.m., there was a flash of bayonets all along the line, and our men got over the parapet, and walked forwards in a beautiful line towards the Germans. I do not think we could have got so good a line at drill behind the lines. So far there were practically no casualties. Then our shellfire lifted, and concentrated on the lines beyond. The front lines of German trenches appeared as a jagged and continuous line of earth. The men broke into a run. Then, even through that unimaginable noise a sound emerged, so faint that I took it for a clapping of hands. I soon realised, however, that it was machine gun fire. The bit of line that I could see through my glasses suddenly began to fall, the falling moving along from right to left. At first I believed they were lying down by order. I did not realise how quickly people could be killed. Then the whole line hereabouts lay down. Some of them advanced again, but I do not think any of them reached the German trenches. On the right, however, our line swept on, and I saw men crouching in front of the enemy's breastwork, one of them signalling with Dietz discs; most of these subsequently got in.

Corporal Ripley was one of the first to climb the German parapet, and from that eminence directed those following to the gaps in the wire. Though it was scarcely possible to recognise 'Highland Laddie' through the noise of gunfire, the pipers played the Battalion in, and a stream of men flowed over the parapet into the trenches beneath, where Ripley, and other section leaders, at once formed them into groups, and led them on into the second line.

At that point they were on their objective, but the attacks on both sides had failed, and the German defences had been deepened since Neuve Chapelle, so that on the Battalion's front as well as both flanks, heavy fire was concentrated. Reinforcements, which had been moving up, were now halted, and the Battalion ordered back. It was small reward for what the Regimental history described as 'one of the finest assaults the Battalion delivered during the war'.

Four miles to the north, a converging attack had been launched across 200 yards of mud, divided by a stream. Two companies of the 2nd Battalion were sent after an earlier assault had failed. The heaped bodies and unbroken wire showed them how hopeless the task was, but, as in the manner of their forebears at Ticonderoga, they refused to acknowledge defeat before an impregnable obstacle until more than half their number had fallen. Parties of men were afterwards found to have reached the German parapet, and Lance-Corporal Findlay led a section of bombers forward until only two of his dozen were left; those he sent back while he brought in a wounded man on his back. Both he and Ripley received Victoria Crosses for the gallantry each displayed on that day. Colonel Harvey also showed courage of a high order, though not of a sort to win medals, when he refused to obey an order to commit his reserve company to a situation which was already far beyond rescue.

To their right, the 4th Battalion, in reserve, sent forward two companies to support the attack of an Indian battalion across the muddy river. Once more the same battle was fought to the same conclusion. The 4th Battalion, drawn almost entirely from Dundee, was justly known as 'a city at war'. Neighbours in a street, and the men of a family, had joined its ranks as Territorials, so that now they mourned their losses with a special poignancy. Among those who died at Aubers Ridge were Private Pyott and Sergeant Troup; at the memorial service after the battle, Sergeant-Major Pyott erected a cross for his son, the private, while Private Troup put up a cross for his father, Archie, the big drummer.

The failure to take Aubers Ridge was largely ascribed to the artillery's lack of success in cutting the barbed wire, or to its failure to subdue the enemy. This reasoning tended to overlook the breakdown in communications which occurred during the battle, and the misuse of reserves to repeat assaults which had failed, rather than to exploit successes. It is true that Sir John French determined to take control of the reserves so that they should not be thrown into battle fruitlessly, but his cure proved worse than the disease.

By the end of May, the three Battalions already mentioned, and the 5th, which was also present at Aubers Ridge, had been joined in France by the last two Territorial Battalions, the 6th and 7th, and by the first Service Battalion, the 8th. As these anonymous numerals proliferate, the identities which they conceal inevitably become blurred, but until the last year of the war, the fact that they were drawn from certain areas of central and eastern Scotland gave each Battalion its own particular personality.

Dundee was the home of the 4th; it was commanded by a Dundonian businessman, and the *Dundee Courier* reported the war through the eyes and letters of Black Watch men who before 1914 had worked in the jute mills and jam factories in the city. In 1915 it was amalgamated with the 5th Battalion, which was drawn in general from Angus (Forfar), and in particular from the fishing villages on the coast – Arbroath, Montrose and Broughty Ferry, villages whose livelihood depended on the caprice of the sea, and the steadier earnings from linen mills famous for their strong brown cloth. Perthshire and the 6th Battalion were inseparably linked; unlike the others, the Jocks of the 6th Battalion were predominantly countrymen, officered in the traditional manner by landowners, most notably Sir Robert Moncrieffe who first became their Colonel in 1893. In Fife, as in Angus and Perthshire, the peacetime social and economic structure had put on khaki and The Black Watch tartan, but the 7th Battalion, which came from Fife, bore especially the imprint of just one industry – coal; colliers, miners, and pit managers gave it a character as distinct as each of the others and, like them, a character that was notably close-knit.

The Service Battalions, raised indiscriminately throughout the recruiting area, cannot be so easily described, but the Scottish Divisions in which they fought provide identifying marks. The 9th Division, in which the 8th Black Watch was the senior battalion, was the earliest division to be formed from Kitchener's First Hundred Thousand volunteers, and its name was, above all, associated with the labyrinth of Arras where it fought for much of the war. When the Second Hundred Thousand came forward, the 15th Division was the first to be formed, and its senior battalion was the 9th Black Watch; in many of its battles, it found itself beside the 9th Division, but perhaps its outstanding honour was that of Loos where it so nearly broke open the German line.

With so many Black Watch battalions in France, it was certain that sooner or later two or three of them would be gathered together in one place, and that certain rites would be observed. The chance came on an autumn day in 1915 at the village of Estaire by the river Lys, where for a day the streets were filled with dark tartan and Red Hackles, and the not-so-distant thunder of the guns was drowned by the thuds, cheers and pipe-music which are the trademarks of a Highland Games. Two days later the Battalions marched up the line to Loos.

At this stage of the war Britain remained the junior partner on the Western Front, and the choice of Loos for a British attack was determined by its proximity to Joffre's autumn offensive in Champagne. Kitchener had wished to postpone operations until 1916, when the bulk of his New Armies would be in the field, but the terrible defeats suffered by Russia in 1915 finally persuaded him to commit those divisions which had already arrived in France.

The battlefields of Loos were, therefore, the first test of the floods of volunteers who had come forward in response to the War Lord's mesmerising poster with its message 'Your country needs YOU'. One year earlier they had never heard the rasp of a sergeant's voice, and scarcely six months had passed since they were first issued with rifles, yet their behaviour at Loos was impeccable. The Scottish Divisions were the first to be committed, and it is a reasonable estimate that not since Culloden had so many Scottish soldiers been in the field as on the 25th September, 1915.

The main assault force of six divisions faced a spur of ground, which rose from left to right, and converged with the right of the British line in front of Loos. The town itself lay in a dip behind the spur, and in front of a hill seventy metres high. Hill 70, as it was called, lay about two miles from the British trenches, and it was nominated as the objective of the 15th Division. On their left, the 1st Division had as its objective the southern half of Hulluch village, which was still hidden by the spur, though here it was only forty metres in height. Opposite the 9th Division, on the left of the British line, the spur was little more than a slope, but it had been fortified by a strongpoint named the Hohenzollern Redoubt.

After a bombardment, which had continued intermittently for several days, the morning of the 25th was calm, with only a slight breeze from the south-west. The wind was important, for a lack of ammunition had forced Haig to rely on gas as a substitute for artillery during the assault. Nevertheless, he was, as always, confident of a convincing breakthrough, and on all commanders it had been impressed, 'Keep going; a constant flow of reinforcements will be following you.' Even the Meerut Division, which included the 2nd and 4th Battalions, detailed to make a subsidiary attack on Aubers Ridge four miles to the north, was warned to expect a complete breakthrough.

At 5.50 a.m., the gas and some smoke was released from cylinders, and gently swirled away towards the German lines. 'The spectacular effect of the drifting cloud of in-termingled whites, greys, yellow and brown, was singularly impressive.' There was a short bombardment by artillery and machine-guns, and, at 6.30, the troops advanced. The 9th Battalion of The Black Watch led the assault of the 15th Division. 'No one present will ever forget that attack. It seemed impossible that these lines of disciplined soldiers had been almost all civilians twelve months before. There was no shouting or hurry. The men moved in quick time, picking up their dressing as if on a ceremonial parade. The distance to be crossed varied from 80 to 200 yards, and, despite the fierce fire, not a line wavered or stopped.'

Their first target was the immensely strong fortification of the Lens Road Redoubt, and it was taken within five minutes. Brigadier-General Thuillier, covering the ground a day or two later, reported, 'In front of the Lens Road Redoubt, the dead Highlanders in Black Watch tartan lay very thick. In one place, about 40 yards square just in front of the enemy's wire, they were so close that it was difficult to step between them. Nevertheless, the survivors swept on and through the German lines.' Over two hundred died there, including three company commanders, and three of the company sergeant-majors.

Two hours after the attack began, the remainder of the Battalion had fought their way down the valley, and into Loos itself, where, in the street battle, they became mixed up with the Seaforths, Camerons and Gordons. As this force began the assault up Hill 70, the 9th Battalion Headquarters moved into the town behind them. There they were attacked fiercely from the right, but runners, stretcher-bearers and signallers turned and helped to repel the unexpected threat. By the afternoon, the flank was held, and advanced parties were digging in on the far side of Hill 70, although its crest continued to change hands as the Highlanders repeatedly stormed it, and were as often counter-attacked with heavy machine-gun fire. The 9th Battalion then numbered barely ninety men; 21 officers and 680 men had been killed or wounded, the worst losses in a single action ever incurred by a Battalion of the Regiment; and 75 per cent of their Brigade were casualties. However, it was clear, to the Germans at least, that the 15th Division had made the breakthrough that Haig had hoped for.

On their left, the 1st Division advanced neither so far nor so fast. In the afternoon, the 1st Battalion, in reserve, was sent up with two other battalions to add momentum, and by nightfall they had succeeded in establishing a front roughly in line with Hill 70, but short of Hulluch village, which was the final objective. On the left of the attacking line, the 9th Division had captured the Hohenzollern Redoubt, with the Camerons leading the left brigade of the attack, and the 8th Black Watch in close support. The two battalions soon became intermingled, but the advance pushed on for half a mile beyond the Redoubt. Owing to the failure of the divisional attack on their left, their flank was open to machine-gun fire and, to this, artillery was soon added. The sluices had been opened so that the trenches were head-high in water, but underneath the walls of a village on the eastward slope of the spur, the Jocks found good defensive positions, where they held on until dark, although the retirement of the brigade on their right also opened that flank to raking fire.

It was at this point that the controversy of Loos began. Every division, except that on the left of the 9th, had taken their first objectives. The 15th had magnificently stormed through every defence, and were close to turning the whole position. Where were the promised reinforcements? In the event, it was shown that most of them had been held some sixteen miles back by the Commander-in-Chief, Sir John French, and when they began to arrive during the night, exhausted and confused in the dark, the German defences were already hardening, and the first counter-attacks were being launched.

The 8th and 9th Battalions were relieved before dawn, and the 1st returned from near Hulluch thirty-six hours later. With mounting frustration the 8th Battalion watched their gains being whittled away, until, by the 27th September, it was apparent that even the Hohenzollern Redoubt was in danger of being recaptured. Captain Bowes-Lyon took up a mixed party of Black Watch and Camerons to rally the defenders, and succeeded in stemming the attack. Persistently, the enemy pushed in under cover of shrapnel fire, throwing stick grenades. Bowes-Lyon was killed, the second of his family to die with the Regiment, and hurriedly the rest of the Brigade was ordered up. With the scarcity of machine-guns – four to a battalion – bombs were vital, but the heavy British variety could not be hurled far, and, going forward to get the range, the Battalion bombers were soon hit. Volunteers were given emergency instruction, and took their place. In close-quarter fighting, nothing would make The Black Watch and Camerons give up their first gains of Loos, and, when night came, the enemy admitted the fact, leaving them in command of the Hohenzollern Redoubt.

Further north, the diversionary attack made by the Meerut Division was also expected to make a breakthrough, capturing Aubers Ridge, then turning south to converge on the easterly advance of the main force. In the Bareilly Brigade, the 2nd and 4th Battalions of The Black Watch provided the two wings of its attack with the 69th Punjabis in the centre, and two other battalions in support.

When the gas was released on this front, a contrary wind blew it back in the attackers' faces, incapacitating many of the 2nd Battalion's officers and men, but at 6.30 a.m. they moved off. The hanging smoke and gas made it difficult to distinguish features, but Major Wauchope had rehearsed the 2nd Battalion on a sand model constructed from aerial photographs – one of the first examples of what later became a standard practice – and when his men reached the German lines, the air was clear enough to see, half a mile up the Aubers Ridge, the two landmarks at which they aimed, a mill called the Moulin du Piètre and a chimney stack fifty yards to its right.

Quickly they cleared a nest of trenches in a salient to their right, with Piper MacDonald playing up on the parapets while the bombers went to work below him; then the Battalion moved on towards the mill. Situated on the extreme left of the field of attack, the 2nd Battalion's flank was open to fire, and, on the right wing of the Brigade, the 4th Battalion, at only half-strength, suffered in the same way, for the attackers on their right were caught in deep wire, and only a remnant of Gurkhas broke through.

Under heavy rifle fire and shrapnel, the attack stormed over four lines of trenches, and by 10.0 the Brigade was established in front of the mill and chimney. Behind them, however, there were gaps on both flanks, with an artillery barrage cutting off communication to the rear. Knowing the importance of making a deep offensive, Wauchope visited the other battalion commanders to co-ordinate the defence of the flanks, and to establish a central reserve for the next leap forward, since the support battalions were tending to crowd into the front trenches. The gaping holes in the flanks could not be closed, and all runners to headquarters were hit before they could deliver their messages. Reinforcements were so urgently needed, however, that Colonel Walker, commanding the 4th Battalion, went back himself to bring them up but, like the others, he, too, was killed. Walker had been a distinguished businessman in Dundee when war broke out, but he led the 4th Battalion through its first year in France with skill and vigour, as though to the manner born.

German patrols now penetrated so deeply through the flanks that the Brigade was under fire from all sides, and at noon the order to retire was given. From an extremely dangerous position, the men fell back, halting and firing in good order, to return to their original position. The historian of the 2nd Battalion, General A. P. Wavell, suggested some reasons for the eventual failure of an attack which began so well, and these reasons serve to explain a situation which Black Watch Battalions experienced repeatedly until 1917, when army commanders began to plan attacks with limited objectives only.

The creation of a deep salient with vulnerable flanks gave a resolute enemy, such as the German always was, opportunities for counter-attack of which he was seldom slow to avail himself . . . In position warfare, trenches on the flank gave covered approach to parties of bombers, and such a form of counter-attack could only be met by counter-bombing. Here the attack was always at a disadvantage, owing to the difficulties of supply of bombs, and the attackers' ignorance of a strange maze of trenches.

Neither the French in Champagne, nor the British at Loos, had made any substantial progress, but on the 13th October it was decided to renew the attack. Only the 1st Battalion was engaged in this attempt to regain the ground east of the Hohenzollern Redoubt, which had originally been won by the 8th Black Watch and the Camerons. It was an afternoon attack which went off platoon by platoon, 'rows of drab figures that ran a little way into the cloud of green gas and sulphurous smoke, and after fifty yards were lost to view'. Communications were disjointed, and successive parties were misdirected on to wire which was reported broken, but had remained intact, and into trenches assumed to be empty, but proved to be occupied. Not until the next morning was the Battalion informed of the true position, that the 1st Division had encountered extensive barbed wire, and had been unable to make headway.

For the second time in three weeks the 1st Battalion suffered 25 per cent casualties (at Loos the Regiment as a whole lost 2,344 men, or well over 50 per cent), and it might be thought that a year of such war would have softened morale. Yet, after Aubers Ridge, the Regimental history recorded that the men returned 'singing lustily', and now, after Loos, 'they came out of action with spirit unsubdued', a judgement which was confirmed when they were billeted at Houchin soon after the battle. The inhabitants greeted them with the sullen morosity of Artois peasants who had seen their fields flattened, their beasts purloined, and, no doubt, their daughters' honour trifled with by the rude soldiery. If the Jocks had not been in good form, it could have been an explosive meeting; as it was they stayed there a week, and that was long enough for them to work their magic, even on such unpromising material. The next time they were billeted at Houchin, they found the villagers competing vigorously for the pleasure of their company.

A similar deduction can be made of the 2nd Battalion, to which was attached the two companies that remained of the 4th Battalion. After refitting, the corps was sent to Givenchy, where a low hill made a salient into the German line. Mines and counter-mines riddled it, and the trenches on both sides had been blown up so often that the sector was a series of overlapping craters. Always keen to hold the initiative, Wauchope ensured that The Black Watch scouts and snipers dominated the lunatic landscape of no-man's-land. 'It was a form of warfare very trying to men whose nerves were at all overwrought, but which appealed strongly to the adventurous.' A week after they arrived, three mines were exploded, and before the mushrooming earth subsided, the Germans were sprinting across the gap which separated the trenches. With the self-possession of men whose nerves were not at all overwrought, the Jocks moved at once to their posts amid the rubble of destroyed trenches, where their steady fire checked, and finally turned the attack.

At the end of 1915, the Indian Corps departed with the 2nd Battalion to Mesopotamia. When they left, the army was settling down to its second winter in France, but under incomparably better conditions than in 1914. Trenches were drained and constructed to give shelter against weather and shrapnel, the art of latrine-siting had flowered, and rest billets were now situated far enough back from the front line to permit some comfort and a greater relief from the stress of trench-life. To adapt a phrase from another war, it might be said that the end of 1915 marked the end of the beginning.

CHAPTER 15

# The Somme, Arras and Passchendaele

During the winter season the British Army at last adopted that organisation of men and munitions with which victory was eventually won. In common with other Territorial battalions, difficulties in recruiting had forced the 4th and 5th Black Watch to amalgamate in late 1915, and, as a result of the insufficiency of volunteers, conscription was introduced in January, 1916. The flow of munitions swelled under Lloyd George's ministrations; there were sufficient shells to satisfy artillery-minded commanders, enough machine-guns to permit the organisation of plausibly-sized machine-gun sections, and the bombing sections were equipped with the Mills grenade. Finally, in the winter lull, Sir John French was induced to resign the command in favour of Sir Douglas Haig. It was as well that Britain's strength was at last channelled efficiently for in February, 1916 the Germans began a campaign of attrition at Verdun which inexorably drained the strength of the French.

If 1915 was the year of the Scottish Divisions, this proved to be the year of the 51st (Highland) Division, one of the first units to notice the effect of Verdun, when it was moved south in March to take over the French sector at Arras. This labyrinth of trenches became familiar ground to the 6th and 7th Battalions; they spent thirteen months of the next two-and-a-half years there. As at Givenchy, the enemy had gone underground, and mines presented the gravest danger. But the 7th Battalion proved to have, in the pit-face workers from Fife, the masters of this kind of warfare. From listening-galleries, they picked up the scratching sound made by German diggers, then drove in counter-mines beneath them. So frequently were German mines destroyed, that the loss of diggers eventually forced them to blow-up their remaining half-completed tunnels. Above ground, the 51st practised a policy of aggressive raiding, which was a habit more common among fresh troops, like the Australians, than the British after eighteen months of war, and suggests that its commander, General Harper, remained confident that he had the sort of troops who could still take the strain.

By the end of June, the British were ready to take over a major share of the burden on the Western Front. Because it was necessary to relieve the pressure on the French, the area of the British offensive was moved south from their own sector in Flanders to the point of junction with their allies, and that was the valley of the Somme.

The belief in massive preliminary bombardment, which had been partially choked by the shortage of shells, now flourished with their plenitude. High explosive, especially valued for destroying barbed wire, was at last produced in greater quantity than shrapnel. Both were available in profusion and, for the sake of morale, some commanders made it a habit to return a dozen shells for each one fired by the enemy. But the price paid for a heavy bombardment was the loss of surprise and, in the wet weather of that July, destruction of the very ground over which British troops were to advance. The line was the form of that advance, and the number of lines was determined by a staff theory crudely expressed as: one line of infantry never takes a trench, two lines may take it, three lines sometimes take it, while four lines usually take the trench.

The battle of the Somme began on the 1st July, a day which saw the capture of many trenches, but cost 60,000 casualties in the lines of infantrymen. The greatest advance was made near the river Somme itself, but further north the gains dwindled away. Thus, in the southern half of the great German bulge into France, the British had created a small, shallow salient. Thereafter the fighting on the Somme was directed towards widening the salient already established.

One of the most successful assaults during this part of the campaign was made by the 9th Division around Longueval, and beyond it, Delville Wood. After a very brief bombardment, the 8th Battalion attacked at dawn, and, with the advantage of surprise, they took a quick hold on the village of Longueval. Patrols sent forward into Delville Wood reported the presence of strong enemy forces, and the counter-attack came in the next morning under a ferocious barrage. The shelling, however, had offered sufficient warning, and the Battalion drove their enemy back with some ease. The bombardment never ceased over the next twenty-four hours, and the following afternoon it became a moving barrage behind which the Germans forced their way back into the village.

On two or three distinct occasions, each Battalion performed feats which stand out for the sheer quality of character displayed, and one such was Longueval. On the outskirts of the village, the 8th Battalion stemmed the German advance, and Colonel Gordon led a counter-attack which regained part of Longueval. With the enemy off-balance, a further charge drove them out of the remaining houses, and back into the wood. Then again the tide turned, and the enemy reserves pushed round to the north of the village to establish themselves in some outlying buildings. There, however, they were held. When the 8th Battalion was relieved on the 19th by the Durham Light Infantry, it numbered only 171, but it had won and held Longueval against the best efforts of the enemy.

The popular myth that the continent of Europe enjoys better weather than the British Isles should have been dispelled for ever by the perpetual downpours of the Somme campaign. The 1st Battalion, engaged in intermittent fighting at Contalmaison and High Wood, found light relief after four days of continuous saturation, when a carrier pigeon fluttered into the Battalion coop during a brief break in the weather with a message from the Berkshires, their neighbouring regiment: 'Floods subsiding; herewith dove.'

In September, Brigadier-General Stewart, whose diary of the Boer War has been quoted here, was killed by a stray shell. The Commanding Officer of the 1st Battalion was promoted to take his place, and Lieutenant-Colonel Victor Fortune D.S.O. was now put in command of the 1st Battalion.

The weight of the Somme offensive was directed northwards, to whittle away more of the German bulge round Bapaume. Two areas in particular were the targets: Thiepval and Beaumont Hamel. Between them flowed the River Ancre, which hitherto had been the northern boundary of the fighting on the Somme. On the 3rd September, the 4/5th Battalion took part in an attack along the river valley, which achieved only limited success. The Battalion's own performance in the battle was remarkable for its ferocity. They

PLATE 19 *The 7th Black Watch marching along the Fricourt–Albert road, August, 1916.*

advanced on an extremely narrow front, constricted to fifty yards by the river on their right, and a railway on their left. Enfilade fire from across the river picked off most of the officers, but the leading companies were led on by their N.C.O.s into the German trenches, where, the Regimental history records, 'the fighting was of a particularly grim and determined nature; men on both sides firing point-blank at each other from twenty yards range.' Two lines of trenches were taken, but it was clearly too narrow a front to be held and, in the afternoon, the survivors were withdrawn.

They had a brief breathing space and then were sent to the Schwaben Redoubt, the last stronghold in Thiepval. The Battalion held its southern face, and the Germans the north, an impossible situation which was resolved on the 13th October by a furious British assault, behind what was now the usual barrage. In their eagerness, some of the men pressed forward on the heels of the barrage, and were wounded by their own shells. But it was an error in the right direction, for the attackers arrived in the trenches before the Germans could recover.

Initially resistance was slight, and one company had pressed forward beyond the Redoubt, before all the officers were hit. Sergeant Hutton, the senior N.C.O., took command; he supervised the withdrawal back to the Redoubt, carried in one of the wounded officers, and then returned to bomb out the last German dugouts. When the inevitable counter-attack came in, the defence was largely conducted by Hutton and other N.C.O.s, and with such success that only their reliefs could remove them from the Redoubt.

In these close-quarter battles, one of the most unnerving jobs fell to the stretcher-bearers, who were required, and never failed, to pick up the wounded beneath the very eyes of the enemy. The runners, carrying messages back to Battalion Headquarters, developed a style of their own to promote confidence in the rear. Having hared over the ground from the front-line, they would stop when they approached Headquarters, light a cigarette, and nonchalantly stroll over the last fifty yards to deliver their information.

The rains still came down heavily, soaking everyone, and arousing the sympathy of a Battalion runner who returned from the trenches to find his commanding officer sitting ankle-deep in mud, in a dripping, shell-shaken dugout. 'I'm sorry for ye, sir,' the runner said consolingly. 'I aye think ye must have been accustomed to something better back hame.' Only an optimist as sanguine as Haig could now have hoped for a successful assault through the quagmire, but the 13th November richly rewarded his optimism. The 4/5th Battalion had a share at St Pierre Divion, south of the Ancre, but most of the glory went across the river to the 51st Division at Beaumont Hamel.

To appreciate the importance of Beaumont Hamel in the mythology of the 51st, a brief description is necessary, both of what was considered an impregnable position, and of the Division's unlucky history in the Somme. They had been the first British troops in the area, having been stationed there in August, 1915. That tour was relatively quiet, although, more than most, they had suffered from the shortage of shells, and the winter had offered them a foretaste of the mud. But in July of the following year, in their first major battle of the Somme campaign, they were committed to an extremely bloody and unsuccessful attack on a strong German position in the High Wood. For their second battle, they were now faced with an even more formidable prospect.

Beaumont Hamel had been repeatedly assaulted during the campaign, contributing more than its share to the Somme's final toll of 420,000 casualties. The reason was not hard to find. Although the village was situated in a hollow, laid open to artillery fire, vast caves and underground cellars protected its defenders, and the uphill slope afforded a good field of fire to their machine-guns. It was wired and parapeted, of course, but its outstanding defence was natural, a huge gash in the ground, south of the village, known as the 'Y' ravine. Running out at right-angles from the German line, it permitted the defenders to enfilade any assault, and was deep enough to be immune to shell-fire.

General Harper had varied the concertina-action of the four-line attack, to allow the waves to pass through each other on to defined objectives, and the Division practised the movement incessantly as the assault was postponed owing to bad weather. The mud became so deep that, on several occasions, the 7th Battalion had to dig out its sentries at the end of their duty. For three weeks, while the rains came down, the shells went up, and the Germans became accustomed to the routine of a prolonged morning bombardment.

On the right of the divisional attack was the 153rd Brigade, made up of Gordons and The Black Watch. Their position placed them opposite the 'Y' ravine, whose capture was their objective. The 6th Black Watch and 7th Gordons were to lead the attack, with the 5th Gordons in support and the 7th Black Watch in reserve.

On the night of the 12th November, the 6th Battalion moved up into the front line, but neither the cold nor the formidable dangers of the morning affected, what Sergeant Mitchell remembered as, the men's 'wonderfully bright spirits'.

In one of our sections an argument started about who would be in the Hun trench first. One wee chap from the 'Pow'* declaring his willingness to bet a whole franc on the matter. About 5 a.m. we had a hot drink served out to us. 'It's rum with some tea in it,' said one man. 'Away man, it's tea with a little rum.' Whatever the concoction may have been, it put a nice heat into us.

Trying to convey an impression of the conditions in which the battle was fought, the historian of the 51st Division wrote, 'Let two teams dressed in battle order [i.e. carrying about 55 lb] play football in the dark on a ploughed field after three weeks' rain, and the

*Local form of 'Pomarium Street, Perth'.

PLATE 20  *The 9th Black Watch celebrating Hogmanay, January, 1917, on the Somme.*

difficulties might in some measure be appreciated.' At 6 a.m. a mine was exploded, and the men set off. In thick mist, the barrage provided the only sense of direction, but, inexorably moving away at 100 yards every four minutes, it soon outstripped the infantry struggling through the torn-up mud. The right of the 6th Battalion and the 7th Gordons' left struck the German trenches in front of the ravine. Some got through the wire, but were surrounded; others were illuminated in the mist by starshells, and violent fire caught them close to the trenches. The machine-guns constantly swept no-man's-land, and, until noon, the men in this sector could do more than hold on.

On the left of the attack, however, two companies were able to advance for some distance parallel to the ravine, despite losing all their officers. One who survived was 2nd Lieutenant Lindsay, who had the nerve-wracking experience of being stuck in a mud-hole for an hour in full view of the enemy. When he finally extricated himself, he brought the first reliable news of the situation back to Battalion Headquarters. It should have been terrible – there was no progress on the right, and on the left the attack was fogbound, mudbound and officerless, a recipe for chaos. In fact, however, the two companies were continuing their momentum, with well-rehearsed soldiers quickly sorting out the inevitable confusion which followed an assault, and moving on to the next objective.

Just after midday, twenty-five men under 2nd Lieutenant Leslie fought their way into the northern side of the ravine. In a battle involving about 100,000 men, it would be invidious to select one particular action as absolutely decisive, but Leslie's brilliant feat quite certainly broke the deadlock on the Divisional right. Liberating The Black Watch and Gordons, who had earlier been surrounded, Leslie's men proceeded to clear out the defences in the west of the ravine, nearest the British line. They bombed out the machine-guns which had dominated no-man's-land, then turned eastward, and with an ever-increasing number of released prisoners, and a support party brought up by Colonel Booth, they swept the ravine clear.

There were so few officers left in the 6th Battalion, that the 7th sent up replacements, together with bombers and two platoons. One of their privates, de Reuter, spoke German and, to considerable effect – he argued an officer and twenty-five men into surrender, and then persuaded the officer to order another sixty men in a strong-point to cease firing and give themselves up.

Meanwhile the subalterns, Leslie and Lindsay, had established a line at the east of the ravine, and in the evening the 6th Black Watch with a battalion of Gordons on either side, moved forward to their final objective, an embankment beyond the last line of German trenches. They were still trenching and fortifying it at 3.0 the next morning, twenty-two hours after they first warmed up. Over on their left, the rest of the 51st had occupied the village of Beaumont Hamel itself, thus completing the capture of that impregnable position. It was a famous victory, and deservedly so, for it demonstrated as much training coupled with high courage in avoiding disaster, as initiative and skill in developing an opportunity so that it finally yielded complete success.

The previous winters had been seasons of consolidation, when little happened to alter the map of the Western Front, but the effect of the Somme offensive, and particularly of its last battles, had so weakened the old German front that, in March, 1917, Ludendorff shortened, and immensely strengthened, his line by withdrawing his troops to the Hindenberg Line. Months had been spent in preparing that naturally forbidding position, which stretched from Arras in the north to the river Aisne in the south, and although the recovery of so much French territory was regarded as a victory by the Allies, the Germans were without doubt far more strongly placed than before.

Their withdrawal occurred too late to check the momentum of Allied plans for a spring offensive. Nivelle, giving voice to the universal dream of a decisive breakthrough, had won the confidence of the French government. He replaced Joffre in command of their troops, and Lloyd George, now leading Britain's coalition government, was sufficiently motivated by the seduction of victory, and his dislike of Haig, to give Nivelle control over the British army as well. Nivelle's plan for total victory called for a British attack at Arras to pull enemy forces away from his intended area of offensive near the Aisne. More than a month before the fighting began, each of the Allies thus had half their battleground pulled from beneath them by the German retirement, but Nivelle, who owed his promotion and unique power to the promise he had held out, could not postpone his campaign without losing his position.

The troops who would be involved had passed a miserable winter, the coldest since 1880. Beyond some raids, there was little fighting, but a steady flow of casualties was taken to the rear, suffering from trench feet and rheumatism. The 6th and 7th Battalions were issued with wellingtons, and 'owing to the mud and cold', wrote their historian, more in sorrow than in anger, 'it was thought right to replace the kilt by trews, but as the authorities forgot to issue braces, the troubles of the men were little lessened.' The wellingtons actually aggravated trench feet, so whale oil was issued as an unguent, adding its pungent smell to the odours of the Western Front. Despite the precautions, the 6th Battalion eventually estimated its losses from disease that winter to be greater than those sustained at Beaumont Hamel.

Its bloody finish notwithstanding, Arras represents a watershed in military tactics on the Western Front. In response to the greater depth of German defences, the wave advance, which the 6th and 7th Battalions had practised before Beaumont Hamel, was further developed so that a battalion now learned to advance in paired companies. When the first pair was on its target, the second passed through to its objective, where it was 'leap-frogged' by the supporting battalion in the same formation. Telephone communication was improved, and counter-artillery fire was brought to a high pitch of efficiency. Finally, the tank, which had first appeared on the Somme, was used at Arras with results for which two Battalions of The Black Watch had reason to be grateful.

The winter became a boisterous spring of sun and storm, and on the 9th April, the day of the First Battle of Arras, a furious gale blew columns of sleet towards the German lines. The battle was fought on either side of the Scarpe, a slow, marshy stream which flowed eastward between spurs of high ground to the north and south. The German withdrawal had disrupted the attack in the south, but in the north, the First Army triumphantly stormed Vimy Ridge. The Third Army, under General Allenby, advanced astride the Scarpe; the left marched along the river valley, but the right, south of the river, faced rising ground surmounted by the village of Monchy le Preux. There had been a relatively short four-day bombardment, reflecting Allenby's belief that surprise would be more important than wire-cutting, and, as the battle developed, an ambitious counter-artillery programme picked off enemy batteries.

The 15th Division was directed at Monchy le Preux, and the 9th Black Watch led their right wing with the Gordons. Allenby's gamble on surprise allowed them to reach the first trenches at dawn with little loss but, in the second line of a deep defence, the entire divisional attack came to a halt in front of a triangle of high embankments. After some severe fighting, a solitary example of the bizarre creation of Colonel Swinton and Mr Churchill, clanked over the embankments, and The Black Watch rushed the astonished defenders to win its first tank-supported action. A new line was quickly established, and the second wave of infantry passed through towards the crest of the hill.

In the valley north of the river, the 8th Battalion achieved similar success, although without the help of a tank. The attack, like that of the 9th, went forward two companies at a time, the first pair meeting little opposition, the second, passing through, having to fight hard for the capture of its objective, a railway cutting. It yielded an impressive harvest of about 250 prisoners, and provided an early sign of the extraordinary success that the day was to bring.

The 51st Division attacked on the left of the Third Army, and to considerable effect, but their gains were rather overshadowed by those of the neighbours next door, the Canadian Corps in the First Army, who stormed Vimy Ridge. Participating in that triumph were all three battalions of The Black Watch's affiliated regiment, The Royal Highlanders of Canada. If it was a notable day for *Am Freiceadan Dubh*, it was equally so for the army as a whole, which made its largest gains of the war to that date – more than 6,000 prisoners and three miles of ground were taken on the 9th April. A week later, Nivelle made even greater gains in the south, but compared to his promise of total victory, and the forces he had employed, they were the cruellest disappointment. The morale of the French Army, which had held through the fiasco of Plan XVII, the Champagne offensive in 1915, and the attrition of Verdun, finally gave way, and mutiny began to show at assembly points in the rear.

While Nivelle's offensive was still in progress, the 51st Division relieved the 9th Division in the Scarpe Valley. The 7th Black Watch took over the position occupied by the 8th Battalion, a hurried relief under heavy shelling which caused casualties in the 7th Battalion. A week later on 23rd April, 1917, Allenby's Third Army attacked again. This time there was little chance of surprise, but to compensate for that, the Battalion was supplied with a tank. Unfortunately it had not arrived when the barrage came down on the enemy trenches, and the leading companies moved off without it. Almost before the barrage lifted off the German line, the Battalion came under murderous machine-gun fire, and, tragically, the wire remained uncut. For four hours before the tank approached, they were pinned down in the open. Invulnerable to machine-gun bullets, the tank tore an opening in the wire, through which the men poured. With this position in their hands, the survivors of the support companies advanced on their next objective, a chemical works from whose tall chimneys, observers directed artillery fire on to the attackers. However, they managed to reach the outskirts of the factory, where they were reforming when large numbers of Germans were thrown *en masse* against them. It was a reversal of roles, in which the Germans suffered against machine-guns as terribly as the British had in earlier battles, and the Battalion's position was not much altered at nightfall.

It had been planned that the 6th Battalion, in support, should pass through the 7th when it had taken the chemical works, but now the hold-up forced them to work their way in short rushes under fire a little to their left, on to the slopes of Greenland Hill. There, like the 7th, they found that massed counter-attacks were no match for their Lewis guns, and the threats to their position were soon broken up. The chemical works, however, remained beyond their power, and that night the 51st Division was relieved.

The same pattern of attacks encountering stiffer defences was repeated all along the Third Army front. On its right, the 15th Division assaulted the village of Guemappe on the high ground south of the river Scarpe, and found that well-designed defences and the torn ground made organised attack slow and costly in lives. However, the ground offered opportunities for small groups, and seventy men of the 9th Black Watch under Captain

Morrison held an advanced and isolated trench for four hours until directed to retire. Two days later, on the 25th April, when a second attempt was made to capture high ground beyond the village, two companies fought their way to the objective, on the left flank of the Camerons, and the 45th Brigade. In the evening, sustained counter-attacks by the Germans drove first the Brigade, then the Camerons, off the ridge, so that by dawn The Black Watch companies were entirely cut off. Through the day the enemy made repeated attacks on them; two platoons were over-run, but the others fought on without food or water, until dark came and a relieving force could approach to take over their defences.

Neither the Regiment, nor the Army, was yet finished with Arras. In his biography of Allenby, Wavell wrote, 'The First Battle had been fought in the sure faith of victory; the Second in good hope of success, but this Third Battle on May 3rd was mere charity.' And the unsoundness of the brass made charity expensive. At the last moment, Haig changed the time of attack from 4.15 a.m., first light, to 3.45 a.m., when there was not a glimmer.

The decision arrived too late for officers to take compass bearings, so that when the 8th Black Watch led off the left of its brigade attack, it had only a general idea of the direction as it stumbled through the dark. Soon the brigade on its left veered into the Battalion's path, causing more cunfusion, and almost immediately after, heavy machine-gun fire broke out from the German defence-line. When dawn came, half the Battalion were casualties, and it was a scene reflected along the whole front. Thus Arras, which had begun so well, ended in failure.

The state of the French army was now so alarming that Pétain, who had succeeded Nivelle, estimated that he had only two reliable divisions between the Germans and Paris, and only unremitting pressure from the British could distract attention from that frail defence. Loos, the Somme and Arras had all been selected as battlegrounds in order to assist French operations in the south, but, once released from that obligation, Haig chose Ypres as the point at which to exert pressure.

There were two reasons for his choice. At the beginning of June, General Plumer had won a notable victory at Messines Ridge, which provided an opportunity to extend the gains north-east along the high ground to Passchendaele. Secondly, the German sub-marines, which had come close to strangling Britain's food supply, operated from Ostend and Zeebrugge, almost due north of Ypres, and a breakout from the salient would put those ports within reach of the army. There were contradictions implicit, both as to the direction and to the extent of the attack, which became apparent as the Third Battle of Ypres developed.

During the three-and-a-half months of fighting, six Battalions of The Black Watch came into the Ypres salient, before fanning out to north, east or south. Certain conditions, however, were common to all. Each suffered the disconcerting experience of any salient, where the enemy, on three sides, could bombard supply columns and rear camps. All the Battalions suffered the unusually heavy rains of late July and August, and most the storms of October and November, although one, the 8th, enjoyed the bright days of September when, on dry ground, Plumer came close to breaking the German army with three successive victories. Finally, each had to learn new methods of dealing with a defence, in which concrete pill-boxes and fortified strongpoints had replaced trenches. Mopping-up parties followed the waves, and the waves themselves more often moved forward in column than line.

When the first attack went forward on the 31st July, there was no suggestion of surprise. The salient was overlooked by high ground – to the east, Passchendaele Ridge, and to the south-east, Gheluvelt Plateau – so that all the preparations could be seen by the enemy, and a fortnight's bombardment had given further warning. One of the official historians concluded, 'No offensive was ever so clearly heralded, or so confidently awaited.'

Nevertheless, the first offensive, designed to drive the enemy off Pilchem Ridge to the north-east, achieved considerable success. The 9th Battalion, leading the 15th Division near the right of the line, found the wire cut and, advancing by section rushes, over-ran most of the defence posts, which the support companies mopped up with the help of a tank. When they were on their objective, the supporting battalion passed through, and as they disappeared over the little rise called the Frezenburg Ridge, it seemed as though the advance was being executed with a watchmaker's precision. Throughout the morning, however, the 9th Battalion came under persistent shell-fire from Passchendaele and Gheluvelt, some three miles to their right, and that part of the attack closest to the guns broke down under the bombardment. This, in turn, forced the advanced brigade of the 15th Division to pull back to The Black Watch line.

What happened on that first day recurred constantly throughout the earlier part of the Third Battle of Ypres. The left of the line, that furthest from the artillery on the high ground, made the greatest advance. This pattern can be seen in the fortunes of The Black Watch Battalions on the 31st July. In the left centre, the 4/5th advanced for almost a mile to the banks of the Steenbeek River. They suffered few casualties up to that point but, on the far bank, they extended in line with two other battalions to their right, and continued the advance. Now the defence posts became more numerous, and more formidable, and the centre battalion stumbled on to a concealed machine-gun nest, which practically wiped them out. The guns were then turned on The Black Watch, almost to rake them, and the rapidly mounting casualties forced them to pull back to the river.

To the left of the 4/5th, the 51st Division also had as its target a line beyond the Steenbeek, representing an advance of about 2,000 yards. It was a well-planned operation, executed almost flawlessly. The 7th Black Watch advanced behind the barrage at a pace of 100 yards every four minutes, their direction marked by drums of burning oil fired from mortars on to the enemy lines. The ground was badly torn by shells, which had, however, made less impact on the concrete pill-boxes, but these defences were stormed, and the ground negotiated at the right speed. When the assault battalions reached their objectives, the support troops, among them the 6th Black Watch, passed through. The 6th Battalion found the opposition stiffening as they approached the Steenbeek River; wire and sandbags converted the ruins of farms into keeps or fortresses, each of which had to be stalked and stormed, each taking its quota of casualties. However, by the afternoon, a company numbering about fifty men under two officers, was constructing a formidable post on the far side of the river. But this was the limit.

Five separate counter-attacks of mounting strength were directed at the post, and beaten off. One of the defenders described the last moments:

Ammunition was running short, and the enemy were massing for another assault, when we received the order to fall back on the German gunpits beyond the river.

Those who came through bear witness that it was one of the most exciting moments of their lives. Stumbling through the mud, falling, rising, pressing on, while the enemy, barely one hundred yards away, stood up and took deliberate aim – one of the memories of the Great War which no length of time will ever blot out.

The banks of the Steenbeek River now marked the northern limit of the salient, and for the 6th and 7th Battalions that first attack was also their last experience of Third Ypres, for the 51st Division was immediately withdrawn, to begin training with tanks in preparation for Cambrai.

Wet as the previous August had been, in 1917 five times as much rain fell during the month. Shell-fire had destroyed the drainage systems, and the water collected in shell-holes, trenches and dugouts; men and weapons were plastered in mud, and a man who ventured off the duckboards and marked routes risked being drowned. Even the marked routes were only relatively safe, for the incessant shellfire broke up the duckboards, and made craters in the road, which the rain filled and camouflaged with slime.

The artillery fire could not be evaded. The 4/5th Battalion, still holding its position on the south bank of the Steenbeek, suffered so many casualties that one company was reduced to six men and an officer, and Sergeant Hutton, who had been so prominent at the Somme, again found himself in command of his company. Eventually they were relieved, and, after a fortnight of re-forming and refitting, they were sent with the 39th Division to the very south of the salient, to take over that sector from Plumer's Second Army. From there, the Battalion could see something of the attack of the 21st August, the last great attempt to break out of the salient to the north-east.

The 15th Division fought on almost the same ground as before, that is, across the Frezenburg Ridge, but the conditions under which they fought had changed entirely. Not only had the ground become a quagmire, but the enemy had sited fresh nests of machine-guns, and built new pill-boxes close to the front. The Divisional attack was halted almost at once, though isolated parties of Seaforths and Camerons managed to work their way to within 500 yards of a particularly troublesome keep called Gallipoli Farm. Two days later, the 9th Black Watch, in reserve, were ordered to send two companies up to make a night attack on the farm. They had no time for reconnaissance, and little for planning, but in the dark they managed to fight their way across a hundred yards of mud, before the intensity of fire made further movement impossible. Out of 120 men 50 were casualties, and by an unhappy stroke of misfortune, a shell exploded in Battalion Headquarters killing 12 of the staff, including the temporary commanding officer.

The loss did not prevent another attack being made on Gallipoli Farm two days later, and this time the companies reached its outskirts, but the keep itself, protected by barbed wire and a hail of machine-gun bullets, remained uncaptured. After each attack, the companies dug themselves in on the ground they had gained, and when the battle ended, the front had been advanced by about 400 yards. Nowhere had much more significant gains been made.

The commander of this first stage of Third Ypres, General Gough, observed, 'The more our left pushed forward, the deeper it became buried in a salient, and the enemy could bring converging and enfilade fire to bear on us from the high ground to our right.' It was now manifest that no further movement could be made to the north-east until

Gheluvelt Plateau and Passchendaele Ridge to the east were captured. That responsibility was given to Plumer and the Second Army, and there was a lull until the 20th September, when the first of three battles took them a mile on to Gheluvelt Plateau. But after the third victory on the 4th October had brought the British to within 3,000 yards of Passchendaele, the rain returned, making porridge of the dusty ground. For another five weeks, the army inched its way up the ridge to Passchendaele.

The 8th Battalion fought a typical battle at Poelcappelle, where, in a landscape without landmarks, all that stood out from the wasteland was the unrelenting courage of companies, then platoons, and eventually sections, moving forward from waterlogged craters and ditches, until they could rush a machine-gun sited in the ruins of a farm. When runners from headquarters were all hit, so that there was no communication, when the only guide to direction was the source of the bullets, and when one slimy shell-hole offered as good protection as any other, to have kept going forward was the supreme victory, beyond the strength or imagination of an individual but possible within the family of his platoon, battalion and regiment.

On November 8 Passchendaele itself was taken, and officially the battle ended, but ten days later the 1st Battalion came into the salient, and fought a brief action to take the last section of the ridge. On the crowded roads to the front, they met The Royal Highlanders of Canada coming back. The latter provided a resourceful guide, who took the 1st Battalion to its trenches via the only route which remained free of crowds – no-man's land. It was here that The Black Watch extended to The Royal Highlanders of Canada the right to wear the Red Hackle, and there could have been no more appropriate place than Passchendaele to recognise the strength of regimental ties, which is implicit in that symbol.

While the battle of Third Ypres was being fought to its sombre conclusion, the 6th and 7th Battalions trained with the 51st Division for an operation with tanks at Cambrai. Planned at first as little more than a raid against the Hindenberg Line, it blossomed in the warmth of Haig's approval until six divisions and over 400 tanks were involved. Since this was to be the first large-scale action with tanks – the lozenge-shaped Mark IVs which had a top speed of 4 m.p.h. – infantry commanders had not yet decided on the most effective tactics to be adopted. Five of the divisions practised advancing in column close behind their tanks, but 'Uncle' Harper trained his troops to move in a spear-head formation, which closed in order to pass through the gaps torn in the wire, and then opened again. They followed 150 yards behind the tanks because, in Sir Basil Lidell-Hart's opinion, Harper distrusted the new-fangled machines. It was a detail which gave rise to controversy after the battle.

A detailed concern for secrecy enabled the tanks to be assembled behind the front line without arousing the suspicions of the enemy. This concern deprived the 7th Battalion of the kilt, and compelled it to conceal its identity, and eveything else, in trousers. Finally, complete surprise was guaranteed when the artillery dispensed with the usual preliminary bombardment, and laid their guns by means of the new survey method, which made registration unnecessary.

At 6.20 a.m. on the 20th November, the guns opened fire, and 250 yards behind the barrage the tanks rolled forward on firm ground which had been neither soaked by rain, nor excessively torn by shelling. Behind them, at the northern end of the line (the left of the attack), came the 5th Argylls and the 6th Black Watch leading the left brigade of the

PLATE XI (above)  *Drummer of The Black Watch in South Africa during the Boer War. Khaki begins to cover the finery . . .*

PLATE XII (right)  *. . . but not altogether. Officer in Review Order 1914.*

*Over page*

PLATE XIII (top)  *Review order for N.C.O.s and Drummers. Notes by Colonel Wallace. 1930s.*

PLATE XIV (bottom left)  *Drawings and water colour by 'Snaffles'. First World War.*

PLATE XV (bottom right)  *R.S.M. Smart of the 2nd Battalion. 'No position he was so proud to hold as Sergeant-Major in The Black Watch.' 1915.*

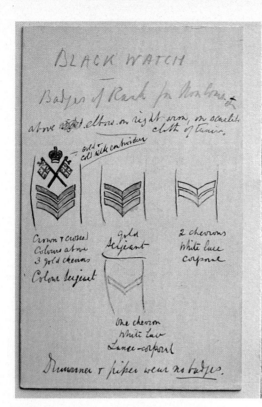

BLACK WATCH

Badges of Rank for Non-coms.

above right elbow, on right arm, on scarlet cloth of tunic.

Gold + Cells with embroider

Crown + crossed Colours above 3 gold chevrons
Colour Sergeant

gold Sergeant

2 chevrons White lace corporal

One chevron White lace Lance-corporal

Drummers + pipers wear no badges.

BLACK WATCH, DRUMMER, REVIEW ORDER

ENLARGEMENT

DRUMMER'S LACE + cord
Red crimson or white worsted

Drummer's uniform is same as fusilier's except that "wings" are worn, + "drummer's lace" on collar, wings + sleeve slang. The cords are red + white.
A dirk, same as pipers', is worn on right side. No sword or bayonet.
When the drum is carried the sporran is not worn.
(Buglers, pipers, + drummers are generally called "drummers".)

A Heilan Lad.

51st Division. As the Mark IVs rumbled out of the early morning mist, some Germans simply fled; others, stunned by the barrage and by the sight of the monsters, made more terrible by the huge bundle of fascines each bore so that Birnam Wood must have seemed on the move, put up little resistance to the infantry and were captured. A few, however, stayed by their machine-guns. On four separate occasions, platoons of the 6th Battalion were briefly held up by machine-gun fire, until a Jock stalked forward to demolish them with grenades. Otherwise, the advance had the precision of a final rehearsal. The spearheads opened and closed like umbrellas; when one wave encountered uncut wire, supporting tanks came up on the commander's signal to perforate the entanglements, and the movement continued, sweeping up large numbers of prisoners. By 8.15 a.m., the leading platoons had reached their objective on the Grand Ravin, a shallow river-bed which belied its name.

An hour later, the 7th Battalion passed through the 6th to begin the second phase which was aimed at capturing the village of Flesquières. At first, there was the same pattern of overwhelming victory, and the Battalion sent back more than 200 prisoners from the trenches it captured. But by this time, the barrage had advanced some distance ahead; it arose from the Hindenberg support line an hour before the 7th Battalion arrived, and it was there that the first set-back occurred. As the Battalion's tanks crossed the ridge, they came under fire from one or more German field guns. It was later established that these gunners had already met French tanks during Nivelle's May offensive, and now they remained cool enough to aim and register direct hits on each tank as it came into view. From Flesquières itself, machine-guns swept the ground, and without the invulnerable tanks to cut them down, the 7th Battalion could only force one more trench before the attack halted.

The official historian blamed Harper's formation, asserting that it slowed the advance and left the infantry too far from the tanks to give support against the artillery. It must be said, however, that it was hard to see how the 7th Battalion, for instance, could have approached close enough to knock out the field-guns except under cover of smoke, which was not available. Nor is any delay apparent in the 6th Battalion's finely-executed advance, except that occasioned by machine-guns, which would presumably have been present whatever their formation.

The set-back appeared more prominent because the rest of the attack achieved almost flawless success, but even Flesquières did not remain uncaptured for long. Patrols sent forward during the night discovered that the Germans had evacuated it, and at dawn the 7th Battalion were firmly established there.

That first day of Cambrai surpassed any gain so far made in the war, except for the first day of Arras when much larger forces had been involved. The formidable Hindenberg Line had been breached, four miles of enemy ground gained, and 4,000 prisoners captured. In London, the church bells rang to celebrate a victory which appeared all the brighter set against the drab patterns of Passchendaele.

Further gains followed, but the confidence of victory seems to have blinded the commanders to the signs of a counter-attack. When it came, on St Andrew's Day, almost all the ground taken in the previous ten days was lost. Last to be taken, Flesquières was also the last to be lost. The two Black Watch Battalions were still there, when the Germans launched their final momentous offensive in March, 1918.

# CHAPTER 16

# From Mesopotamia to Megiddo

If the year had ended indecisively on the Western Front, the East at any rate was glowing with victory. As a Christmas present to a weary nation, Allenby had captured Jerusalem, and the 14th Black Watch, which until recently had been the Fife and Forfar Yeomanry, mounted guard over the holy places, the first Christians there since the Crusaders. In Mesopotamia, the Turks had been driven from the country by a campaign which had started two years before with a string of bitter defeats.

When the 2nd Battalion disembarked from a Tigris river-boat on the 5th January, 1916, it was immediately thrust into a desperate race to rescue General Townshend's army, besieged in the town of Kut, some fifty miles away. Transport, artillery and medical equipment were all lacking or in short supply, for such was the need for haste – Townshend had asked for relief before the 10th January – that equipment was abandoned rather than delay the movement of troops. In the valley of the Tigris, the Battalion met rain and mud, as bad as in the worst of European weather, and the Turks, defending entrenched positions, proved a skilful and stubborn enemy.

The day after landing, the 2nd Battalion marched twenty miles upriver and, on the 7th January, it was thrown against the Turkish position at Shaikh Sa'ad. Haste was the keynote of this stage of the campaign, and it was allowed to obscure the otherwise glaring weakness of the Turkish army there. The river Tigris split their army, leaving about 6,000 men on the south bank, and twice that number on the north. Each part might have been defeated in detail, but, duplicating the unsoundness of the Turks, the British attacked simultaneously on both banks.

The 2nd Battalion, in reserve on the north bank, had been sent to breakfast, when their brigadier ordered them to advance to fill a gap in the attacking line. Colonel Wauchope asked for time to make arrangements for communications and ammunition supply, and enquired what his objective was. The brigadier replied that the attack must be made immediately, and 'the objective was the enemy's trenches, and the direction, wherever the bullets were thickest.' There was little artillery and no infantry support, nor could the enemy lines be seen half a mile away, for the mirage obscured all detail.

The Battalion advanced at great speed, each company receiving its orders for direction on the move. As it came under fire from front and flank, it extended into line, all manoeuvres being made without pause, so that it soon passed the leading battalions on either side. The plain was entirely flat and open, allowing shrapnel and rifle-fire to take full effect. The Colonel and three company commanders were hit, and when they were still about 300 yards from the Turkish line only six unwounded officers and about 120 men were left with the Battalion. At that point the order was given to halt, and dig in. Lying out in the open, the survivors kept up a well-controlled fire, though their targets could only have been muzzily seen through the heat-haze, and when dusk came they were withdrawn from their exposed position.

Throughout the men had displayed a praiseworthy sense of cohesion and discipline, and the Regimental historian wrote, with some self-restraint, 'The pity was that so fine a Battalion should have been so reduced without an opportunity of striking back.' The aftermath of battle provided further evidence of the ill-effects of haste, for there were only 250 hospital beds available for 4,000 casualties, whose sufferings were thereby needlessly aggravated.

On the south bank the attack, moving over more broken ground and a shorter distance, achieved complete success, and, with their position turned, the Turks withdrew from the north bank twenty-four hours later. After a second, short battle, the enemy finally took up an immensely powerful position, between a salt marsh on their left, and the Tigris on their right, and, although the front was less than a mile wide, it was defended in depth.

The Black Watch, numbering about 250 men, were detailed to lead the assault on this position, along the river bank. Since they were so few in number, Major Hamilton-Johnson commanding them, suggested that the support battalion should move close up to take immediate opportunity of their break-in. The battalion's commanding officer agreed, but, unfortunately and for no apparent reason, they were over-ruled. At dawn on the 21st January, The Black Watch attacked in the same perfect order as at Shaikh Sa'ad. Through river mud, and a concentrated fire which broke the battalions to their right, they swept into the Turkish trenches. There was a brief, fierce struggle, then Piper Crichton was playing along the captured trench, with the enemy in flight, losing heavily as they ran. But the support battalion, starting their attack nearly 1,500 yards away, were fiercely shelled and shot at from the rear trenches, and had no chance of reaching The Black Watch.

It was not long before the enemy realised how few their attackers were, and the counter-attacks quickly swelled in strength and number. The Jocks soon found that British grenades rarely exploded, but, for two hours, hurling Turkish grenades which had been left behind, firing Turkish rifles and machine-guns when their own ammunition ran out, the remnants of the Battalion held on. Only when they were almost surrounded, did they begin to give ground, and then so grudgingly that they halted at an advanced trench, closer to the Turks than the British. But when they were relieved at nightfall, only ninety-nine men, wounded and unwounded, answered the roll-call, and a subaltern commanded them.

For the first time since they arrived in Mesopotamia, the Battalion had some respite from fighting, and during the period of quiescence, it was decided that the survivors of The Black Watch should be amalgamated with the Seaforths, who had suffered exceptional losses at Shaikh Sa'ad, to form a Highland Battalion.

In Kut, Townshend's army of 12,000 still held out, and, at the beginning of April, the relief force, considerably strengthened since January, made a fresh attempt to force the Turkish position between the salt marsh and the Tigris. The Turks had retreated a little deeper into their natural fortress and were now situated, perhaps more strongly than before, at Sannaiyat. The first assault was supposed to be by night but, in confusion like that at Magersfontein, the attackers were found at dawn, in close formation and some distance from the trenches. Out of 1,800 casualties, the Highland Battalion's losses accounted for 200. A second attempt was equally disastrous, but by now the Kut garrison was *in extremis,* and a third, final attempt had to be made to breach the Sannaiyat line at any cost.

Heavy rain and the flooding of the Tigris had reduced the ground to such a quagmire, it was estimated that it would take seven minutes for the attacking troops to cover the 400 yards between the trenches. However, the Highland Battalion had proved an exceptionally happy marriage of regimental traditions, and it went into the attack with such dash that the Jocks reached the enemy trenches within four minutes. They flung themselves into the mud until the guns had lifted. Then they sprang over the first trenches, so flooded that they were unmanned, and advanced on the second line, exposed all the while to a pitiless fire of bullets and shrapnel. Wading through water-logged communication trenches they worked their way close to the third line, when a huge counter-attack was launched against them. Seeing the Highlanders enveloped, an officer in the supporting battalion which had just started to come up, ordered his men to retire. But the Highland Battalion doggedly held on to its position, and more. A pilot, who was flying over the battle, later reported, 'I saw small parties of men on three separate occasions make attempts to get into the Turkish third line. In each case, all the men were knocked out, and not one came back. To make one attempt was all right, but for men to make two more, knowing that almost for a certainty their efforts must fail, showed to my mind a bravery, a devotion to duty, which must be considered wonderful.'

By misfortune, the order to retire reached the Indian regiment on the Battalion's right, and the Highlanders were now entirely unsupported. It was obvious that the attack had failed, and finally the survivors were forced to fall back.

With that last, magnificent effort, the hopes of the Kut garrison finally disappeared and, a week later, they surrendered. Almost three years of captivity awaited them, but for the Tigris army there was a better turn of fortune than they had hitherto known. Under a new commander, General Maude, and without the pressing need for haste, the army could regain its balance, and reconstitute its terribly depleted battalions.

The Highland Battalion, which had been less than lucky in the field, but deeply successful as a corps, was split into its constituent parts and, for the rest of the year, Colonel Wauchope, now recovered from his wound, trained up the new 2nd Battalion in the spirit of The Black Watch. By December, 1916, it had become so proficient in one aspect of its craft, that a brigade order ordained that scouting and reconnaissance was to be carried out only by The Black Watch. As to its shooting, the evidence is more ambivalent. On a route march, a skein of northening geese was seen passing overhead, and Lance-Corporal MacKintosh, in a fine display of presumption, skill and luck, brought one down with a single rifle-shot; that prompted a Battalion fusillade through which the rest of the skein flapped serenely on without scathe. If the incident does not say much for their marksmanship, it is good testimony of their morale, after a campaign which had twice seen the Battalion reduced to company strength.

In February, 1917, the Turks were at last evicted from Sannaiyat, by a turning movement south of the river, followed by an attack on their line. 'None of our men will forget the scene on that clear morning, nor the feeling of freedom and elation, as the companies gained trench after trench. The Sannaiyat position which had held us back for ten long months was now in our hands.' Kut was by-passed, and Baghdad became the target.

On one of the long, wearing marches, Wauchope, riding in a Ford, offered a lift to an elderly sergeant. The N.C.O., who had served in Egypt in the 1880s, refused the offer indignantly, remarking that he had been marching through desert long before Fords were thought of, and that he would still be marching long after that particular model had broken down. Like those of other Black Watch battalions, the N.C.O.s of the 2nd were men of stern will, and outstanding character.

There was Kennedy, who arrived in France as Company Sergeant-Major, and three years later was a Lieutenant-Colonel commanding a battalion; Sergeant MacDonald, past editor of the *Cherat Times*, and, after retirement from the Army, sometime employee of the Military Governor of a province in Central China, but who returned by devious means to his old Battalion when war broke out; Company Sergeant-Major Palmer, who retired in 1912 to take up sheep-farming in Patagonia, but paid his own way back to rejoin his Regiment; Regimental Sergeant-Major Smart, who turned down a commission with the splendid boast that there was no position in the British Army he was so proud to hold as Sergeant-Major in The Black Watch; and finally there was Company Sergeant-Major Houston, former heavyweight boxing champion of India, who did take a commission, and on the 11th March, 1917, led one of the first patrols to enter Baghdad.

Houston penetrated into the heart of the city, where, with considerable daring and some violence, he captured intact the vital railway station. This started rather a habit of station capture, culminating, on the 23rd April, with the taking of Samarrah Station, whose bell was presented to the Battalion, and is now inscribed, confusingly, but with some justification, 'Baghdad'. But the winning of Mushaidie Station was the most notable feat of the three.

The Battalion's battle began at sunset on the 13th March, when with the rest of the 7th Division, it was ordered to make a night march towards the western flank of the Turkish defence line. This was sited on a low ridge, which ran east-west across the railway line, and ended at its western extremity in a sugar-loaf hill. In the clear dawn, every detail was visible of the first advance along the east of the railway. When this was halted, in the early afternoon, The Black Watch received orders to make an assault west of the railway, with the Gurkhas on their left.

Formed up in four extended lines, the Battalion moved off at 3.30 p.m. across some 1,500 yards of almost open desert. Some low-lying sand-hills broke the flatness of the ground, and, in their lee, the final orders were given, before the Battalion went forward again. Figures began to fall in growing numbers, and it was apparent that the most damaging fire came from Sugar Loaf Hill. To meet it, the Battalion extended to the left, the support companies coming up to fill the gap. Such losses were sustained that it seemed the attack must lose its momentum, but all along the line small sections continued to rise from the ground, rush forward thirty or forty yards, then fling themselves down, weaker perhaps by two or three of their number. One platoon lost five commanders in as many minutes, but a Lance-Corporal led them on with the same gallantry. Finally, nearest the railway line, the right of the Battalion burst into the Turkish trenches, and at once began a sweeping fire of the rest of the ridge. Artillery, which so far had been out of range, was brought up to make a precise and brief bombardment of Sugar Loaf Hill. When their fire began to slacken, the setting sun suddenly gleamed on fixed bayonets, as The Black Watch rose like one man from their trenches, and rushed the hill. There was a brief flurry, then the last Turks fled from their defences, and the Jocks tasted the sweet satisfaction of occupying Sugar Loaf Hill.

Already they had been on the move for twenty-four hours with little water, but almost at once the order came for the Battalion to push on alone for Mushaidie Station four miles further. The remaining ammunition was distributed, and the 300 survivors were organised in three companies. At 11.30 p.m., the companies deployed as they approached the station, then charged once more with the bayonet. There was little work for them. The Turks fled from their midnight visitation, leaving some prisoners, stores and a fully operational Mushaidie Station to the Battalion. There the exhausted Jocks finally slept, closing a day which must rank as one of the most outstanding in the Mesopotamian campaign, and one which is commemorated by the pipe-tune, 'After the Battle'.

Thrust out of Mushaidie, the enemy now fell back, offering little resistance until he reached the ancient ruins of Istabulat. On the 30th April, the Battalion and the Gurkhas led the attack on an entrenched position between a canal and the Tigris. In characteristic fashion, The Black Watch made a very fast advance, which took their leading companies into the Turkish redoubt, some way ahead of the support companies and Gurkhas. At once, there was a furious counter-attack, which threw the Jocks out. 'The smallest hesitation, the slightest wavering, and the Turks had made good their success. But there was no hesitation, and, though only one unwounded officer remained, there was no wavering. The bombers dashed forward, every available man followed, and within fifteen minutes of its loss the redoubt was recaptured.' It was a ferocious quarter of an hour, epitomised by the exploits of an old soldier, Private Melvin of Kirriemuir. His bayonet was damaged so that it could not be fixed on his rifle. Flinging the rifle aside, he grasped the bayonet, and rushed on a group of Turks. Three were felled by fist or bayonet, and another six, stunned by the violence, quickly surrendered, and were brought back as prisoners. For this action, which represented those of so many others, Melvin was awarded the Victoria Cross. That determined struggle so impressed an artillery officer, whose guns could not be used for lack of range, that he wrote, 'That day the Highlanders, without help, won a victory that only those who saw it can realize was one of the most gallant gained in the war.'

Istabulat proved to be the last major resistance that the Turks offered in Mesopotamia; by the middle of the year, all possible reinforcements for the battered Turkish army were being diverted to meet the threat of Allenby's advance up the Eastern Mediterranean seaboard. In December, the 2nd Battalion left Mesopotamia to join Allenby's forces. Briefly there were two Black Watch Battalions, the 2nd and 14th, engaged in the raiding and skirmishing through the Judean hills, which pushed the Turks back from Jerusalem. In April, 1918, however, the 14th Black Watch were part of the force detached from Allenby's strength to make good the losses on the Western Front. The 2nd Battalion remained to take part in the masterpiece of Megiddo.

To troops who were accustomed to fight for every yard of ground, the objectives laid down were astonishing; the Battalion Headquarters was expected to move forward 5,000 yards in an hour. But the plan was simple and the complex preparations thorough. Allenby's strength was concentrated secretly against the Turkish right in the coastal plain.

There the infantry, including the 2nd Battalion, were to break open a gaping hole, through which the cavalry would ride, passing to the very rear of the Turkish army where they might fall upon the disorganised enemy.

Secrecy had been so well-maintained that the Turks had no suspicion of the coming battle. Weeks earlier, when the Battalion first moved into the area, enough tents had been pitched for a force twice their number, so that when another battalion was sent up to join them shortly before the battle there was no evidence that the troops had been doubled in strength. In the early hours of the 20th September, as the Battalion lay waiting to attack about 500 yards from the enemy lines, they could hear the unsuspecting Turks engaged in no more war-like activity than shouting insults at their fellow-Muslims in the Punjabi regiments. Then at 4.15 a.m., a massive bombardment broke out, and immediately the Battalion was on the move, for Allenby trusted more to surprise than to high explosive, and his barrages were brief. Entering the southern end of a long salient, platoons successively branched to the left to mop up its western side. They drove through an elaborate, and well-manned system of trenches, without stop or pause, taking about 1,000 prisoners. By 8 a.m. the last platoon had rejoined the Battalion Headquarters, 5,000 yards from where they started. This was only the start, for they now had to drive the broken enemy into the cavalry at the rear. The 2nd Battalion finally slept at midnight, having covered another seven miles, stormed up a steep hill, and fought a second fierce battle at its summit.

After Megiddo, the Turks could offer little more opposition. On the day following the battle, Lance-Corporal Kelman of Perth was killed, the last man in the Battalion to be killed during the war, although, sadly, malaria and flu accounted for many others. On the 30th October, the Battalion was approaching Tripoli, not far from the Turkish frontier, when news came that an armistice had been signed with Turkey. For the 2nd Battalion, the Great War was over.

Compared to the Mesopotamian extremes of disaster and triumph, the campaign in Salonika seemed to be a limbo, void of victory and defeat. The 10th Battalion had arrived there in December, 1915, and disembarked in a snowstorm. Seven months later, they were broiled by the sun and bitten by mosquitoes. Pioneer Sergeant Duncan of the 13th Battalion, who joined them in the summer of 1916, wrote, 'The mosquito is the chief enemy. The female as usual being the more dangerous of the two, as it bites and spreads malaria. For this reason, in the summer, the troops had to go to the hills, and only a very thin line was left in the Struma valley.' As a precaution against bites, sentries were dressed like bee-keepers, in veils and gauntlets, but the weather kept everyone in a state of indecision about the proper headgear; at one point, the men wore slouch hats, and carried in their packs a khaki bonnet, steel helmet, pith helmet, waterproof cover for the bonnet, and a cap comforter. Their objective seemed equally indeterminate. Neither guarding Macedonia against Bulgarian invasion, nor threatening attack themselves, could be properly done in winter snow or malarial summer, so they built dugouts and roads, and occasionally raided across the Struma Valley.

In their digging, the 10th Battalion became amateur archaeologists, turning up some Tanagra statuettes, copper ornaments, and a ten-foot long tusk. For their part, the 13th Battalion, converted from the Scottish Horse in October, 1916, formed a hunt from sundry mongrels which was followed by anyone who could borrow a mule. The Bulgars proved most understanding about whipping in over-enthusiastic hounds which crossed the front while hot on the scent, but what manner of beast left the scent seems, like so much else, to have been undetermined.

In May, 1917, an attempt was made to resolve the situation by an attack on the Bulgarian position south of Lake Doiran, an enormous expanse of water, which then lay some distance inside the Greek frontier, although it is now part of Yugoslavia. The 10th Battalion made a night attack with no support on a very dispersed frontage. Despite some of the confusion, inevitable in such an attack, their front line, reached the enemy wire, separated but more or less intact. There they found the wire uncut, and, while they struggled with it, the barrage lifted from the enemy trenches. The Bulgars came out of their shelters, and opened fire on the Jocks caught on their barbed wire. However, some men in each company managed to break through to the enemy line, but reinforcements were so thin by the time they came up, that no further ground could be gained, and what they held was untenable when daylight came.

The very lack of success at Doiran stimulated organisation and planning, which produced victory in the spring offensive of 1918. By then, however, the 10th Battalion was in France, but by bitter irony they had no part in the victories there either. In late September, the Battalion received orders for disbandment, and its men were distributed through the rest of the Regiment.

# CHAPTER 17

# Retreat and Victory

On the Western Front, the first months of 1918 were dominated by the growing awareness that the Germans intended to mount an offensive in the spring. The collapse of Tsarist Russia had released the divisions fighting on the eastern front for service in the west, and all Germany's strength would be concentrated on defeating Britain and France before the American armies could be built up.

Although forewarned, the British were by no means forearmed. Lloyd George was convinced by the 400,000 casualties sustained at the Third Battle of Ypres, that Haig was a butcher, whose blood-thirstiness could only be limited by denying him men. Reinforcements were hoarded in England, while the number of fighting troops in France actually dropped to less than the total of twelve months earlier.

In The Black Watch, the approaching German attack was common knowledge, but trench warfare concentrated the mind on immediate sensation: a comfortable billet, an extra loaf of bread produced by an ingenious ration party, the farmyard smell where the battalion horses and mules were stabled, the bitter chemical stink of supposedly deloused shirts, and the almost immortal lice themselves. In a pleasant conceit, Private Linklater mused on the origin of his, picked up in an old barn.

> Beside a rusty nail, whereon I hung my helmet, I read by matchlight a name carved in flowing script: Joannes Baptiste Vansteene 1816. A barn of decent age, and Joannes, I thought in the gliding minutes before sleep, may have talked with Wellington's men, the valiant of Hougomont, and cat-scarred veterans from the Peninsula. Perhaps, I thought a little later – waking to scratch – these lice that are afflicting me, were bred in primogeniture from a pair in Joannes armpit that were young when Picton hid his wound at Quatre Bras . . . Joannes' lice had been prolific. The whole floor was alive. . . . Old soldiers, tough as saddlery, rose cursing and afraid, and we youngsters were ravished more deeply, and far more often, than Lucanian girls by Spartacus' insurgent gladiators.

Lice were not specific to The Black Watch, but another of Linklater's memories, the 4/5th Battalion leaving the Ypres salient through torrents of rain in January, 1918, clearly is. 'A highly intelligent company commander had told us to take off our kilts, and wear them as capes about our shoulders. So we said good-bye to Passchendaele with a flutter of grey shirt-tails dancing behind our bums.' Even that nineteenth-century Colonel, old Cameron of the 79th, could hardly have relished a more exhilarating native bracer. For Ypres mud, the 4/5th substituted that of the Somme – 'a paler, more sympathetic mud than the dark and evil mud of the Salient' – and there, in March, they met the German attack.

The pattern of it was repeated against all the Battalions; machine-guns and light artillery were brought up to fire from the front-line, while the infantry probed the weak spots in the defence, then poured *en masse* through the gaps. The front was no longer defended as a line, but in depth after the German model, yet unlike the Germans the advance posts were strongly held, and, as a result, the troops there were almost immediately surrounded.

On the 22nd March, a clear and sunny day, the Regimental history recorded, 'the enemy put down a most astounding barrage, under cover of which they attacked, and by the sound of the firing it seemed as if every second German had a machine-gun.' As the forward posts were bombarded, the support companies and headquarters were simultaneously attacked from flank and rear. There was and could be no communication. When the commanding officer ordered a withdrawal, isolated groups remained behind. Companies, battalions, and even divisions became inextricably mixed. But within that confusion rolling westward, there were rocks of disciplined fighting which gradually wrecked the precision of the German advance.

In the extreme south, the 8th Black Watch withdrew, companies passing through each other's line, sometimes to maintain alignment with other corps fighting an enemy beyond the Battalion's sight, sometimes encountering stiffer opposition in the rear than the front. Close to them, the 51st Division fought stubbornly at Cambrai, the 6th and 7th Black Watch shoulder-to-shoulder. Even when swirled apart, isolated parties formed themselves round resolute individuals, and resisted with such distinctive courage that the Germans dropped a message by aeroplane, 'Good old 51st, still sticking it.' 'Sticking it' was the vital quality of that week. The 9th Battalion, who fought superbly in defence of Arras, were told by their Corps Commander, 'I knew you could be relied upon to stick it out to the end . . . I want the honour of holding Arras to be yours alone.' The cost was terrible. The 9th was so reduced that it had to be amalgamated with the 4/5th, and the 4/5th themselves numbered only thirty men when the German advance was at last halted. But Eric Linklater remembered that, as they came out from the Somme, they passed the fragment of a Guards battalion, and their piper began to play 'Highland Laddie'. 'We were a tatterdemalion crew from the coal-mines of Fife and the back-streets of Dundee, but we trod quick-stepping to the brawling tune, kilts swinging to answer the swagger of the Guards, and the Red Hackle in our bonnets like the monstrance of a bruised but resilient faith.'

In April, the Germans attacked again, this time in the north, and the combined Battalion met once more an enemy who swirled round their posts from all sides. When Haig announced that 'We have our backs to the wall,' his message was received with rude laughter in the 4/5th, for, on the day before, the Battalion had beaten off a German attack which came in, not towards the parapet but against the parados, or backside of its trenches, and a wall behind it would have been warmly welcomed. At Givenchy, the 1st Battalion fought a battle of hellish invention through darkened tunnels which honeycombed a hill jutting into the German lines. Two companies were trapped inside, and died or were captured by the enemy using flamethrowers and grenades in the confined space. Outside, two keeps manned by the Battalion were surrounded, bombarded, then attacked. 'The lift of the barrage was seen in the nick of time, and the platoon turned out while a stream of shells was still falling. The enemy was forty yards away, but a Lewis and Vickers machine-gun were brought out, and the attack died away under the stream of bullets.' With the help of the Camerons and the Northamptonshire Regiment, the Battalion held on to its position until – as the Regimental history put it – 'the enemy were no longer in the mood for attack.'

By the end of April, the German effort was exhausted. Three months later, on the 20th July, the 51st Division began to carry the fight back. Through hilly, wooded country near Rheims, the two Black Watch Battalions alternated in leading the attack of their brigade. Frequently the fighting resolved itself into surprise encounters and hand-to-hand fighting in forest clearings, but through a week of continuous pressure the Germans were slowly pushed back. It was hoped that a final attack might break them, and, on the 28th, the 6th Battalion was directed to capture the village of Chambrecy. For 800 yards they advanced without opposition, then at close range a barrage of shells and heavy machine-gun fire from the flanks came in on them. Gaps appeared in the ranks, but without hesitation the Battalion quickly closed the distance to the village, and not only cleared it of Germans but fought their way out the other side. There were only 140 survivors, but it was significant that, although they were far ahead of the nearest support, a French battalion on the left, there was no German counter-attack to challenge their success. Carried out under the eyes of the French, the 6th Battalion's feat was judged to merit their highest distinction, the Croix de Guerre, for, as the citation emphasized, an attack which would have been remarkable by rested troops, was carried out 'après sept jours de combats acharnés'.

On the same day, the 4/5th Battalion took part in another Franco-Scottish attack to capture the village of Buzancy. With the snap of fresh troops, a mixed force of Black Watch, Seaforths and Camerons rushed the village, and the high ground beyond, but this was to be one last, tragic instance of unsupported success turning to failure. On their right, the French could make no progress, and a fierce counter-attack in the evening forced the Jocks to pull back. A week later, Black Watch patrols found the enemy in retreat. As the tide rolled back, the French came to occupy Buzancy, and the vivid evidence of the Highlanders' courage moved them to erect a monument on the spot where they found the body of the soldier who had advanced the furthest, a man of the 4/5th Black Watch. Commemorating that latest sacrifice for the ancient alliance, the memorial was inscribed, 'Ici fleurira toujours, le glorieux chardon d'Ecosse parmi les roses de France.'

The 51st Division likewise was moving forward, and familiar names began to reappear on what was known as 'The Advance to Victory': Greenland Hill and Monchy le Preux were recaptured, and beyond them, the troops found themselves in open country for the first time since 1914. The change forced all Battalions to learn one final variation in their method of advance; lines and columns were abandoned, and in their place came unmilitary formations like blobs and snakes, which were taught to follow the contours of the countryside rather than grid lines.

On the penultimate day of September, the army attacked the Hindenberg Line, and the 1st Battalion encountered the last, well-fortified trench system of the Great War. Under an indescribably dense barrage, they entered a maze of defences protecting the western banks of the St Quentin Canal, and swept up its dazed and demoralized defenders.

It was a duty which cost them the honour of being the first across, but they followed the next day.

In this last month of the war, there was no shortage of fighting; battles followed closely on each other as the enemy was driven from one stronghold after another. There was no spectacular breakthrough, and, although the support arms of aircraft, artillery and armour reached heights of unparalleled efficiency, the strain of marching, fighting, clearing-up and marching again, told heavily on the infantry. When news of the Armistice on the 11th November reached the 1st Battalion, the men, dulled with weariness, received it with relief rather than rejoicing. They had fought what they hoped was the war to end wars, they had fought past the furthest conceivable limit of human endurance, they had fought until their enemy capitulated. That was enough.

# Peace and Palestine

There had never been anything in history to compare to the Great War. But if its suffering was – and still is – beyond imagination, there was this to be put in the balance – the scope of comradeship, which grew as intensely and pervasively as the war itself. Some 30,000 men had entered the family of The Black Watch; 7,993 had been killed, and about 20,000 wounded. For many of the latter, the days of peace were very bleak, and the Regiment, which had encompassed their lives during the war, determined that, so far as it could, it would continue to look after its own. As a memorial to those who had died, a spreading Victorian mansion, Dunalastair House was bought and endowed, where widows and the families of the wounded could take an annual holiday without care or charge. Where little else was being done for soldiers returning to the land, which Lloyd George had promised would be 'fit for heroes', the Regiment's memorial to its dead gave practical meaning to the spirit which they had sustained while they lived.

The title of the Regiment underwent its penultimate metamorphosis in 1922 and became The Black Watch (The Royal Highlanders) until, in 1937, the bracketed title reverted to that given in George II's proclamation of 1758, the 'Royal Highland Regiment'. In passing, it may be noted that the Royal Highland Regiment was specifically required by that proclamation to have a piper in each Battalion, a right not shared by the other Highland Battalions for almost a century, during which their music had to masquerade as that of fifes, the only instrument officially recognised in the army.

If it was a time for the revival of old traditions, a new one also came into being, when King George V became Colonel-in-Chief. It was a duty which he exercised with more than official care, and the Regiment obviously valued the honour of having as its immediate head the Sovereign to whom its ultimate loyalty was due. On the King's death, Queen Elizabeth (now the Queen Mother) became the Colonel-in-Chief. Five of her family, the Bowes-Lyons, have served in the Regiment, and her brother and cousin were both killed in the Great War. It is impossible to describe the affection that The Black Watch bears to its Colonel-in-Chief, but it is well-merited. Not only has she invariably been present to bid it farewell on its departure for war, in the convulsive changes of peace, her frequent visits have revived good humour and hope when they have been most needed.

In the immediate years after the war, The Black Watch gradually adjusted to prosaic peace. After twenty years abroad, the 2nd Battalion returned to an excited welcome in Perth, and promptly departed for Silesia, where a plebiscite was to determine how the province should be divided between Poland and Germany. Its pre-war station in India was taken by the 1st Battalion, and the 'incorrigibles' left in the Regimental area settled down to serious work in the Territorial Army.

Perhaps the least corrigible of them was Sir Robert Moncreiffe, who first commanded the 6th Battalion in 1893, and took it to France in 1914. A year later he was
invalided home, but now he briefly took up the reins again until 1922, when the 6th and
7th Battalions were amalgamated in common with the 4th and 5th. As always, the
Territorials withered first in the frost of military penury, but the Regulars soon felt the
cold as well. The economic slump cut army wages in 1925, and again in 1931, when a
cartoon appeared, in the *Red Hackle* magazine, of a tombstone inscribed, '10% – in loving
memory of a soldier's pay, which after a long illness fell into a decline 1/10/31 – we miss it
most who had it longest.'

However, as pay fell, recruiting increased, a paradox which was explained by the state
of industry in the Regimental area. When Churchill, as Chancellor of the Exchequer,
revalued the pound, Fife coal, most of which was exported, was priced out of the
international market, and the mine-owners reduced wages and laid off workers. The jute
industry was undercut by Indian produce, and, in Dunfermline, linen manufacture almost
came to a halt. Only the shipyards at Burntisland remained as serious competitors for the
employment of young men, and The Black Watch, in habitual fashion, contrived to take
the best. Rather to the concern of senior officers, there was also a steady flow of recruits
from England, but, by the invisible magic of the Regiment, these too became Jocks. By the
beginning of the 1930s, the Regiment had recruited almost to full strength – a state
equalled by few other regiments in the army – but, as a result, it had to find many others in
1938, to replace those who had served their time.

The 2nd Battalion came back from Silesia in 1924 with gloomy forebodings. 'Will the
Poles benefit by their accession of territory?' wrote an officer. 'Many of us doubt it, and
some even prophesy that within this generation the German flag will again fly from the
Rathaus.' It was a percipient conclusion to come to, a decade before the dream of German
expansionism was translated into votes for Hitler's National Socialists. The British
government was rather more dull in its response, but in that it merely reflected the general
mood.

Military matters were not popular, and the military budget left little money, after the
fixed charges of pay, pensions, etc., for the development of new weapons. Indeed it was not
until 1937, when the 2nd Battalion was in the Maryhill Barracks in Glasgow, that The
Black Watch witnessed the end of the equine era, so far as their transport was concerned.

The coming of the lorry brought into being the Motor Transport section, who joined
the Machine-Gun company and the Signals and Intelligence sections as specialists.
During the instruction period for specialists, companies were now frequently reduced
to skeleton groups and this problem was complicated by the tendency of more officers to
spend more time away from the Battalion on courses, so that it was rare for a company to
have the same officers for more than six months. When loyalty to individuals was thus
strained, the over-riding loyalty to the Regiment assumed new importance, yet it was at
this period that a move started, which gathered strength after the war, to dilute the
regimental system by cross-posting officers between different corps.

The courses, specialisation and training, all represented, in different fashions,
attempts to restore to the infantry its mobility in battle, which had been hobbled by the
machine-gun. There were, in general terms, two solutions. The infantry could be
motorised and protected by armoured vehicles and, secondly, the dispersed, stalking

movement of Sir John Moore's Light Infantry could be revived, so that, as Wavell vividly put it, the infantryman was 'poacher, burglar and gunman'. Except for an annual exercise, the theory of these matters, being cheaper than the practice, tended to dominate, and 'Tactical Exercises Without Troops', more commonly known as TEWTS, flourished like starlings. As it happened, however, the 2nd Battalion was no sooner motorised, than it was called upon to exercise all its latent talent for the illegal skills which Wavell enumerated.

In 1937, the antagonism between Jew and Arab in Palestine, bubbled over into widespread violence, and the 2nd Battalion was transported from Glasgow to reinforce the troops already in the country. During the first six months that it was in Palestine, the Battalion came under the authority, civil and military, of two of its former officers, General Wavell and Sir Arthur Wauchope. Having served for five years as High Commissioner, Wauchope was convinced that the two races could live together in harmony, and it was his personal misfortune to accept a second term of office, during which that conviction was overwhelmed by violence. Since the Diaspora, Palestine had been occupied by the Arabs. The first Jews to arrive there, after Balfour had declared it to be their National Home, were able to settle in peace, but with the flood of refugees from Hitler's Germany, friction rapidly grew to explode in bomb-throwing and assassination. For centuries, the Turks had been the overlords of Palestine but, by Allenby's victory at Megiddo, their suzerainty had passed to Britain and was so confirmed by mandate of the League of Nations. *Force majeure* had determined the course of the country's history, but now *force minima* was the policy, and The Black Watch was called upon to perform the duty for which it was originally raised and named, acting as armed police.

The Battalion moved up to Jerusalem in November, and, almost at once two privates, Milton and Hutchinson, were murdered. They were both sons of the Regiment, shot in the back and left lying in the gutter, where the blood gradually stained their white, blancoed spats. By dusk the trail of the murderers had been followed to a village which was cordoned off during the night. Wavell had only the Battalion at hand for the cordon and the search next morning, but the murder of their comrades had put the Jocks in dangerous temper. During the afternoon, they had tried to break out of barracks, but were halted by the presence and tongue of Regimental Sergeant-Major Finlay. Now they waited for dawn before closing in on the village, and neither their commanding officer, Colonel MacLeod, nor General Wavell knew how they would react. Wavell wrote, 'I must admit I spent an unhappy night, as I knew I had taken a certain risk. There were a great number of people, both in Palestine, and at home, who were only too ready to accuse British troops of atrocities, and I did not want my old regiment involved in what might well be a serious incident.' [*Wavell*, by John Connell].

Shots were fired at them as the police entered but, with impeccable discipline, the troops made no reply. One soldier was ordered to fire a warning shot past a villager crossing the cordon, which unfortunately winged, or to be accurate, bummed him. Iodine, cigarettes and sympathy were pressed upon him with their varying effects, and soon, between the murderers' neighbour and the friends of their victims, there was a cheerful amity, which prompted an eyewitness to remark that 'Jocks are good forgivers'.

Jerusalem was quiet thereafter, so that in the spring the Battalion was moved to Nablus, where twenty years before it had helped to round up the Turks after Megiddo. Now, reinforced by 200 men from the 1st Battalion which was returning home from India, patrols were sent out to search villages for armed men and weapons. With Zionist and Arab eyes watching, it was a considerable, if frustrating, responsibility for a young subaltern. 'The hidden wells, threshing-floors, and the sanctity [*sic*] of Arab women, made the search for arms, and the checking of the male register rather fruitless, though some men were collected.' Soon the motor patrols were being ambushed, and from that evolved the tactic of allowing one platoon to be fired on, while another went haring round the back of the boulder-strewn hills to ambush the ambushers. On the whole, it was exhilarating activity, which required junior officers and N.C.O.s to make quick decisions on their own responsibility. In the early days, however, they could still be flummoxed, as was the individual who, on a moonlight night, summed up the situation at a glance, and ordered, 'Those on the right of the moon fire to the right, those on the left fire to the left.'

Impartially they searched for Arab gunmen in Nablus, and Jewish bombers in Jerusalem, and suffered with both the rains of which the Bible had complained somewhat earlier. In the hills, December and January were cold, soggy months, when roads were washed away and tempers briefly cooled; then in spring the cycle began again. In such circumstances, the soldier can only hope to contain the antagonists until the gentle drip of politics can melt their prejudices away. Long before that could happen, The Black Watch was distracted by more pressing duties.

When the 1st Battalion arrived home in 1938, the prospect of war dominated the country. It was a rude change from the undisturbed peace of India, for the rising tide of nationalism in the continent had hardly touched the Battalion during the years it had spent there since 1919. Naturally, there were very few who had spent all that time in India. Most Jocks served the customary four-year tour, which a needy government usually extended to five (the extra being known as 'the buckshee year'), but the pattern of life scarcely altered from one military generation to the next. They generally lived in huge barrack bungalows, the size and height of warehouses, where they could expect the *punkah-wallah* to keep his fan creaking through the night, until dawn brought a barber to the bedside, and reveille brought the *char-wallah* and his urn. With daylight came a host of sundry cleaners, sweepers and latrine attendants so that the Battalion could live in a style to which it quickly became accustomed. Even these luxuries could scarcely compensate for the drawbacks of service in India: prickly heat which often became so intolerable that a man would scratch until the blood came; insects which stung; flies that covered the food in swarms if a prowling hawk did not lift it off the plate first; and dust which floated everywhere on a route march, and settled on sweating skin where it turned to itching mud. In India, The Black Watch was an instrument of law and order, but it served the purpose by its presence, rather than by action. Coming home in 1937, it spent a year in the Sudan, but in that superbly administered colony their duties were largely ceremonial, and, before they left for Britain, 200 men were transferred to the 2nd Battalion in Palestine.

In March, 1938, the evidence of Hitler's militarism at last provoked the government to reaction; apart from a belated increase in the military budget, the Territorial Army was doubled in size. The 4/5th and 6/7th Battalions were separated from their Siamese embrace, and resumed their independence, but the sorry state in which twenty years of cheese-paring had left the Regular Army was on view at the August manoeuvres, attended by the German and Italian military attachés. The 1st Battalion had twenty-two Bren guns instead of fifty; lengths of gas-piping stuck into pieces of wood were anti-tank rifles; a man holding a blue flag was a carrier; and imagination supplied mortars. To make matters worse, the Battalion only numbered about 300; apart from those transferred to the 2nd Battalion, 120 men were on training courses, and about the same number had left the Colours after coming home. There was much work to be done in the next twelve months.

# CHAPTER 19

# The Second World War

When the 1st Battalion sailed to France in September, 1939, there were inevitably echoes of that magnificent Battalion which had gone to France twenty-five years before. It was not just that it was once more part of a British Expeditionary Force sent to fight with the French against German invaders; some of the very names in the Battalion recalled that earlier force. The sons of Colonel Grant-Duff and Captain Rowan-Hamilton both travelled with the 1st Battalion in 1939, and many of the Jocks were following in their fathers' footsteps. They were only echoes however, and in two important respects the Battalion differed considerably from its predecessor.

The more obvious difference was in dress. On the eve of their departure, a bitter blow fell when orders were issued to exchange the kilt for trousers. In the course of two centuries, the kilt had proved to be healthier garb than trousers in all but extreme heat, and its effect on the wearer's morale was incalculable but, on the pretext that the Regiment might be identified, it was now discarded. Company Sergeant-Major MacGregor expressed the general response to that, when he exclaimed, 'But damn it, we *want* to be identified.' However, there could be no argument, and the loss was sadly accepted.

The other difference was less apparent. For the previous twelve months, while the barometer veered wildly between flap and calm, the 1st, like the Territorial Battalions, had trained hard, especially the Reserves who were required to master the intricacies of the Bren gun, introduced only in 1938. The 1st Battalion was certainly ready for war, but its state was not to be compared to the high polish of its forebears. The nine months' duration of the phoney war was therefore employed to the full in making good their deficiencies.

After a short spell in the Saar portion of the Maginot line, the Battalion spent the next six months near Lens, opposite the largely undefended Belgian frontier. Then, in January, 1940, the 51st Highland Division, which included the 4th and 6th Battalions, arrived in France under the command of General Victor Fortune. It was an entirely Territorial division, and, in a minute to the War Office, Churchill expressed the fear that their part-time training had not sufficiently prepared them to face an experienced, well-drilled enemy. So in February each brigade was ordered to take in a Regular battalion at the expense of a Territorial, with the result that the 1st Battalion replaced the 6th.

In his history of the Highland Division, Eric Linklater wrote: 'To the Highland Territorials who composed the 51st Division in the earlier German war, a strange thing happened; regimental loyalty was to a large extent replaced by their pride in the division.' They returned now with fair confidence of adding to the division's fame, and their commander was the reboubtable Fortune who had fought for three uninterrupted years on the Western Front. It was a good pedigree, and the introduction of Regular troops was an unnecessary spur to their pride.

Through the spring of 1940, all three Battalions trained, patrolled, and dug trenches, which at that stage were still on the 1914 model of three feet across and six feet down. The Highland Division found more elaborate defences when they moved to that part of the Maginot Line in the Saar with which the 1st Battalion was already familiar. There is no fortification which cannot be improved, and the Division duly brought the defences up to their specification. But it was not to be another static war. In May, the Germans entered the Low Countries, and by-passed the Maginot Line, though their southernmost wing rustled against the 4th Battalion, losing several feathers in the process.

Further north, the 6th Battalion, now part of the 4th Division, experienced a trying month, with which The Black Watch of 1914 would have sympathized. First came the swift advance into Belgian territory, as far as Louvain on this occasion, followed by the discovery that they were in danger of envelopment by vastly superior forces, and then the not quite so swift retreat. But there was no Marne in 1940; instead of the swing south, the Germans made straight for the Channel ports. On the 24th May, when the 6th Battalion was some twenty miles from Fontenoy, they heard over the BBC that Boulogne was occupied, news which meant that their route to the coast would take them through the rear, or part of the rear, of the German army.

The Lys canal barred their movement north, and along its far bank German troops could be seen advancing. For a whole day, the 26th May, the 6th Battalion raced the Germans westward for possession of the first bridge; at nightfall, the leading Black Watch company reached it 1,500 yards ahead of the enemy, and still found enough breath to keep the Germans at a distance. Through the night and a heavy counter-attack the next day, the Battalion guarded the crossing while the 5th Division passed through to Dunkirk, and by evening it was occupying an honourable, though unsought, role as rearguard. When they drew off under cover of night, they passed through crowded roads and confused rumours to arrive on the coast at Nieuport, a long way east of Dunkirk. There the crumbling perimeter soon left them as rearguard again. On the last day of May, they were ordered to prepare for embarkation, and since that was impossible from the beaches at Nieuport, there was no choice but to cover the twenty miles which lay between them and the smoke pall over Dunkirk. Close to the port, they were ordered to split up, and little parties of Jocks made their separate ways to the ships, four regimental police paddling themselves out with the butts of their rifles, and a young second-lieutenant marching his platoon briskly in step along the quay to the ship he had chosen, with every man singing

> You may talk o' the First Royals, the Scots Fusiliers,
>     The Aiberdeen Milishy and the Dundee Volunteers,
> But of a' the famous regiments that's lyin' far awa' –
>     Gae bring tae me the tartan o' the gallant Forty-Twa.

### 1ST AND 4TH BATTALIONS

The successful evacuation of Dunkirk was aided by the Germans' concentration of effort on their main front, which by the 1st June had left the port far behind, and lay along the Somme River – from its mouth to Amiens, and thence to the old battlefields on the Aisne –

but still the thrust was to the north of Paris rather than at the city. Near the mouth of the Somme, the Germans had established a small bridgehead across the river at Abbeville. The French had made two attempts to break their hold, and on their second attack a company of the 1st Battalion went with them. This too failed to break the Germans' position and a few days later, with attack threatening further south in the line, the French Armoured Division was withdrawn from Abbeville. In that short space of time, however, an important link was forged, to which General de Gaulle, commander of the Armoured Division, bore witness: 'I can tell you that the comradeship in arms experienced on the battlefield of Abbeville, between the French Armoured Division, which I had the honour to command, and the valiant 51st Highland Division under General Fortune, played its part in the decision which I took to continue fighting on the side of the Allies.'

When de Gaulle's division was withdrawn, the Highland Division, with the French 31st Division on its right, remained holding a front of about twenty-five miles, with no armour other than the light tanks of the Lothian and Border Horse. On the 5th June, four days after the evacuation of the 6th Battalion from Dunkirk, the Germans attacked along their entire line. The fighting during the next week took place in a green countryside closely resembling the south of England in fine sunny weather, and the Highland Division fought throughout in a rectangle whose width, from the coast inland, was rarely less than fifteen miles, and whose length, from Abbeville to St Valéry, was about sixty miles.

On that first day, the 1st Battalion held a line in the hills above Abbeville, which measured some two-and-a-half miles, but the 7th Argylls, further to their left, were even more widely dispersed, and it was against them that the Germans moved, pouring through the gaps. Behind the Argylls, the 4th Black Watch was still digging in when the first German troops appeared. A forward platoon was surrounded, but held off the enemy until support arrived to extricate them; at the same time, showing that their defence could be thoroughly offensive, a company surprised and broke up a German movement passing their extreme left.

The 4th Battalion was prepared to hold their position longer, but it was ordered to fall back on the river Bresle, and, like the 6th Battalion a few weeks before, it had a race for the nearest bridge across. On the far side, it took up its new position, but the river was shallow and the front wide, and the enemy streamed through the spaces. On the night of the 8th June, the Battalion was ordered back to the village of Arques, near Dieppe. Here it was made part of a scratch force, named Ark Force, detailed to prepare Le Havre for the evacuation of the Highland Division but, when they reached that port, news came that the Division was surrounded, and that it would be taken off at St Valéry. Ark Force itself was lifted from Le Havre, leaving its vehicles burning in the streets, and was taken first to Cherbourg, and then to England.

The 1st Battalion retained its position overlooking the Somme until the night of the 5th June, when the Highland Division began to fall back on the river Bresle. In those words 'fall back' are contained the swirling, disruptive confusion of last minute orders – and later counter-orders, out-of-date information, missing transport, and unmapped roads, often choked with French troops. To the south of the Division, the Germans had broken through the French line, so that on the 8th June, when the Highland Division was six miles from Dieppe, the enemy were already in Rouen, well to their rear. General

Fortune asked for permission to evacuate his troops from Dieppe, but his request was refused; while France still stood, the last of Britain's troops would support her.

On the 9th June, for the fifth night in succession, the 1st Battalion was moved back from a position which it had prepared for defence throughout the previous day. On the river Varenne they paused, fighting a mortar battle with the enemy who was crossing an inadequately blown bridge. As evening drew in, they were ordered to hold their place, though the battalion on their left was over-run. At night, they were withdrawn to the village of St Pierre-le-Viger, six miles from St Valéry. The next day, the 11th June, from an insecure position on the forward slope of a hill, they watched stragglers from the French army streaming past, and at their heels German infantry, and later tanks. These were part of General Rommel's force, and against their weight of armour and gunpower, the tanks of the Lothians and Border Horse had a grim time. 'Ca' they things tanks?' asked a Jock disparagingly. 'They're knocking them oot three a penny up the road.'

There was little fighting until the evening of the 11th. During this lull two companies and the wounded were sent back into St Valéry to prepare for embarkation, while the remainder were told that they would be taken off that night or the next. Some dismounted French cavalry arrived as the Germans attacked with tanks, and side by side the French and Scots fought this last battle of the old 1st Battalion. When night came, the survivors of the two companies under Lieutenant Bradford withdrew to a hill on the east of the St Valéry perimeter, but the fog which had shrouded the harbour on the previous night came down again so that the Navy could not send in the ships waiting to take the Division off. At dawn, the German guns commanded St Valéry, its harbour, and its perimeter, and Rommel's tanks had broken in on the west.

At 8 a.m. on the 12th June, the French divisional commander capitulated, followed by General Fortune. Major Rennie of the Regiment brought the news to Bradford's companies as they were preparing to fight off a morning tank attack. For a week the men had been without proper rest, yet now, surrounded by Rommel's troops, with no hope of escape, they heard with incredulity Rennie's order to surrender. Some mortars were fired off, and indeed part of the Battalion was still fighting three hours later, but General Fortune's decision was not only right, it showed great moral courage, for though the Jocks remained ready to fight, their deaths would have gained nothing. Some men escaped by the cliffs, and a few, including Rennie and Bradford, from the roads on the way to Germany, but, for most of the Highland Division, St Valéry spelled captivity.

It is conventional wisdom that the soldiers of the eighteenth and early nineteenth century were tougher, more robust than their successors, yet, under the hardest test, prolonged retreat, it is only necessary to look at Corunna and Burgos to see into what disruption these soldiers fell. In 1940, the 1st Battalion was inadequately prepared, without sufficient tank support, and deprived of rest, but it remained throughout a force which was responsive to command and capable of fighting to the very end. Their predecessors might have been surprised by their endurance and discipline, but they would not have been ashamed.

2ND BATTALION

The old phrase, 'every British campaign begins with a retreat', also held true for the 2nd Battalion. Palestine remained their territory, and Palestinian terrorists were their enemy until May, 1940, but by then Italy had entered the war, offering a change of scene and opposition. The Battalion was uplifted by way of Suez and the barren rocks of Aden to Somaliland. A joint French and British defence of their Somali colonies had been planned against an expected Italian invasion from Abyssinia. The capitals lay in a coastal plain separated from the hinterland by a crescent of bare, rocky hill, and it was estimated that the enemy could be held in the passes while the French blocked their progress along the coast. This plan collapsed when Vichy France withdrew its troops, leaving the British flank open.

On the 12th August when the Italians began to advance along the coast from French Somaliland, the 2nd Battalion was digging in at a pass in the Barkasan hills forty miles from the sea, while Major Rusk of the Regiment, commanding the King's African Rifles, was already engaged with the enemy at a pass further inland. The weakness of the British position made a swift evacuation inevitable, and the 2nd Battalion was required to hold Barkasan until the ships were ready to take them off.

Their position was almost two miles wide, forcing the Battalion to disperse embarrassingly; two companies were sited on the low hills on either side of the road, with the single Bofors gun directly behind the road-block, while the other two companies lay further back, in reserve, and ready to prevent outflanking movements. After Rusk and the King's African Rifles had passed through, the Italians appeared on the morning of the 17th. There was a certain tentativeness to their first attacks, directed at Captain Rose's company on the right of the roadblock but, as reinforcements built up, they grew bolder. At length one assault burst into company headquarters. With bayonet and Bren they were driven out, but large numbers remained just below the position. There was no ammunition for the mortars, so, in a scene which the anonymous private at Corunna would have appreciated, Rose led his Jocks in a roaring bayonet charge down the hill. Whether 'ilka man gat his birdie' is a matter of doubt, for the astonished Italians scattered before them, leaving the vicinity of Rose's company markedly unoccupied for some time thereafter. But both flanks were now being worked round, though the road block itself remained undisturbed by Italian armour owing to an extremely accurate Bofors. Behind them, the evacuation was almost complete, and in the evening, the Battalion was ordered to start back for the coast. Like the evacuation itself, the battle had been skilfully conducted, and when Churchill queried the necessity of evacuation in the light of such small casualties, Wavell was amply justified in replying, 'A large butcher's bill is not necessarily evidence of good tactics.'

From the flinty hills of Somaliland, the 2nd Battalion moved to Cairo, where lights were as low as spirits were high. The Jocks had come through their first battle well, and their confidence was just right to appreciate the heady splendours of Crete when the Battalion was ordered there in November, 1940. They found the island to consist largely of a 150-mile mountain range crowned by the perpetual snows of Mount Ida, but the hills were serrated by fertile valleys growing vegetables, fruit and grapes. The Cretans they discovered to be amiable and incurably gallant, and during the six months that they were there the Jocks acquired such Greek as was necessary for social life, thus, just as 'kallimera' meant 'Good morning' and 'krassi' meant 'wine', so 'krassied up' meant one too many. It was a pleasant interlude.

Three weeks after the Battalion landed in Crete, Wavell's troops under the command of General O'Connor won an outstanding victory at Sidi Barrani, but, even as they drove westward, the demands of Wavell's other campaigns magnified; the Sudan, East Africa and, from March, 1941, above all Greece. In that month, The Black Watch moved from Suda Bay to Heraklion in the centre of the north coast of Crete, where they were brigaded with the 2nd York and Lancaster, under Major Alastair Gilroy of the Regiment, and the 2nd Leicestershire. The Battalion was concentrated on an airfield, built to support the campaign in Greece, and on a low range of hills running east from it roughly at right-angles to the runway. There, under the command of Colonel Hamilton, they dug themselves in.

As the situation in Greece deteriorated, air-raids on Heraklion intensified. In their slit-trenches, the Battalion suffered few casualties, and Hamilton had succeeded in camouflaging his defences so well that no German maps pin-pointed them. There was, however, a sad dearth of material. Wavell's supplies came via the Cape, and not until Greece had fallen did Crete have prior claim on his slender resources. Through the first weeks of May the expectations of attack mounted but, when it came, on the evening of the 20th, its size was far beyond the wildest estimates. Wave after wave of transport planes, guarded by fighters, droned in from the north, and over Heraklion spawned a cloud of floating parachutes. 'Every soldier picked his swaying target, fired, and picked another. Many Germans landed dead, many were riddled as they hung in trees and telephone wires, some tangled with each other and fell like stones, and many fired their tommy-guns as they floated down.'

For two hours the parachute drops continued. Those who reached ground safely, gathered their equipment cylinders, and holed up in buildings beyond the foot of the runway or in fields below the hills, and individual platoons were sent after these parties. The last flight, it was observed, dropped its contingent well away from Heraklion, on to a table-topped mountain beyond a valley to the east. The next evening more paratroops were dropped, and a routine emerged, which Captain Barry described. 'During the day the valley would ring to the volleys of rifle and machine-gun fire sent hurtling across it by both sides, but after darkness shooting ceased; by tacit understanding no firing took place after dark, it would have inconvenienced both sides equally. For this was when the casualties were evacuated, the dead were buried, the rations and ammunition distributed, and the men were able to walk about and stretch their legs.' As the days passed, grim determination replaced the high spirits, for there was no prospect of relief. Captain Hamilton told his men, 'The Black Watch leaves Crete when the snow leaves Mount Ida,' and for him, as for the others killed on the island, it was true. But though the build-up of German forces beyond the valley continued, there was no thought of failure. Not a yard of ground had been lost, and the ferocious battle had cost the Germans enormous losses in men, planes and equipment. The Major of a German parachute battalion, captured a year later, described the situation from his side. 'I had never experienced such bitter fighting. Had it been any other regiment but The Black Watch – any other – all would have been well. I had 80 men left out of 800, little ammunition, no food – the Jocks were eating our food.'

On the west of the island, however, the Germans had succeeded in capturing the airfield at Maleme to which they could fly in troops, and under intense bombing the defence began to crumble. German supremacy in the air made it impossible to supply the defenders, and on receiving General Freyberg's message that the garrison was *in extremis*, Wavell ordered it to be taken off.

On the morning of the 28th, the 2nd Battalion was ordered to be ready to leave. In the course of the day, the heaviest parachute-drop of all came down, and the Battalion headquarters were heavily mortared. When night fell, the Jocks crept away from their trenches down to the harbour. The wounded and some soldiers who had been cut off were left behind, but the rest boarded the four destroyers and two cruisers in the harbour, the largest party of 240 on H.M.S. *Dido*. As everyone had anticipated, German bombers came with the dawn. H.M.S. *Orion*, one of the cruisers, was struck by three bombs, killing over a hundred of those on board. The other cruiser, H.M.S. *Dido*, received two hits, the second of which exploded in the lower decks where most of the troops were jammed. Many were killed instantly, and few of the injured survived, for fire broke out and the area had to be flooded. Of the Regiment, 103 died, and those bodies which could be disentangled from the wreckage were buried at sea. As the cruiser limped into Alexandria at dusk, a piper in a tattered kilt climbed up beside the bridge, and began to play the Battalion in. The Navy picked him out with a searchlight, and held it on him, while the ship steamed up the harbour, bringing back the defenders of Heraklion to the only music which fitted their pride and its price.

Even as the Crete battle was being fought, Axis activity in Syria and Iraq forced Wavell to send troops to that area, and simultaneously the planning for an offensive in the Libyan desert had reached an advanced state. Troops in the Middle East were perforce kept fully occupied.

In August The Black Watch was ordered to Syria, where, in the bewildering world of the Middle East, their enemies were now the Vichy French, and their particular task was an assault on a depressingly formidable position close to Damascus. Fortunately, the political wind shifted just before their attack, and an armistice was concluded between the Vichy forces and the Allies. In place of battle, the Jocks found that they had been granted a brief period of holiday, and during it Colonel Rusk returned from the campaign in Abyssinia to take command, and Pipe-Major Roy, wounded and captured in Crete, walked in by way of Greece and Turkey. Their arrival deserves to be noted for each was about to be matched to the hour.

In October, 1941, the 2nd Battalion sailed to Tobruk, as part of the force relieving the Australian garrison. All that Nature had contributed to Tobruk was the harbour, the rest was artificial; it was a flat segment of desert surrounded by a twenty-five mile perimeter of wire, mines, trenches, and deep, galleried pill-boxes, four-fifths underground. The Battalion found that garrison life was composed of equal parts of boredom and discomfort. Water was scarce, and bully beef, sardines and biscuits soon palled. There was still some warmth in the sun, but, when it set, the cold was bitter. For the patrols who went out every night through the wire, the only diversions were the searing patterns of tracer and anti-aircraft fire in the sky above them.

Early in the year, Rommel had swept past Tobruk to the frontier of Egypt. A

PLATE 21    *Pipe-Major Roy and mascot in North Africa, May, 1943.* ▷

premature counter-attack, code-named 'Battleaxe', had failed in the summer but now, in November, another attempt was to be made to drive the Germans back, and it would be aided by a sortie from Tobruk. In Major Barry's words, 'Our role will be to give them [the Germans] a kick up the backside as they pass.'

The road which their targets might be expected to travel ran along a plateau that rose steeply from the desert floor, some seven miles from the perimeter. Between this escarpment and the Battalion's position, the flat featureless ground was scattered with German strongpoints, wires, sand-bagged, and defended with machine-guns. Six had been picked out, whose capture would present a threat to the disorganised enemy retreating along the road. The Battalion's objective, codenamed 'Tiger', lay about 4,500 yards away, with 'Jill' as an immediate point, and the strongposts on either side of 'Jill' allotted to three other battalions. A battalion of tanks was to support the assault; one squadron was to make straight for 'Jill' with a company of The Black Watch on its tracks, while another squadron circled to the rear of 'Tiger' to coincide with the assault on it by the remaining companies. That, at any rate, was the plan.

On the 18th November, the Eighth Army began its attack, and two days later the Battalion moved out from its trenches, and lay up through the night behind the minefields. At 6.30 a.m., an eight-minute bombardment began but, though the Battalion was in position, the tanks were late and, when they arrived, they crossed in the wrong place and became mired in a minefield. The leading company could not afford to wait for them, and set off across the open at a fast pace. They had covered several hundred yards, when the German machine-guns opened up with a monstrous explosion of fire. Immediately men began to fall, but with a series of rushes the company kept going forward, though with each rush its numbers were reduced. It felt like pressing against a wall of lead, and it seemed impossible that anyone could live through it. But the momentum was never lost, and at last the survivors went into the strongpoint with the bayonet. 'We drove the Jerries afore us,' said a sergeant, 'like Christ clearing the money-changers from the Temple.'

The first support company came up and passed through 'Jill', going on for 'Tiger', where a German machine-gun battalion was positioned with mortars and light artillery. Everything was fired at the figures approaching across the sand. Behind the first company came the others including Company Sergeant-Major McKinlay with the ten survivors of the capture of 'Jill', and with them came Pipe-Major Roy and Pipe-Sergeant McNicoll. The pipes had been silenced in garrison, but now they played the Battalion on, with 'Highland Laddie' the Regimental March, 'Lawson's Men', commemorating the Mutiny stand against overwhelming odds, and 'The Black Bear', that tune, punctuated by shouts, which is played when the men are weary. An officer, lying wounded on the ground, later wrote, 'I heard "Highland Laddie" as I lay, and it was the tune that got me on my feet, and advancing again.' The signal for the stretcher-bearers was a rifle stuck in the ground by its bayonet, and reaching back to 'Jill' and beyond was a forest of rifle-butts.

Eventually, the Battalion, or what was left of it, came to a halt. At Loos and in Mesopotamia, the Battalion had fought such battles and, now as the Battalion lay out in the open, Colonel Rusk, with his experience of that 1914–18 war, turned the balance. He had seen the absolute necessity of the tanks and, though two vehicles had been blown from beneath him, he commandeered a third to search out, and bring back the tanks. 'Standing up in one of them like a policeman, he returned to the companies, and ordered the survivors on.' The men rose from the ground, and resumed the attack beside the tanks. Without further pause, they stormed into 'Tiger' and occupied it. Of the Battalion, 632 strong when it had started, 168 were left to man the position.

The summing-up of what they had achieved is best left to an eye-witness, a Major of the Royal Horse Artillery, who observed the battle and wrote, 'I class this attack of The Black Watch as one of the most outstanding examples of gallantry combined with high class training I have seen. Not one of us who was there will ever forget such supreme gallantry.' Such was the fierceness of the battle that the other objectives had been abandoned and, for a few days, the Battalion's gains remained precarious until the salient was widened out. The Eighth Army's offensive had been less successful than planned, and instead of relieving Tobruk, its troops came pouring into the perimeter, accompanied by their commander, General Godwen-Austen, who wittily signalled, 'Tobruk is not half as relieved as I am'. But at last the British advance flowed west past Tobruk, and in January, 1942, the Battalion returned to Egypt. It was a sombre journey, for many friends were left in the sands of Tobruk.

# CHAPTER 20

# War Round the Mediterranean

Of the disaster at St Valéry, Eric Linklater wrote, 'To Scotland the news came like another Flodden. Scotland is a small country, and in its northern half there was scarcely a household that had not at least a cousin in one of the Highland Regiments.' But the response was in due proportion to the disaster. A new 51st Division began to form round a nucleus provided by the 9th Scottish Division. The Regiment immediately started to re-form its 1st Battalion, and the two Territorial Battalions, the 5th and 7th, came forward to fill the places left empty by their sister Battalions; after its evacuation from Normandy, the 4th Battalion had been posted to Gibraltar, while the 6th remained as before in the 4th Division.

The Highland Division, which thus contained three Black Watch Battalions, started its new life under Major-General Ritchie of the Regiment. Soon he was called to join Wavell's staff in the Middle East, and it was under the command of Major-General Douglas Wimberley that the Division hit its stride. In June, 1942, it sailed for North Africa, and arrived there two months later, more or less simultaneously with Generals Alexander and Montgomery, and, as it then seemed, just ahead of Rommel. The offensive, which had released the 2nd Battalion from Tobruk, had come to a halt in early spring and, throughout the summer of 1942, the Germans gradually regained the ground they had lost, and more.

Depressing as Qassassin Camp appeared to the Highland Division, it should have been seen as a good omen, for it was from there that the Highland Brigade had started for Tel-el-Kebir exactly sixty years before. This invigorating thought was probably lost in the welter of training for desert conditions to which the Jocks were immediately committed. On the 30th September, when the German advance was finally stopped at the position Auchinleck had chosen at Alam Halfa, the Division was preparing what would have been the last defensive line in Egypt beside the Canal. Thereafter Rommel's star, which had grown in brightness since St Valéry, began to dim.

For the coming battle, the Highland Division was instructed in the technique of desert patrolling by the 9th Australian Division, that same which the 2nd Battalion had relieved in Tobruk, and in the desert behind the Alamein lines they practised the attack they were soon to make. In one of those training assaults using live shells, five Jocks and the second-in-command of the 1st Battalion were killed, when a round tragically fell short. On the 22nd October, the Division moved up to its position in the El Alamein line, between the Australians on their right, and the New Zealanders on their left.

In front of them lay a five-mile depth of minefields and wire, defended by machine-guns, mortars, and above all by the Afrika Korps' armour and anti-tank guns. Since there was no flank to be turned, the plan of attack required the infantry to make a frontal attack through the minefields and wire, and open up the way for the British tanks behind. It was only with this initial phase – in Montgomery's words, with the break-in and start of the dog-fight – that the Regiment was concerned.

On the extreme right of the Highland Division, the 5th Battalion stood shoulder to shoulder with the Australians, as the 7th Battalion did with the New Zealanders on the left. There was a bright moon, one night before the full, when the bombardment began at 9.40 p.m., on the 23rd October. At 10.0 p.m. the 1st and 5th Battalions went forward with the leading wave, moving close behind the barrage. When a company of the 5th Battalion encountered wire early on, the company barber moved up with wire-cutters. 'Get a bloody move on, Jock,' shouted a voice impatiently. 'You're no cutting hair now.' Once through the wire, however, the casualties from Spandaus began to mount. Piper McIntyre, only nineteen-years old, was hit three times as he played; dying on the ground, he continued to play, and when he was found the next morning, the bag was still in his oxter, and his fingers on the chanter. All along the Highland Division's line of advance, that emotional, traditional music could be heard through the thunder of the artillery. The first two companies of the 5th Battalion reached their objective on time, and the next pair passed through to reach their target by 1.30 a.m. Hours of training had emphasized the importance of staying close to the barrage, and keeping well dispersed, and the lesson had been learned well. In the 1st Battalion, the pattern of attack was very similar, but the second wave of companies found the defence growing stiffer with every yard. On their very objective was a machine-gun post, but they raised their speed to a charge which knocked out this final obstacle. As each battalion arrived on its objective, another passed on forward, and the 7th Battalion was in this leap-frogging wave.

Opposite the New Zealanders and Highlanders, the Mitereiya Ridge provided a conspicuous target. At its northern end protruded a feature named 'The Ben', and this was the 7th Battalion's objective. By now the artillery barrage was considerably dispersed, and the defenders well prepared. Even before they reached the ridge, all companies suffered heavy casualties, but at the foot of the hill Captain Cathcart collected a small group, which he led up towards 'The Ben'. The moon had long since been obscured by smoke and dust, and it was through the dark, occasionally lit by flashes of fire, that Cathcart's party fought their way up the rocky ledges to drive the enemy off the ridge. As dawn began to show, thirty survivors occupied their objective. Brigadier Kippenberger from the New Zealander Brigade on their left wrote

> I went across to see if there was a proper tie-up in the inter-Brigade boundary. Our neighbours on the right were a very depleted Black Watch company in good touch with us. Their casualties were very heavy, but they had all their objectives. I returned by the right-hand route, seeing an extraordinary number of dead Highlanders. In front of one post there was a whole section, a corporal and seven men, all on their faces. [*Infantry Brigadier*, by Brigadier Kippenberger].

The Battalion's position was perilous, situated on the western slope, exposed to the enemy beyond, and only they and the New Zealanders were on their final target, so that part of the ridge was still held by the Germans. Behind them, the armour, following the narrow paths cleared through the minefields, began to jam up, and in the daylight it looked, in one officer's opinion, like 'the Purple Car Park at the Aldershot Tatoo'. Without room to manoeuvre, they were extremely vulnerable to anti-tank fire, and their casualties were high.

For over a week, The Black Watch dug in, patrolled, and suffered the mortaring and shell-fire which was the common lot of the infantry. On the 25th, the 5th Battalion occupied a forward position, 'Stirling' on Mitereiya Ridge, and their experiences typified the conditions of the dogfight. By day they were shelled and shot at from a further fold of the ridge, little more than 400 yards away, and by night they patrolled, and tried to stalk down the artillery which tormented them during the hours of light. Such was the confusion of the battle, that several German vehicles, including an armoured car, drove into the 5th Battalion's post, and were captured. On the 31st the 7th Battalion was withdrawn from its exposed and honourable position, and three days later the others followed suit.

By then Montgomery had recast his battle in a new mould. The Australians had driven the mighty 90th Light Division north, and against the gap which had been left, Montgomery concentrated his considerable superiority in tanks, guns, and men for a second assault, 'Supercharge'. On the night of the 3rd November, the 4th Indian Division and the New Zealanders, with two brigades of the Highland Division made a clean break through the minefields, and in their wake came the armour, able at last to operate in open country.

The casualties at El Alamein consisted largely of riflemen who, by the nature of the attack, had been required to open up the path for the mortar, carrier, and anti-tank platoons. Together with the specialist sections – intelligence, medical, signals – these support units accounted for almost half the battalion by this stage of the war. In the First World War, a full strength company would contain 200 riflemen, but now the number was less than 100, and losses among them, especially of the magnitude suffered by the 7th Battalion, had a disruptive effect on a battalion's attacking strength. Thus, in the weeks following the battle, companies had to be restructured, while the pursuit of Rommel was maintained.

It was a chase which exhilarated the spirits, and mottled the backsides of those thrown about in the back of the trucks. Sometimes the Division would be squeezed Indian-file on to a track through a ravine or a salt marsh; at others, a billowing mile-wide dust cloud marked their advance. The day started in the chilly dark, but soon after the heatless sun had appeared, they halted to brew up breakfast over a myriad of petrol fires, then faster and hotter the pursuit continued, with only one more halt before they dug in at nightfall. Three of the divisions that had made the breakout at El Alamein, the Highland, New Zealand and 7th Armoured, led the chase.

Benghazi and Tobruk were passed, then on the 8th December the first contact came at Mersa Brega, a village astride the coastal road. There too they met anti-personnel mines, which looked like twigs on the sand, but which, if set off, twanged high in the air firing a shower of metal in all directions. The wild pace of the previous days slowed abruptly to a tense crawl, which could not prevent casualties as the Division patiently pressed in on the Mersa Brega position. On a night of agonising frustration, the 1st and 7th Battalions attempted to circle round the village, and cut the road beyond. The 7th had a relatively trouble-free night march, but found that the road had been heavily mined, suggesting, as was later confirmed, that the Germans had already left. The 1st ran straight into a minefield, and its progress in the dark was punctuated by explosions and casualties. They were still short of the 7th Battalion when dawn came, and their patrols brought back news only of their own grievous losses to mines, and an absence of enemy troops.

The buried mines laid a huge stress on everyone, but for the stretcher-bearers they provided one of the worst ordeals of the war. An explosion was usually the signal for them to begin picking their way through the hidden menace to the injured man. As was traditional, they were nearly all bandsmen; Sergeant Orr, a first class musician with the 1st Battalion, and an incurable creator of dance-bands, recorded a melancholy list of trumpeters, trombone players, and drummers who became casualties in the Battalion's journey acrosss North Africa.

In the rolling wave of the Divisional advance, all three Black Watch Battalions spent the triple festival of Christmas, Hogmanay and Red Hackle Day nearer the wake than the crest. It was now that Colonel Rennie of the 5th Battalion took another step towards the moment of personal and Divisional revenge, and was promoted to the command of the 154th Brigade, containing the 1st and 7th Battalions. They started moving again on the 5th January, along the booby-trapped trail of the German retreat. Its conduct by Rommel was extremely skilful, and time and again his troops slipped out of the bag.

The pace of the advance had slackened considerably, when suddenly storm damage to Benghazi harbour threatened to halt it altogether by choking their supply line. From the 17th January the race to Tripoli really was a race – against time. When the 1st and 7th Battalions bumped against a rear-guard post, and sent out a patrol to discover its strength, they were peremptorily ordered to attack at once. The patrol, commanded by Lieutenant Fortune, the General's son, was returning with information of formidable defences, when it saw a strong raiding party heading straight for disaster. Fortune bolted across the open, and had just warned the tanks of their danger, when he was shot down. The infantry walked into the fire, but with good luck found shelter under the walls of an old fort.

The fort surmounted a hill commanding the road, and the whole position, justifiably named Edinburgh Castle, was held by the German 90th Light Division. A more considered assault was launched at night, when the 1st Battalion moved in against the Castle, while the 7th circled round to cut the road behind. With the 7th started tanks, artillery, Argylls, and Seaforths, but the natural hazards of a dark night, exceptionally rugged terrain and deceptive landmarks reduced the size of the force to The Black Watch, Seaforths and some tanks. When dawn came the leading company was scrambling into position near the road, with the rest of the Battalion further away. A convoy of vehicles came racing down the road from the direction of Edinburgh Castle, and the Battalion opened fire. Almost immediately, they realised that the vehicles were British, and the firing ceased. But the original impulse proved to be correct, and the Germans, quickly recovering from their surprise, turned every weapon they had on the Battalion. The company nearest the road succeeded in capturing some of the enemy, but were at once the object of an overwhelming counter-attack. When it seemed as if the entire Battalion might be in danger, machine-gun fire from their left announced reinforcements, and the Germans abruptly made off down their escape route.

The 1st Battalion's task which had seemed so formidable proved, in the event, to be simple for, as they went into Edinburgh Castle, the defenders went out the other side. It was only the beginning of three hectic days. While the 7th Battalion drowsed by the side of the road, the 1st had been chivvied out of the Castle, and were hanging somnambulently on to the back of anything that was driving in the direction of Tripoli. Early the next morning, a crater in the road forced them off their vehicles, and on to their feet. They stumbled round the detour, and were dropping off by the verge of the road, when Wimberley appeared among them, pointing Tripoli-wards, and ordering, 'Lorry-hop, lorry-hop!' They lorry-hopped as far as they could, before the threat of German attack slowed up the rush. The 1st Battalion was pushed forward to make the rough places smooth by searching for Germans and filling up craters, and as the armour entered Tripoli, it passed a little group of sleeping Jocks at each levelled hole.

Of their month in Tripoli, the Regiment had two outstanding memories: work in the docks unloading the gigantic quantity of supplies required for an army on the move – in Churchill's phrase 'they are unloading history', though the Jocks may have chosen a less grandiose description – and secondly, the great parade on the 4th February, when to the massed pipe bands of the Highland Division the Eighth Army marched triumphantly past the Prime Minister. The Regiment provided a composite Battalion from the three in North Africa, and succeeded in impressing even the New Zealander, Brigadier Kippenberger. 'As they turned into the square, they caught the skirl of the pipes, every man braced himself up, put on a swagger, and they went past superbly. I had climbed on to a tank to watch, and for almost an hour was intoxicated by the spectacle.'

The route ahead swung northward round the Gulf of Gabes. At the Gulf's most southerly point, the Matmata Hills approached the sea, squeezing the coastal plain to a width of twelve miles. The gap itself was blocked by the deep Wadi Zigzaou, which had been further fortified with an anti-tank ditch, wire and the ever-present mines. In mid-February, the Highland Division moved towards this formidable obstacle, named the Mareth Line.

The Germans did not remain on the defensive, but made a strong attack on the 5th March, of which a part managed to over-run a ridge looking down on the 1st Battalion. In the evening Major McKinney took his company up the ridge, marching at its head with a big stick in his hand. They quickly cleared the enemy out, and McKinney duly reported his success over the radio, accompanied by a mournful plaint, 'But I've only caught one Panzer Grenadier, and he's so wee I doubt he's not worth keeping.'

In the breaking of the Mareth Line, the main burden fell on the 50th Division, making a frontal attack with enormous courage on the Wadi itself, while the 4th Indian Division crossed the Matmata Hills to make a flank attack from the south. Although the 51st Division was moved up to support the 50th against the most bitter opposition encountered since Alamein, Montgomery swung his main force into the flank attack which turned the enemy from his position.

The 51st, remaining on the coastal road, was now on the inside track as the coastline turned northward. There was only one major obstacle left between them and Tunis, and again it was caused by that combination of ridge and wadi. Almost parallel to the road and about three miles to its left, rose the Roumana Ridge. From its slopes the Wadi Akarit scored its way to the sea, cutting across the road at right-angles. An infantry attack on this position was required, while the armour broke through on the landward side of the ridge.

PLATE XVI (above)    *A Battalion disembarking in France in the First World War.*

PLATE XVII (below)    *'The Return from Heraklion' by Noel Syres. H.M.S.* Dido *entering Alexandria. 1941.*

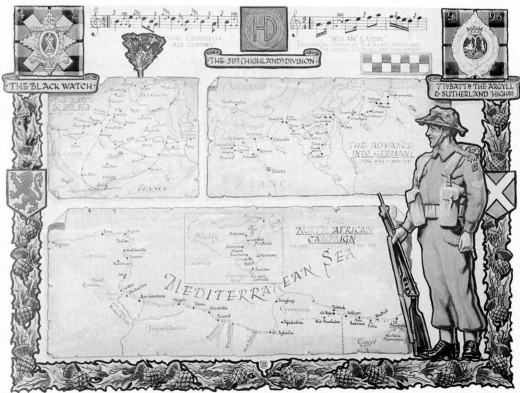

PLATE XVIII (above)    *Briefing for El Alamein. The Commanding Officers of the Highland Division: Lieut.-Col. J. A. Oliver, 7 B.W. (left foreground); Lieut.-Col. T. G. Rennie, 5 B.W. (sixth left, back row); Lieut.-Col. W. N. Roper-Caldeck, 1 B.W. (third right, back row).*

PLATE XIX (below)    *The Highland Division's victorious path from 1942 to 1945.*

PLATE 22    *The 5th Black Watch on Valentine tanks north of Gabes, April, 1943.*

On the 6th April, the brigade which was sent to capture the ridge found its initial advance gradually being thrust back in a fierce, grenade-throwing battle among the peaks and crevices. The 5th Black Watch, in divisional reserve, was sent to reinforce them, which it did with spectacular *élan*, the leading platoon storming on to the crest in the nick of time to relieve the Seaforth platoon holding the summit of the ridge. As night came, they worked their way towards the north end of the ridge, but there the enemy was well ensconced.

Down by the road, the Argylls were to cross the Wadi Akarit and, when they had established a bridgehead, the 7th Black Watch were to follow them across the wadi, then turn west towards the Roumana Ridge. Under Colonel Lorne Campbell, the Argylls soon opened the bridgehead and, behind their guard, the 7th Battalion executed their turning movement. Their right flank, nearest the enemy suffered so severely that all its officers, and most of its sergeants became casualties. However, by 9.30 a.m., they had reached the foot of the ridge, but instead of linking up with friends on the heights, they were met by heavy fire. They took cover in the enemy's own trenches, and settled down to fight it out. Behind them, the Argylls were being pressed hard in a ferocious battle which won for their Colonel the Victoria Cross, and artillery fire on their position prevented the 7th Battalion's support weapons coming through. The anti-tank guns were sorely missed in the afternoon, when a squadron of tanks appeared round the corner of the ridge and over-ran two companies.

On all three fronts, the ridge, the foot of the ridge, and the Argyll's bridgehead, pressure was so great that it seemed that something must give. At the foot of the ridge, the situation was so tense, that the 1st Battalion was ordered up to support the 7th. However, the demands of the Argylls were too insistent to be ignored, and only one company of the 1st Battalion came up. Its commander, McKinney, was badly wounded, so it was brought on by Captain Taylor, who by a happy chance had started his soldering as a private in the 6/7th Territorials.

With the coming of dark, the pressure eased, although enemy troops infiltrated the 7th Battalion's lines, causing it to be drawn back some distance from the ridge. But when the sun came up, the extent of the German defeat could be seen in the mass of material, guns and ammunition discarded in their retreat. When the Highland Division advanced, they found the road clear of mines, a novel experience, for, as General de Guingand said, until then the Division 'more or less lived among mines'. The battle of Wadi Akarit provided almost the last contact these three Battalions had with the enemy in North Africa, for the last cracking of the nut was passed to other divisions in the Eighth Army, and to the First Army advancing from the west.

4TH BATTALION

When Operation Torch landed the Americans and First Army in North-West Africa, it seemed to offer the 4th Battalion a chance of release from their sojourn in Gibraltar. Shipped there in 1940, they had spent their time in hard labour, riddling out tunnels, galleries and caves from the rock, and using the rubble to convert the racecourse into an airfield. Spain's belligerent neutrality meant that they were as strictly confined to the Rock as the 42nd had been in the early nineteenth century. Before Corunna, men of the 42nd had helped to build the New Mole which allowed the Navy to use Gibraltar as a base: now the compliment was repaid, when the Navy helped to relieve the monotony by offering unofficial cruises, patrolling the Mediterranean or hunting the Bismark. A firm friendship grew up, particularly between the Battalion and the ill-fated Ark Royal, a friendship which even thrived on the mighty snub offered by a sentry to Vice-Admiral Sir James Somerville when he came to visit the Battalion. Observing the stranger's doubtful uniform, the sentry refrained from saluting when he passed. Mildly, the Admiral suggested that the ships in the harbour and the three gold rings on his arm entitled him to a salute, but the Jock was not altogether convinced. 'Ye may be a sergeant,' he said at length, 'but you're no a sergeant in The Black Watch.'

If not tactful, the Battalion sentries were certainly alert, and when, late in 1942, ships began to assemble in the harbour and planes on the runway for Operation Torch, the Jocks were on their toes, and a wide-mouthed American in civilian clothes found scrambling over the cliffs was quickly hustled away to the guard-room. The fact that the Battalion was given no part in the North African landings probably had nothing to do with jailing the supreme commander – Eisenhower was a notably broad-minded man – but, for soldiers who wanted to be back in the field, the frustration was enormous. But, deprived of their Division they remained administratively out in the cold, and when they returned to England, it was only to take on a training role. Finally, late in 1945, the Battalion was shipped to the Mediterranean, and there it was disbanded. It may be said that the 4th Battalion never really escaped from St Valéry.

### 6TH BATTALION

The 6th Battalion joined the First Army when it was approaching Enfidaville, the last position before Tunis. In a last gamble to hold on to North Africa, Hitler had sent out some of the divisions which had invaded Russia and, when the 6th Battalion made a night attack on the village of Sidi Medienne, it met units from the redoubtable Hermann Goering Division. One after another The Black Watch companies were committed to the attack. The noise of the conflict was orchestrated to 'a hubbub of grenades and machine-guns, with an obbligato of pipes above all', and the battle hung in the balance until the last company was committed. Even with the village in its hands, the Battalion had to fend off two sustained counter-attacks, and their prisoners confessed that the fighting was as bitter as anything they had experienced in Russia.

The battle for Enfidaville brought a joint attack by the First Army, and by divisions of the Eighth. The front was so crowded that the same track through the wire was allotted to the 'A' companies of both the 6th Black Watch and the Duke of Cornwall's Light Infantry. For some time as the men streamed through, an officer from each battalion stood by the fork in the path, hissing '"A" company this way', and confusion would have been complete, but for the inevitable Jock wearing his bonnet instead of a helmet. Colonel Madden spotted his Red Hackle going the wrong way, and with some difficulty the 'A' company cocktail was unmixed. In the battle itself, the Battalion found opposition light, and over the next ten days it scoured the last Germans out of North Africa. On the 13th May all resistance ceased.

### 1ST, 5TH AND 7TH BATTALIONS

When the Allies crossed the Mediterranean, the three Black Watch Battalions in the Highland Division again took up the running, while the 6th Battalion paused in North Africa. On the 10th July, Sicily was invaded in typical Black Watch weather, a strong wind blowing up tall, stiff-backed waves. One man actually died from sea-sickness, and the landing itself took place through heavy breakers. But the foul weather had relieved enemy fears of invasion, and, so far as the Regiment was concerned, the first days of their advance from the southernmost tip of Sicily saw little fighting. The country was mountainous, cut through by broad valleys. At the confluence of several roads was situated Vizzini, perched on a conical hill, and looking like 'a fairy castle in a Disney film'. In stifling noon-time heat, a battalion of Gordons and the 5th Black Watch were sent forward across the open to the outskirts of the town. Skilfully using what cover was available, the Battalion reached the outskirts of the town with few casualties, and a brisk street-battle gave them a firm lodgement in Vizzini before nightfall. The Gordons had similar success on the other side and, threatened by a Highland pincer, the Germans departed under cover of darkness.

The advance now debouched from the hills into the Catanian Plain, which stretched north to the slopes about Mount Etna, and east to the sea. The Highland Division, however, operated along its western edge, where it touched the central mountains of Sicily. Rivers from the hills cut across their passage, offering good defensive positions, but the Highland Division drove on without halt until they came to Gerbini. 'Emboldened by the speed at which we had gone forward,' Wimberley wrote, 'we were now too hasty, and took rather a bloody nose.'

The strength of the defences was badly underestimated, and for three nights and two days, Rennie's brigade of the 7th Argylls and 1st and 7th Black Watch battled to capture a bewildering complex of roads and railway. The greatest success fell to the 7th Black Watch who passed through the German lines under cover of night, and took up position round the Gerbini airfield. At dawn, the Jocks heard all round them the unsuspecting noises of an army waking up, which quickly turned into hostile machine-gun fire and clattering tank manoeuvres. While they fended off their enemy, the 1st Battalion and the Argylls fought two dogged but unsuccessful battles to take the station and barracks. Of the courage shown, that of Private John Travena can serve as an example. When the order came to withdraw, Travena carried with him a wounded Argyll officer, but the distance was too great, and, five-hundred yards from the 1st Battalion's line, he hid the officer in a dugout and stayed there with him through the day. Twice he went out to fetch water despite the danger from German patrols, and, when night came, he made his way to The Black Watch post to get help in bringing the officer back.

Eventually, Montgomery decided to switch the whole direction of the attack to the west, and all three battalions were withdrawn from Gerbini, the 7th returning in the same light-footed way in which it had advanced, through the ranks of its enemies.

The last fighting of the Sicilian campaign took place round Mount Etna. South of the volcano, the Sferro hills rose up from the plain, and overlooked the German stronghold of Adrano. As the other Battalions were fighting at Gerbini, the 5th Battalion and the Gordons broke into Sferro village, and for ten days this toehold in the hills was maintained while the Americans made up ground in the west. Above them two peaks dominated the position, and for the capture of each a brigade was employed. From Rennie's brigade, the two Black Watch Battalions assaulted the west peak with clockwork precision but, pushing further on, the 7th Battalion was ambushed. One company was cut off, from which only four survivors came back, and a German counter-attack threatened the others on the crest. With each side struggling for possession of the hill, the battle continued into daylight, and then the Battalion, firing mortars and anti-tank guns at point-black range, at last forced the enemy to break off.

The capture of the Sferro hills turned the last line of defence, and thereafter the Division concentrated on scouring out the last spots of resistance. The 154th Brigade crossed the straits of Messina to set foot briefly on the mainland of Europe, but in late October the entire Division sailed for Britain. It was a year, almost to the day, since El Alamein – an *annus mirabilis* in their history.

## 6TH BATTALION

The Italian campaign continued without the benefit of the Regiment's participation, until the Allied advance ground to a halt in the Liri Valley underneath the tall outcrop of rock which carried the monastery of Monte Cassino. In March, 1944, the 6th Battalion was haled out of its limbo in Suez, and sent to hold a bridgehead in the hills south of the Liri Valley. Among the crags and corries, the Jocks looked over, and were over-looked by, the German positions. Each side mortared, shelled and sniped, but on the Battalion's side roofed-in sangars provided good protection. Compared to North Africa, where neither side exposed themselves at all in defence, it was a novel experience, but this proved only to be a period of acclimatisation. The real impact of the Italian war came when they were moved across the valley into the town of Monte Cassino, lying at the foot of the monastery's hill.

The town had been almost completely levelled by gunfire. Where a half-destroyed building remained, it might house a patrol, but otherwise the companies in the town led a troglodytic existence, in the Cathedral crypt, cellars and basements, all of which were covered in rubble. Half of the town was still held by the Germans, so that during the day all movement ceased. Many of the streets had been flooded by a mountain stream which had overflowed its banks, but, though there was water everywhere, every drop for drinking, like all other supplies, had to be brought in by porters. The moment of their arrival was the most frenzied of the day. Artillery, which had fired explosive through the day, now fired smoke shells to camouflage the hurried rush of ration parties through the ruins. It was one of these smoke shells falling short which put an end to the soldiering of Sergeant Wilson. A direct descendant of one of the original soldiers in the Independent Companies, Wilson himself had begun his career in 1908; he was severely wounded in the Great War, but persuaded those concerned in 1939 that he was young enough and healthy enough to be given a second chance. As he was carried away from Cassino, he sent a message to Colonel Madden, apologising 'for falling out without permission'.

The stress of life in the lunatic world of Monte Cassino wore men down quickly, and there was general relief when, in May, they were withdrawn to take part in the crossing of the Rapido. The river joined the Liri just below Monte Cassino, and it was hoped to cross it higher up and thus create a bridgehead in the mountainous country behind the monastery. It was confidently expected to be an extremely bloody battle.

To say that fortune favours the brave is frequently only an elegant way of saying that the brave make the most of their opportunities. Certainly, the 6th Battalion had two enormous strokes of luck in the next month, but not everyone would have exploited them so triumphantly. The first stroke came on the day after they crossed the Rapido.

Thick fog rolled over the hills before dawn, but the Battalion started forward although it was almost travelling blind. When companies seemed in danger of losing touch, Madden formed them in squares round their tanks. They pressed past veiled woods and German guns and, when occasionally there was a burst of fire, the tanks would roar out of their squares to deal with the offenders. Unable to see where they were going, the Battalion simply continued until the ground began to fall away in front of them, and there they dug in. As the fog began to lift, it gradually revealed that the 6th Battalion had stumbled on to an extremely strong position, for they had passed through nests of machine-guns and mortars, and in the midst of their trenches, they found an anti-tank gun with a shell in the breech.

The same revelation came to the Germans, and for forty-eight hours the Battalion had to withstand continual heavy shelling until two other battalions edged forward to secure their flanks. After a week, in which Cassino itself at last fell, the Battalion was relieved. They had suffered over 240 casualties in the fighting around Monte Cassino, with particularly heavy losses of officers and N.C.O.s and, although drafts arrived to fill the gaps, there were hereafter more often three companies to the Battalion than four.

Many of the new officers came from an affiliated regiment, the Transvaal Scottish, but this was not the only South African favour that the Battalion received. With the fall of Monte Cassino, the road to Rome was theoretically open, although in practice the country around was still held by the enemy. On the 8th June, Sergeant Dickson appeared. He was a South African prisoner-of-war who had just escaped through the enemy lines, and knew all their positions and the undefended tracks through them. With his guidance, the Battalion threaded its way through the hills to a point so far advanced that the brigade headquarters was frankly disbelieving.

Then the Battalion's luck seemed to evaporate. In the hard, skirmishing pursuit from Rome to Florence, there were six changes of commanding officer due to wounds, and heavy casualties among the N.C.O.s. Lord Douglas Gordon caught fortune in a more benign mood when he led two companies into a vital and extremely sensitive part of the enemy line with the prosaic name of Corbett. The reaction was fierce and, for two nights and a day, the companies helf off repeated counter-attacks and withstood an endless stream of shells. Inadvertently, but successfully, they practised the technique of calling in their own artillery fire on their position, and the barrage demolished the last assault only yards from their trenches.

With the fall of Florence, Italy lost its appeal for the Allies and, as troops were drained off for the landings in Normandy and the South of France, the diminished army switched its attack east into the open spaces of the Po Valley. In the suburbs of Forli, the Battalion encountered the most severe fighting they had known since Monte Cassino. Every building housed a machine-gun, and each had to be cleared individually against resistance which was that of desperation.

Urban warfare was the staple diet of the 6th Battalion in the last months of the war for, in December, 1944, they dropped out of the fight against Fascism, and took up the struggle against Communism in the streets of Athens. Their particular battleground was the suburban motorway linking the capital with Piraeus and the airport, which the Jocks named 'Mad Mile'. Their enemy was ELAS, the Communist force which had led the resistance to the Germans in the countryside, and was now attempting to spread its power to the towns.

After three weeks of sniping, ambushes, and bomb-throwing, ELAS decided that its luck would be better in the countryside, which represented a crucial defeat, for their Stalinist theoreticians had forecast that the revolution must come through the urban proletariat or not at all. Two years later, the 6th Battalion returned to Edinburgh, and there passed into that War Office limbo called 'suspended animation'.

# CHAPTER 21

# The Second Battalion in Burma

One truth that military philosophers had discerned in the turmoil of war was that the increasing complexity and number of support arms for the infantry – armour, artillery, communications, etc. – had made the division the most crucial unit in battle. It was to the twentieth century what the regiment had been to the nineteenth. As an interpretation of events, it was based rather selectively upon the experience of large, set-piece battles.

By a fluke of circumstance, the experience of the 2nd Battalion ran counter to the general thesis. In Somaliland, it had operated independently; at Heraklion, since guns and tanks were almost entirely lacking, each battalion in their brigade effectively fought on its own; the sortie from Tobruk was planned as a brigade action; but Burma was to provide the most famous contradiction.

In 1943, the fame of the Chindits and the personality of Wingate persuaded Churchill that it was worth repeating on a larger scale the experiment of operating a force behind enemy lines. The 70th Division, of which the 2nd Battalion was part, had been stationed in India since February, 1942, and it was now dismembered to provide troops for this second Chindit force. When he heard of the munificent reinforcement, one well-known Chindit was moved to quote the story of the Highland minister who, after a long drought, prayed for rain, and was answered with a downpour. 'Oh Lord,' said the minister, 'I ken fine I prayed for rain, but this is fair ridiculous'. More forcefully that comment was echoed by senior Divisional officers, but the 2nd Battalion found welcome relief from the policing duties which had occupied it since its arrival in India.

The Battalion was reorganised into two columns, and with a proper respect for history the senior column was numbered 73, and the junior 42. Then for six months, they trained to acquire the skills of jungle-fighting, and the initiative to use them. The means were rigorous, but the end was to produce Wavell's 'poacher, burglar, gunman', who could live and fight with little support from anyone but himself.

Although the Japanese occupied all Burma, the only large conflict at this time was in Upper Burma, where General Stilwell was pushing south from Ledo. It was hoped that the Chindits would disrupt the flow of men and supplies to the Japanese near Ledo, by seizing strategic points round Indaw. In February, Brigadier Calvert established his strongpoint 'White City' across the Japanese line of communication and, at the end of the month, Brigadier Fergusson of the Regiment, having marched 450 miles into Burma, opened an airstrip, which Wingate christened 'Aberdeen'. The 2nd Battalion flew into 'Aberdeen' in March to be greeted by Wingate's good-humoured congratulations on being 'the first Scottish battalion to land at a Scottish airport in Burma'.

Tragically, the plane carrying him back to Imphal crashed and, with Wingate's

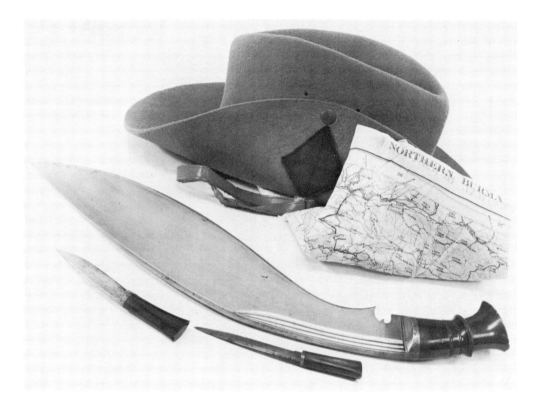

PLATE 23    *The Burma kit of Wavell's 'poacher, burglar, gunman'.*

death, the original concept of the Chindits' role changed, and modifications of it followed so rapidly that 14 Brigade, which contained 73 and 42 columns, expended enormous energy marching and counter-marching. 'This ought to confuse the Japs,' Colonel Green remarked optimistically. 'We don't even know where we're going ourselves.' An additional embarrassment, as they moved away from 'Aberdeen', was caused by the large numbers of British troops in the area and, for most of one tense day, 73 column under Colonel Green played hide-and-seek with what it took for a Japanese column, but which turned out to be equally nervous Gurkhas. Once out of the ruck, however, they demonstrated the justice of Wingate's belief that enormous damage could be wreaked in the enemy's rear. Early in April both columns ambushed a convoy on the Indaw road, and a week later 42 column under Major Rose destroyed a fuel dump – employing a Chindit 'first' in tactics by calling in an air-strike as the Jocks attacked. Air support, in fact, gave them enormous mobility; their supplies came by plane, their sick and wounded went out by plane, and planes were their artillery.

Otherwise the Jocks were on their own. When a soldier came down with appendicitis, the medical officer operated successfully using mess-tin handles for clamps and someone's sponge as a swab. They chose to base their way of life on good Presbyterian standards. The padres said family prayers on most nights, and there was a service at Easter. They shaved regularly, refusing to follow Wingate's louche practice of growing a beard. And a disapproving paragraph in the *War Diary* noted: 'Litter and north country newspapers indicate a column here before us. What a bivouac! My platoon again has something dead in its area – a mule this time. Jocks shocked at litter and refuse after our own strict litter discipline.'

Near the end of April, it was at last decided that the Chindits should leave the Indaw area to join Stilwell's forces in the north. To help Calvert break out of 'White City' the Black Watch columns laid ambushes as a diversion and, in their biggest action in Burma, Colonel Green broke up a convoy of some 1,200 Japanese with a force of 200 Jocks. In May, however, the monsoon broke, and from then on their most deadly enemies were ill-health and the weather. The jungle trails became as slippery as eel-skins, the saddle-girths on their mules rotted away, and as they neared the Indawgyi Lake they had to climb up through steep passes defended by the Japanese. During their march, seventy men died of typhus, but in the depths of illness and exhaustion, the columns fought innumerable small actions. Food rations were inadequate, and the men deteriorated physically to such an extent that in July only fifty were deemed fit enough to stay in the jungle another month. Nevertheless, on the 6th August, both columns went into battle one last time, played in by Piper Lark on a set of pipes dropped to him by parachute, and from a well-entrenched position near the railway their enemy was thrown out. Two days later, a patrol near the station met the first men of the 36th Division advancing from India, and before the end of the month the remaining Jocks were savouring the luxuries of dry clothes and fresh food back in India.

Not the least of the tragedies resulting from Wingate's death was that, by obscuring the role of the Chindits, it also obscured the successful operation of Regular troops, such as the 2nd Battalion, in a hazardous, irregular situation, for which specialist, volunteer units were generally called. After it had recovered from its ordeal, the 2nd Black Watch further displayed its versatility by converting into a parachute battalion. The worst problem they encountered was over the matter of headgear. General Montgomery, the last person, it would have been thought, to complain about unorthodox hatting, ordered them to discard their bonnets and Red Hackles in favour of red berets. The Battalion, however, had friends in high places, and the commanding officer wrote a report on the matter for the Viceroy, sending it, with a nice touch of finesse, by way of General Montgomery himself. Viceroys trump Generals, and from Vice-regal Lodge Wavell immediately cancelled the order. Thus the 2nd Battalion could claim that it ended the war as it had begun, under the command of its former subaltern.

CHAPTER 22

# The Highland Division Returns

Between 1942 and 1944, most graffitisti, offered a chalk and a blank wall, would have lost no time in scrawling 'Second Front Now'. The implication of dilatoriness used to annoy Churchill intensely, since the invasion of France had the over-riding priority in Allied plans, as its codename 'Operation Overlord' suggested. The formidable nature of the administrative details required time, and troops such as the Highland Division needed to learn new tactics suitable for Europe, and to master new weapons like their improved mortar, and the Wasp flame-thrower. When D-Day came, the Division was sent to support the Airborne Division in the eastern salient between Caen and the coast. If Caen was the hinge round which the Allied armies would swing, this area, containing the villages of Bréville and Colombelles, was the very screw which held the hinge in place.

The 5th Battalion was the first to land, on the afternoon of the 6th June, and almost immediately tasted the quality of the fighting. They were holding the Chateau de Bréville and its environs with orders not to fire until ordered. In gun-pits about the grounds and in the huge, empty rooms of the castle, the Jocks heard and saw the Germans approaching, but they held their fire until a voice shouted, 'Come on Jock surrender; there are more of us than you.' The reply was a burst from a Bren gun, and the battle was on. The castle offered a conspicuous target for enemy mortars and artillery, but their troops were too close not to suffer enormous casualties. One section of the Battalion was over-run, and the survivors shot, but the remainder kept up a steady fire and held their ground. After an hour of close-quarter fighting, the shooting began to die away as the enemy fell back from the castle grounds.

For three weeks, the battle in this sector remained static. The 7th Battalion, holding a forward position in the Bois de Bavent, was tormented by a battery of multiple mortars, alias 'Moaning Minnies', whose shells splintered the trees and caused vicious wounds. It had not even the comfort of being with its own brigade, for the Division was being committed to battle piecemeal, and a general unhappiness began to spread through its ranks. Faulty information often resulted in a company being committed to an action which required a battalion, and a battalion to that which required a brigade. An attack on Colombelles by the 5th Battalion and its brigade was driven back when, from tall factory chimneys, observers called in artillery fire on the infantry, and a strong Panzer force knocked out their tanks. To capture it eventually required the employment of two divisions.

At the beginning of July, there was a change of command and of fortune. General Rennie took over command of the Division, and resistance round Caen eased as the Americans worked their way down the west side of the Contentin peninsula. South of

Caen the countryside opened out into wide, rolling fields but, in sunken roads and behind thick hedges, a stiff defence might still be expected. While American forces circled round from the west, the Highland Division, now part of the Canadian Corps, drove south to nip that salient round Falaise where Hitler had ordered his army to resist at all costs. 'Drove' is the operative word, for the 1st and 7th Battalions more or less motored into battle, riding in eviscerated self-propelled guns, the first armoured personnel carriers. Under artificial moonlight created by shining searchlights on the clouds, and following the direction given by tracer fire from the flanks, they moved deep into the enemy position to attack villages in the second line of defence. There was a sharp battle for possession of the houses but, so swiftly had the Battalions arrived, that men and guns were captured in enormous quantities. Dawn brought back more traditional warfare, in a counter-attack on the 1st Battalion and mortar shelling for the 7th, but it was noted with satisfaction that the victorious pattern of North Africa had returned. As though in confirmation, the 5th Battalion pushed in a perilous attack on a horseshoe range of hills beyond the river Dives, a battle which its companies conducted largely without benefit of direction from head-quarters for heavy shelling had almost destroyed it, and had wounded the command-ing officer, Colonel Bradford. But at the crux of the struggle for the hills, Bradford reappeared, bandaged and sitting on a tank, which he urged on to the slopes to tighten the hold his men had established.

Finally, after a fortnight of almost continuous fighting in the first half of August, the German forces round Lisieux were destroyed so completely that the Division seemed to enter a vacuum where there was no resistance to their advance. In this period of relative calm General Montgomery turned the Canadian Corps from its eastward advance and, with shrewd understanding of the psychological effect, diverted the Canadians on to Dieppe and the Highlanders to St Valéry. It was fifty-one months since disaster had struck the original 51st; in that time, their successors had exacted revenge in North Africa, in Sicily, and most lately in Normandy under the command of Tom Rennie, General Fortune's former staff officer. When the massed Pipes and Drums beat the Retreat at St Valéry, there was cause for remembrance and pride alike.

The momentum of victory carried the Allies into Holland by early October, but the Highland Division was delayed by the hook-back needed to take Le Havre, and a spell in the siege-line round Dunkirk. When the Division arrived the Allies were still fighting to broaden their corridor which stretched as far as Nijmegen on the Meuse (Maas) River and, in that low-lying country, furrowed by river and canal, winkling out the enemy called for a rare blend of quick reaction and considered expertise. On the day that the 1st Battalion moved into the area, a company headquarters was raided and, after a brief, contrapuntal exchange of grenades and bullets, the Germans made off with three prisoners. They were dangerous passengers for, when the raiders bumped into an outlying platoon, the three Jocks killed the German officer in the confusion, and few of his men survived the expedition. Travelling with an advanced patrol in a Kangaroo, Lieutenant Donaldson encountered a self-propelled gun at point-blank range, and took the immediate and destructive course of ramming it into the ditch. The expertise was demanded by the recurrent obstacle presented by rivers which webbed the land. At St Michelgestel, the only bridge over a small river was blown up as the 7th Battalion approached, but some boats were found, and a platoon surreptitiously ferried itself over to the far side. After dark, the Battalion pioneers put a bridge over into their tiny bridgehead and, as reinforcements began to pass over it, more bridges were added, so that when day and horrible reality dawned on the Germans the entire Battalion, its guns and armour, and most of the 1st Battalion as well had crossed into their territory. The bridging feat was repeated a few days later by the 1st Battalion, under cover of smoke, to turn yet another defensive position, and by the end of November the Allied side of the Meuse had been cleared.

The invasion of Germany could not long be delayed, but the threat to their homeland provoked the fiercest response from the enemy. The sluice gates of the lower Rhine were opened, and all three Battalions, stationed on The Island, low-lying country between two arms of the river, had the unnerving experience of seeing the water rising higher by the day, while they exchanged shots with the Germans from farm-buildings and such high ground as still emerged. The last Jock waded out just before Christmas, and by then the enemy had launched their last convulsive attack through the Ardennes on the Americans. In biting cold, which the men transferred from the 2nd Battalion in India felt keenly, the Highland Division was pulled back into Belgium. The set-back was short. Back in the Nijmegen bridgehead, the Division prepared for the attack on the Reichswald. On the 8th February, after an eight-hour bombardment by 1,000 guns, the 1st and 7th Battalions led the attack into Germany, and the satisfaction of leading the first Allied troops into the enemy's country fell to Major Taylor of the 1st Battalion, who had begun his soldiering as a Territorial private.

Coming behind the 1st and 7th Battalions, the 5th wheeled southward to widen their bridgehead, and elegantly manoeuvred itself into Genepp village without suffering a casualty. Then the Germans erupted with a barrage of mortars and heavy counter-attacks, so that eventually the whole Battalion and the Gordons were involved. In this fighting in the Reichswald, there were no easy battles, but consistently the Battalions made swift, almost unscathed assaults to gain their position, and were then subjected to ferocious shelling and counter-attack. In mid-February, Hekkens, in the heart of the Siegfried Line, was rushed by the 1st and 7th Battalions who took 300 prisoners for negligible cost, but then, inevitably, the enemy barrage came down. They held on to their gain, however, and the hole in the Siegfried Line widened until the Line was destroyed, leaving only one more obstacle to be crossed – the Rhine.

Every device that technology could produce was employed for the protection of infantry in the crossing of the Rhine. A sixty-mile smoke-screen was laid along the river, and the 1st and 7th Battalions were carried over in amphibious Buffaloes beneath the most concentrated barrage of the war; but at the heart of the matter was the courage of the individual soldier. In the breakout from the Rhine, the last great battle in which the Battalions were engaged, the superb orchestration of air, artillery and armoured support must be ignored in favour of two pictures of the individual in action.

The 7th Battalion was the first to consolidate across the Rhine, but the 1st, following through to the villages of Klein Esserden and Speldrop, ran into a deep minefield when they were counter-attacked by armour and, in the village of Speldrop, an advanced platoon was cut off. Taking a patrol back to extricate them, Second Lieutenant Henderson, nineteen-years old, was fired at from across the road by a machine-gun, which knocked his weapon from his hand. Without hesitation, Henderson pulled the spade from his pack, dashed across the road and killed the machine-gunner before he could fire again.

PLATE 24    *51st Division buglers sound the Last Post at St Valéry, 1944.*

Then he regathered his patrol and led them into Speldrop, where they held out against attacks by grenades, artillery and armour, until the advance caught up with them in the evening.

Having crossed further upstream than the other two, the 5th Battalion was sent in to take the village of Rees, Accurate bazooka fire forced their tanks to pull back, and the Jocks had to fight unsupported from shops and street-corners. Early in the battle, casualties among the officers put Corporal Greaves in command of his platoon. To his company commander, he confessed that he did not know much about the job, 'but show me where to go, and I'll go.' The battle continued through the night, and wherever Greaves was told to go, he went and his platoon went with him. He was wounded, but when the last German surrendered, Greaves was still there to report 'All Correct'.

In the breakout from the Rhine there were many casualties, but that which saddened the entire Division was the death of General Rennie who was killed on the eve of the battle

PLATE 25    *Pennant from Jeep in which Major-General T. Gordon Rennie was killed.*

for Rees. From St Valéry to the Rhine his career could be described as the very personification of the rising fortunes of the Highland Division. His death came at the moment of victory for, although there was still fighting ahead, the Germans' last defence had been broken. As the Highland Division was streaming across northern Germany word came that the enemy had surrendered unconditionally.

The record of The Black Watch in the Second World War can well end with the emergence from the prisoner-of-war camps of the survivors of the original 1st Battalion and 51st Division. Their war had been bleak, but the qualities they showed in a bitter situation were exemplified by General Fortune, who for his activities as a prisoner was deservedly knighted. Despite ill-health, he won for his fellow-P.O.W.s most of their rights, a rare degree of respect, and so dominated his situation that, in Bernard Fergusson's words, 'he led captivity captive'.

More than thirty years afterwards the victory of 1945 still looms large in the perspective of history, and certainly among the achievements of the Regiment its part in the war must rank supreme for no other conflict demanded from it such a variety of military skills. Yet the quality which underlay those technical proficiencies was the same as it always had been – the collective will to resist and overcome – and the value of the Regiment in developing that quality was as clearly evident as ever.

# CHAPTER 23

# The Post-War Era

During more than two centuries of existence, The Black Watch could claim equal familiarity with the extravagance of victory and the penury of peace, but, in the aftermath of a victory greater than any since the defeat of Napoleon, came penury sharper than any since 1815. The Territorial Battalions passed into the dismal void of 'suspended animation' before being amalgamated to continue their activities as the 4/5th and 6/7th. That might have been expected, but the disbandment of the Regiment's Second Battalion in 1948 was an event without precedent since Napoleon was exiled to Elba.

The sad science of economics was in part to blame, for Britain was impoverished by war, but its impact was the greater on infantry regiments because of the advance of technology. Before the Second World War, the infantry represented more than half the army, but the rise of units which were concerned with armour, transport, supply and communications had, by 1945, reduced the proportion of infantry to less than a third of the total. To these must be added a third factor, the passing of British rule in India, whose support had required the presence of the 2nd Battalion for forty-six years of its life.

Independence had been bubbling during the war, but when peace came the ferment began to boil over. Early in 1946 part of the Indian Navy mutinied, a situation which would have explosive repercussions whether it were allowed to spread or suppressed with bloodshed. As part of the Airborne Division, the 2nd Battalion was directed to capture the naval base on Manora Island, near Karachi. It was put ashore at dawn. The barracks were surrounded and rushed, and without a shot being fired, the mutiny there was ended. Then to rub it in, the Jocks beat the mutineers at football. In a situation where rivalries, racial and religious, were becoming homicidal, that game is a detail worth preserving.

After the Great War, the 2nd Battalion had supervised the plebiscite in Silesia; it now moved north to perform the same duty in Peshawar, where the people were to decide whether they wanted to be part of Moslem Pakistan or Hindu India. When the Battalion arrived, the situation was so tense that it was estimated that three-quarters of the inhabitants were carrying rifles, but the next day there was not a weapon to be seen, 'testimony enough,' wrote an officer, 'to the respect in which the Pathans held the Jocks'.

The Battalion had been stationed in that mountainous area before the First World War, and many of the inhabitants still held chits from the officers of that time. In the 1860s, the Jocks and Pathans had exchanged shots when the 42nd patrolled the North-West Frontier, and not far way at Cherat were the graves of those who had fallen victim to cholera in 1867. If past reputation were not enough, the Battalion had a potent weapon in the Pipes and Drums, which on several occasions defused an explosive scene, not least when protesters lying on the railway line came to their feet to hear their music. The Black

PLATE 26    *Lord Wavell and the 2nd Battalion at the Vice-regal Lodge, April, 1945.*

Watch was to be the last British regiment to serve on that myth-laden North-West Frontier for, as disorder increased elsewhere, the government accelerated the date of independence, settling at last for August, 1947. Late in 1946, the 2nd Battalion returned to Karachi, and in their absence the nightmare of murder and massacre spilled over into Peshawar.

In their last months in India, the Jocks, as impartial guarantors of security, were more popular than ever before. An enormous, emotional crowd came to say good-bye when the Battalion marched to its ship with pipes playing and colours flying, and, in his speech of farewell, General Akhbar Khan expressed the feelings on both sides when he said, 'Your departure breaks an old association of friendship and comradeship.' On the 26th February, 1947, the 2nd Battalion sailed from India, the last British battalion but one to leave the sub-continent. It was appropriate that India should have been the last post of the 2nd Battalion for it was there that it had begun its history one-hundred-and-sixty-seven years before; much of its life had been passed there, fighting to spread or sustain British rule; and now both the rule and the Battalion ended together. It was formally amalgamated with the 1st Battalion at Duisburg in 1948.

The independence of India, coupled with the changed composition of the army, had persuaded the government that the Cardwell-Childers system no longer suited the needs of the British Army. Specifically that regimental arrangement, exemplified by The Black Watch with its two Regular Battalions and four Territorial Battalions based upon a training depot at Perth, would have to be radically altered. The process took about a quarter of a century and, during that time, the Regiment's fight to retain its identity, and even its existence, was a constant and disquieting theme.

The 1st Battalion remained in Germany after the end of the war, where its style of life was largely determined by Montgomery's order forbidding all contact with the Germans. To the irritations of non-fraternisation were added those of a dull and meagre diet, and a rigidly controlled supply of cigarettes which could never satisfy both personal cravings and the needs of the Black Market. A demand for wood to help the home-building drive led to 'Operation Woodpecker', in which units of the British Army of the Rhine turned lumberjack in the north German forests, but otherwise there was a sense of purposelessness while the government decided its policy for the army.

Despite these handicaps, the Regiment had little difficulty in recruiting; indeed, Lord Wavell estimated at the time of the 2nd Battalion's demise, that The Black Watch had recruited well enough to sustain three battalions. It was not so in the rest of the army, and by 1947 recruiting had dropped so alarmingly that the government was forced to introduce National Service in order to maintain an army of adequate size.

The 1st Battalion was selected as a guinea pig for the first batch of National Servicemen to go abroad after two months' basic training. The relief from indecision was welcome, and everyone threw himself into the preparations. An elaborate training schedule was worked out, which included Highland dancing, woodwork and language classes (to which reading and writing later had to be added), as well as the more obvious weapon-training and drill. Soon after the recruits arrived, they were sent for a week to live rough and fight mock battles – 'scallywagging' Wavell called it – so that they could appreciate how their performance could be improved by discipline and training.

It was an imaginative curriculum, which seems to have left more good memories than bad among its alumni. After two months' basic training at Fort George, 'it was a different world,' wrote Private McDougall. 'Our training Sergeant and Corporals treated us like human beings – the Sergeant even cracked a joke with us.' Compared to that benign N.C.O., the most nerve-wracking part of the ordeal for most of the young men was the medical inspection by Major Prendergast. In an obituary, Bernard Fergusson wrote a vivid description of his remarkable medical officer. 'Skilful, quarrelsome, friendly and passionately pro-Black Watch, she quickly wove herself into the regimental tradition. Lord Wavell granted her permission to wear the Red Hackle in her bonnet, and a Black Watch tartan skirt, and all the protests of the R.A.M.C. failed to induce her to surrender this privilege . . . Officer and Jock alike were proud, fond, and slightly nervous of her.'

The major drawback of National Service was its conspicuous consumption of the time and energy of trained soldiers, for, to the efforts of The Black Watch, must be added those of the battalion stationed at Fort George which gave basic training to all the National Servicemen drawn from the Highland region. The results, however, justified the cost. There was particular satisfaction when Black Watch companies of National Servicemen won the British Army of the Rhine (BAOR) drill competitions against Regular companies of the Guards, but, more importantly, in Berlin, Korea and Kenya, the 'Nashies' proved to be excellent soldiers.

The Cold War reached melting-point in July, 1948, when the Soviets cut the road and rail routes into Berlin. The news reached the Battalion after a day of Highland Games, culminating in a spectacular night parade through the Duisburg woods of the Pipes and

Drums preceded by torch-bearers. The Ball that followed seemed to one observer at least uncommonly reminiscent of the Duchess of Richmond's, but the expected conflict with the Soviet Union was avoided and, as the airlift into Berlin continued, the tension gradually eased. When the Battalion moved to the city in 1950, there remained only a chilly threat; the blockade, however had produced one vitally important result in the creation of N.A.T.O., which has since then given direction to Britain's defence policy in Europe.

In Berlin, that display platform of the West, the standards of smartness were not less than immaculate, and the Battalion had to work hard to recapture a parade-ground shimmer which had been neglected in coping with the National Service rush. But even while the Jocks went through their white-belted, ceremonial guard duties in front of the Bradenburg Gate or Hess' Spandau prison, the Communist invasion of South Korea had begun.

From a shallow toe-hold in the south of the Korean peninsula, the United States, in the guise of the United Nations, drove the Communist north to the Yalu River border with China, then abruptly recoiled before Chinese forces, not halting the retreat until they were south of the 38th parallel. There the line rocked to and fro. The arrival of the Commonwealth Brigade made greater sense of the term 'United Nations', although the British contingent was never large compared to the Americans. The talking war had started across the table at Panmunjon, when The Black Watch arrived in July, 1952, but the shooting war still continued.

The Battalion made its first acquaintanceship with The Hook in August. Unlike most of the hills in the neighbourhood, it was bare of vegetation. Shaped like a camel's hump, it ran north and south, with smaller ridges running northward down to the Chinese line. One company held The Hook itself, while the others and Battalion Headquarters occupied smaller hills on the flank and in the rear. The Black Watch's first visit lasted a month; it was shelled, and rain turned the dusty earth to mud. There were casualties from shelling and mines, but it could not be called more than an overture. The performance proper opened in November when they returned. On the night of the relief, a heavy bombardment fell on the position, but Major Irwin, commanding 'A' Company on The Hook, had his men deeply dug in, and the shelling caused no casualties. A strong Chinese raid, heralded by a cacophony of whistles and gongs, briefly over-ran an advanced post before being forced back. As they left, they booby-trapped a wounded Jock with a grenade; it proved potent medicine, for he immediately sprang into life and hurled the grenade after the retreating enemy.

In military terms, if there was one Chinese quality more impressive than their use of the dark for movement and attack, it was their ready acceptance of huge losses in order to capture a position.

In the early hours of the 18th November, both qualities were in evidence. Under a phenomenally concentrated bombardment, which landed about 4,000 shells in an area of 300 square yards, the Chinese came on through their own shells, but from dugouts and tunnels the Jocks thinned the ranks of their attackers, and an artillery strike helped to turn them round. Soon Irwin's company was mopping up the last pockets of resistance. Twenty minutes later, a blare of trumpets announced a second assault as something like a thousand Chinese stormed forward on a very narrow front. An advanced standing patrol

PLATE 27    *Roll call of 'A' company after the Battle of The Hook, 19th November, 1953.*

under Second Lieutenant Black, a young National Service officer, was over-run, but his platoon fought back, furiously hurling grenades and then, as succeeding waves closed in, with bayonets and fists. Although he was surrounded, Black remained in communication with his company commander, and his platoon continued to be a point at which a counter-attack could be aimed. From further up The Hook, there came heavy fire from the Battalion's Browning machine-guns, and both the artillery, and Centurion tanks, perched on neighbouring hills, joined in.

At Headquarters, the scene was a remarkable amalgam of frenzy and calm. There were reports rioting out of four telephones, and seven W/T sets, from companies, Brigade Headquarters and artillery and tank networks, but the problem of their interpretation, and of determining at which point to commit his reserves, rested with Colonel Rose, an officer who could call upon a wealth of experience spanning the bare hills of Somaliland and the Burmese jungle. With 'D' Company holding a hill on the flank, he had only 'B' Company in reserve when Major Irwin reported that The Hook was inundated with Chinese. Rose called down an artillery strike on the position and, as the shells and 'howling ripples' of rockets came down on The Hook, he sent forward 'B' Company with a tank and two platoons from 'D' Company. His own position was now wide open, but the moment was well chosen. Disrupted by the shelling, the Chinese were bundled off the crest of the ridge, and then Irwin directed a counter-attack to relieve Black's platoon. By dawn, The Hook was clear of all but a hundred dead Chinese, and even they were only a fragment of their casualties, for the enemy was meticulous in carrying off their dead and wounded.

The battle on The Hook was not the Battalion's last encounter with the Chinese. In April, 1953, it returned to find the hillside bright with azaleas, and almond and cherry-trees blossoming in the valleys. Aggressive patrolling brought in the first prisoner taken on the front for seven months, and in May The Black Watch repeated the trick with three more Chinese taken in an ambush on one of their raiding parties. The last battle of the war took place on The Hook, a week after the Battalion had been relieved by the Duke of Wellington's; again the Chinese were repelled, and in July the Panmunjon Truce was signed. The Battalion left for home in the same month with a pleasant compliment from General West; when the Battalion was in the line, the General said, his commanders would comment, 'The Black Watch is on our right flank, so that flank's all right, now what about the left?'

The journey home was protracted, for on the way The Black Watch was diverted to Kenya. A more striking contrast with the alternately bleak and blossoming landscape of Korea would be hard to imagine than that of the Aberdare Mountains in Kenya. They were layered with trees – cedar and wild fig, thick with undergrowth on the lower slopes, and above them bamboo, densely packed, rotting and slippery on the ground – only on the crest was the forest replaced by heather and tall trees. The Aberdares, traditionally the refuge of the Kikuyu from the Masai, now sheltered the Mau Mau from police and troops. A campaign of murder and mutilation, culminating in the massacre of eighty-four Kikuyu, had forced the Governor to call in British troops, and The Black Watch was the fourth battalion to arrive.

Initially, they were posted near Thika, and from there they sent patrols into the jungle to hunt the Mau Mau gangs. The thick undergrowth was best penetrated by the animal trails through it which a patrol would follow until, close to the suspected hideout, it could lie in ambush for the returning Mau Mau. It was in such an attack that the Battalion suffered a most grievous loss in Kenya, when Major the Viscount Wavell, the Field Marshal's only son, was killed by a Mau Mau gang. Having surrounded some fifty or sixty terrorists in a gully, he was standing up to direct operations with the same unthinking courage which had cost him the loss of his right hand in the Second World War, when he was shot by a single bullet.

However, the Battalion's success in patrolling soon pacified the Thika district, so that in January, 1954, it moved to the pasture-land between the Aberdares and Mount Kilimanjaro. Here the Mau Mau practised cattle-rustling, and the ever-versatile Jocks learned to track them to their camps, sneaking right inside before opening fire. Reflecting on the various crafts he had picked up in Korea and Kenya, an officer wrote, 'One thinks of training days in Colchester, and finds it hard to think of any patrol which required more than a few minutes' thought. Then one thinks of the past two years; full-scale fighting patrols with a battery of tanks, artillery, mortars and machine-guns at call; of five-day endurance patrols in the Aberdares; of lying doggo within a few yards of enemy trenches.' That experience was further widened by a sweep for Mau Mau in the streets of Nairobi, which successfully broke their power in the city, and two rather less successful drives in the Aberdares and Mount Kenya. When The Black Watch returned home in 1955, the

PLATE 28  *General's visit to Thika in Kenya, May, 1954.*

trouble was still simmering, though without real menace, but the result of the military effort was now secondary to the political and diplomatic moves, which were eventually to lead to independence.

The disparity of influence between military and diplomatic operations was most starkly illustrated by the abortive invasion of Suez. As a direct result of that fiasco, the troops of the Middle East strategic reserve were stationed in Cyprus, a concentration which helped to blow into flames the island's smouldering Enosis movement. Stationed in Germany, The Black Watch was spared both Suez and the worst of EOKA terrorism, and when it did arrive in November, 1958, a United Nations debate on Cyprus was pending, so their reception was distinctly *piano,* stones rather than bombs. The Regiment deserved better. This was its second visit to Cyprus and, like its first, it augured a fundamental change in the island's history.

The Jocks had paid their earlier visit in 1878, when they arrived in the train of Sir Garnet Wolseley, who bore a firman, or directive, from Lord Beaconsfield and Sultan Abdul the Damned of the Sublime Porte, by which the island passed from Turkish hands to British. On the same day that the Union Jack was hoisted for the first time, that legendary hero, Sergeant Sam McGaw v.c., died of a fever, and was entombed in a marble sarcophagus of Byzantine splendour. His death was only the first of a flood which, within two years, had reduced the Regiment to a shadow of itself. Nevertheless, British rule had been established and it had lasted for eighty years, when The Black Watch returned to supervise its dissolution and the inauguration of an independent Cypriot republic. They landed at Limni, remarkable at the time for its mud, but when the London Agreement was signed in October, 1959, paving the way for independence, they were patrolling the Troodos Mountains where Grivas had his headquarters.

The next phase of the island's troubled history, the outbreak of violence between Turk and Greek, again called for the Regiment's presence. In 1966, The Black Watch joined the United Nations peace-keeping force, and donned the blue beret in place of the bonnet. A single platoon, which had been sent to Cyprus two years before, had already experienced the symbolic effect of the change in headgear; one day they were spat on in the streets, the next they were cheered. Although the Cypriots may not have had much reason for the first, they had good reason for the second. In Limassol, a predominantly Greek town with a small, fearful Turkish population, the Battalion's presence, and stealthy good works, were so effective that, when they left, the United Nations commander could claim that tension in the area had ceased.

A detachment of a hundred Jocks in a mixed Scottish, Irish and Swedish force in Kophinou had a more gruelling experience, for the town was Turkish and a standing temptation to the Greek National Guard nearby. The stoning of a Greek bus offered the Guard the provocation they wanted and, in the subsequent gun-battle, The Black Watch contingent, which manned the Green Line separating the two sides, found itself completely cut off. The Jocks lived in sangars and trenches sited on a bare hillside across which bullets whistled randomly from Greek and Turk. Since their presence alone prevented the two sides from getting at each other's throats, the Jocks could not move from their exposed position, and their reliefs and all supplies had to come in by helicopter.

This latest variation of military duty demanded an extraordinary degree of patience and self-discipline, but, testing as the situation in Cyprus was, it hardly compared with that of the next trouble-spot to which The Black Watch was sent. In Northern Ireland, the Battalion was called upon to perform a role akin to that for which the Regiment was raised, that of establishing the rule of law in an armed society where law-breaking was overtly or covertly condoned by a large part of the population. The connection between the eighteenth-century Highlands and the streets of modern Belfast may seem tenuous, but almost every link in the chain is touched upon in the Regiment's long involvement with Ireland.

CHAPTER 24

# Ireland

When The Black Watch was first posted to Ireland in 1746, after the battle of Fontenoy, it found a society with which it must have been immediately familiar. In both the Highlands and Ireland, primitive cultivation of poor land supported a small population at a level close to or at subsistence, depending on weather and birthrate. The common root of their culture could be seen in the Gaelic which both peoples spoke; and in religion and politics, each was, for the most part, Catholic and Jacobite. In the Highlands, however, the clan system ensured that landowner and tenant were of the same religion, whereas in Ireland Catholic tenants held the farms of Protestant landlords and the irritations between the two boiled into violence whenever poor harvests or rising population brought the tenants close to starvation. Unlike other troops, the Highlanders of The Black Watch brought a special understanding to the Irish problems, and it is not surprising that Stewart of Garth should write: 'In this delicate service the Highlanders were found particularly useful, both from their knowledge of the Language, and from their conciliating conduct towards the Irish.' They stayed there for eleven years, and returned after the Seven Years' War, when if anything the similarities between soldier and peasant had increased for, as the improving landlords moved into Perthshire in the latter half of the eighteenth century, the tenants found their rents racked higher, and their tenure rendered as insecure as that of the Irish.

That sympathy of language and interest persisted into the nineteenth century, but by then a subtle change had taken place, for the improving landlords had begun to produce benefits to compensate for their destruction of the old Highland society, and the Regimental diarists were not only reconciled to social change, but strongly advocated it. In particular, Anton, who had seen the new towns of Keith and Insch being built in Aberdeenshire to provide employment and a market for agricultural produce, thought that if the government undertook similar schemes in Ireland the evicted tenants and small farmers would earn enough to stave off famine and refrain from outlawry. In similar vein, Sergeant Wheatley condemned the conservatism of Irish peasants, and their resistance to the methods of 'obnoxious Scotch farmers' whose improvements offered a release from the threat of famine. These flights of thought were occasioned by the 42nd's experience in Ireland from 1818 to 1825.

The Regiment arrived first in Armagh and Newry, where the 2nd Battalion had been stationed nine years before, 'and in consequence of the good feeling that had existed between the inhabitants and the soldiers,' wrote Anton, 'we were welcomed with no ordinary rejoicing.' In Northern Ireland, their duty was to preserve the peace between Orangemen and Catholics, but in 1818 the terrible famine provoked widespread disturbances, and the 42nd moved south to Limerick to combat the Whiteboys' murder campaign against magistrates and landlords. The Whiteboys were only one of several terrorist groups which, as they grew in size, fragmented when the more extreme element split off to form a new organisation. Witnesses to murder were intimidated, so that convictions were impossible to obtain, and at last the Insurrection Act was passed, imposing a curfew and martial law, with savage penalties for offenders.

The Regiment was sent out to search for arms. 'A duty harassing to the military, and annoying to the inhabitants, for those visits were generally made at night. Beds were turned up, and bayonets made use of to probe the floor lest any concealment of arms had been attempted. Paragraphs appeared in the papers boasting of the quantity [of arms] brought in as a sign of returning tranquillity, but out of a hundred not four were serviceable.' As the famine grew more severe, Colonel and Mrs Dick's generosity in relieving destitute families won the grudging respect even of the Whiteboys but, while kindness and arms-searches might contain the violence, they could not cure it, and perhaps the last comment on this unhappy time can be left to an officer commanding a detachment in Kilkenny. They were trying to keep two hostile factions apart, and when both sides began to stone them, the soldiers protested. 'Silence,' said the officer. 'What else did you expect on being brought here?'

There are so many resemblances to the 1970s it is tempting to pass over the next 150 years, but the underlying situation changed entirely in that time, as the next three visits of the Regiment demonstrate. The emancipation of Catholics in 1829 gave them some political power, and when the Regiment returned in 1838 for two years, Ireland was peaceful, and O'Connell was working for land reform in Westminster. The 2nd Battalion arrived in 1885, to witness the last round of the tenant/landlord battle, in which the tenants wielded the weapon of ostracism, against land-agents such as Captain Boycott. When disturbances broke out in the north the 2nd Battalion sent a detachment to pacify them but, during their next eight years there, the country was quiet, as the British government reformed most of the tenants' grievances. But 1885 also saw the introduction of the first Home Rule Bill, and that marked the beginning of the Irish split when the Protestants in the North joined the Unionists to oppose separation from Britain. By 1905, when The Black Watch returned to Ireland, the prevalent theme in the North was 'Ulster will fight, and Ulster will be right'. Although passions did not break out during the 1st Battalion's tour of duty, in 1912, the year after it left, the Ulster Covenant was signed, and the Ulster Volunteers were formed, to be followed in the South by the formation of the Irish Volunteers who later became the Irish Republican Army, the I.R.A.

The murky doings of the I.R.A. have no part in this history until 1968, when it insinuated itself into the civil rights movement in Northern Ireland. Marches to draw attention to discrimination against Catholics in housing and employment provoked a Protestant backlash, and the army was called in. The Black Watch was then in Germany but, in 1970, it paid two fleeting visits: the first to Belfast for the 12th July Orange Day parades, when a company burst into the local headquarters of the I.R.A. while the committee was in session; later it visited Londonderry for the march of the Apprentice Boys ('whose ages range from 17 to 70 so far as one could see'). When the Jocks turned back a Protestant mob attempting to storm past into the Catholic Bogside, they could claim to have shown due impartiality. A full four-and-a-half month tour early in 1971 was spent in the border area around Armagh, where the detailed care demanded by border-patrols and searches for weapons in cars, houses and derelict areas often stretched the Jocks' day to sixteen hours. Their good humour and politeness, however, drew favourable comment, despite the frustrations both sides encountered, which the *Red Hackle* illustrated with the story of a mythical Farmer Donnolly. He is stopped at a road-block on his way to market by a patrol which finds his car filled with suspicious objects: bales of hay and sacks of animal feed, all of which might contain explosives, a bag of nails which could be used for making nail-bombs, and a can of petrol – essential for incendiary devices. A thorough check is necessary before the Jocks are convinced that each item is innocent, and allow Donnolly through. To escape this inconvenience on his return, he then takes a route along mud tracks and small lanes, where a helicopter spots him and lands a section in front of his car. This time the search is even more painstaking, and by the time the section is convinced of Donnolly's guileless intentions everyone's time and temper have been tested.

The farmers at any rate returned to comfortable homes, whereas the accommodation of the soldiers was not much different from 1817 when Sergeant Wheatley was in Armagh with twenty-four people packed into a room; in 1971 the number was reduced to eighteen in one small hut. The standard further deteriorated in October when the Battalion squeezed in a two-month tour before leaving for Hong Kong; on that occasion some of the Jocks were housed in double-decker buses.

The Black Watch was then stationed in Belfast, and it experienced a curious mixture of tedium and stress during the tour. A routine quickly developed of patrolling the streets in Land Rovers and personnel carriers, of guarding key points such as telephone exchanges and power stations, and of maintaining vehicle check points, but in August the Government had introduced internment and the I.R.A. had reacted with a campaign against the army. Amid the plethora of bombings and shootings, several incidents stood out: two gun battles in the night with snipers, the dispersal of a stone-throwing mob with rubber bullets, and the death of Corporal Charnley – the Battalion's only loss in Northern Ireland – who was killed by a sniper. This was perhaps the most testing of their tours in the province, yet the Jocks' morale appeared to get higher each week they were there. The military operation, however, could only be deemed to be effective if it permitted the political debate to take over. While the Battalion was in Hong Kong, that moment seemed to be reached with the Sunningdale Agreement, but its breakdown in the face of a strike by Protestant workers brought the cauldron back to the boil.

When the Battalion returned in 1974 after two years in Hong Kong there was, nevertheless, a marked change from earlier tours. Its patch was Andersonstown, a Catholic enclave in a Protestant area, dominated by the Provisional I.R.A., and, although internment was still in force, the emphasis was on a return to the normal procedure of criminal arrest and trial. Instead of confrontation, the Jocks faced a hostile but relatively quiet population; there were still incidents such as an attempt to lure a patrol towards a booby-trapped car, or the approach of a sniper hidden by a sympathetic crowd which suddenly opened to allow him to shoot – an attempt frustrated by the Jock's instantaneous return of fire – but by comparison with their earlier experience the violence was much diminished, and, with well-developed intelligence and a reputation for toughness and no nonsense, the Battalion maintained the uneasy quiet.

In the streets of Belfast a nineteen-year-old corporal with a four-man section shouldered as much responsibility as a company commander in more military fields. Where an arrest or house-search could cause a riot, these young N.C.O.s were diplomatic, even searching their own patrols before entering a house to show the inhabitants that nothing was to be 'planted' inside; where a weapon might be hidden in undergrowth, huts, even sewers, the Jocks were meticulous in covering every yard of ground; and when a sniper fired or a bomb was thrown, their reactions were immediate. But in the battle for the will of uncommitted people, their sense of justice and proportion were the fundamental weapons, and, in a world where morality was turned on its head and murder became a virtue, it was more than ever essential that the soldier's sense of personal responsibility should be strengthened by the undeviating ties of regimental tradition and comradeship.

# CHAPTER 25

# The Survival of the Regiment

When Highlanders were first regimented into the British Army, they brought with them a language, a sense of community, a form of dress and a style of behaviour that was entirely their own. Gradually most of these distinctions have disappeared, in common with the society from which they were derived, and now it would be absurd to claim that The Black Watch is radically different from the rest of the army. Like most soldiers the Jocks tend to marry young and so leave the barracks for married quarters, and in any case they may spend much of their careers away from the Regiment, so that its hold is hardly as exclusive as it used to be; but it would be equally absurd to assume that there was, therefore, no difference, for the original Highland character left a tribal imprint which the years have, if anything, deepened. It does not command much sympathy in the War Office or Ministry of Defence for it thrives on intangible or inconvenient items such as tradition, family links, uniform and loyalty to a name rather than a function but, on the other hand, it does give several hundred soldiers cohesion, pride and a standard of conduct which no amount of training could inculcate.

In more sweeping terms Wavell was accustomed to say, 'The regiment is the foundation of everything', but from 1945 that foundation was severely shaken by a quarter-century of internecine warfare between the regiments and the War Office. The case against the regiments was largely administrative, and particular objection was taken to the variety of promotion rolls among them, with consequent disparities in the seniority of officers and N.C.O.s. Newer corps like the R.E.M.E (Royal Electrical and Mechanical Engineers), R.A.O.C. (Royal Army Ordnance Corps) and R.A.S.C. (Royal Army Service Corps), which had standardised promotion rolls, reinforced the War Office's determination to introduce a similar system among Groups or Brigades of infantry regiments. The drawback was that, to eliminate differences in seniority within a Group, N.C.O.s and officers would be posted to and from different regiments, which, besides causing individual hardship, would have diluted the particular qualities of each corps. The scheme might have been acceptable elsewhere, but in The Black Watch it was fiercely resented.

When the first notice arrived in 1948 about the cross-posting of N.C.O.s, Colonel Fergusson, commanding the Battalion, explained to the Sergeants' Mess that if an individual wished to stay with the Regiment he might have to be prepared to accept a drop in rank and, consequently, in pay. Out of fifty-two warrant officers and sergeants, all but four said they would prefer the drop to being posted away, and two of the four had large families which precluded their taking a cut in pay. Nevertheless two sergeants were posted against their will; both bought their discharges and re-enlisted in The Black Watch as privates.

When the same principle was applied to officers, Colonel Fergusson had to invoke the aid of Lord Wavell, as Colonel of the Regiment, before the depredations ceased. It was the last but not least of the services which Wavell performed for the Regiment, before his death in 1950.

All this, however, might be seen as no more than a battle between tradition and progress, were it not for the sudden embrace, in 1951, of tradition by progress when the Korean War demonstrated the need to expand the army. Almost at once attempts at cross-posting dwindled away, territorial links were strengthened, the Perth Depot took over from Fort George the basic training of Black Watch recruits, and the six strongest regiments were authorised to reform their 2nd battalions. Beneath the cloak of progress, it appeared, mere expediency lurked.

The Black Watch was one of those authorised to raise a 2nd Battalion, but its story was brief. After two years in Germany, it was sent in 1954 to British Guiana where continual riots had caused the suspension of the constitution. Peace had returned, however, by the time the Battalion arrived, and it passed its last active service in that least demanding of military roles – maintaining a Presence. On its return to Europe in 1956, the 2nd Battalion was once more amalgamated with the 1st, although many of its officers and men were drafted to units engaged in the Suez operation.

The most significant aspect of the Guiana incident was that, for the first time, The Black Watch travelled by air. The ability to move troops rapidly across the world was a powerful argument – almost as powerful as financial stringency – in favour of a smaller army. In 1957 Duncan Sandys accordingly announced that National Service would end in 1960, to be replaced by a volunteer army of 180,000 men, of which the infantry would provide a quarter. The Highland Brigade was to be reduced from six regiments to four, which was effected by transferring the Highland Light Infantry out of the Brigade, and by amalgamating the Seaforths and Camerons, and it was further recommended that the Brigade should have a common depot, promotion roll and cap badge. Taken with the reorganisation which occurred ten years later, Sandys' reforms constituted the most profound change in the regimental system since that of Cardwell and Childers eighty years before.

However, it is instructive to see how a regiment holds on to the essential pillars of its identity. When news of the changes was heard, an officer wrote, 'We can only trust that some means will be found to overcome the introduction of a brigade badge to replace the Red Hackle. The thought that our own special emblem is now threatened is almost unbelievable and is probably the hardest part to bear.' A compromise was arranged by which the Brigade badge was to be worn on the blue bonnet, while the Red Hackle remained on the khaki tam o' shanter, and it is no surprise to discover that the tam o' shanter is worn now on all possible occasions. Similarly the common promotion roll was honoured more in the breach than the observance, although promotion within the Regiment was slow. Nothing could be done, however, to save the Queen's Barracks at Perth which had been the Regimental Depot for eighty years, and in 1960 it was closed.

For the army as a whole the next ten years were a traumatic decade. The regular concussion of multi-megaton hydrogen bombs seemed to suggest that a conventional army was an irrelevance, and, on a less theoretical level, recruitment became extremely difficult after the end of National Service, due partly to full employment, and partly to the

PLATE 29 *President and Mrs John F. Kennedy with Major Wingate-Gray of The Black Watch in Washington, D.C., November, 1963.*

swinging tenor of the times in which the military image seemed out of place. Even The Black Watch received only a trickle of recruits, and this despite the enormous public appeal of the Pipes and Drums, which had made a phenomenally successful tour of the United States, inspiring such headlines as: 'Black Watch Kilt Them at the Garden', New York; 'Black Watch Struts – 10,000 pulses stir', Minneapolis; and in Seattle, 'Where does an American go to enlist in The Black Watch?' In Britain the response was more muted. The Pipes and Drums returned to the United States in 1963, when they played before

President Kennedy, shortly before the fatal journey to Dallas, and at the special request of his widow they played once more at the head of his funeral procession.

Uncertainty continued to cloud the future of the Regiment until 1967 when the second phase of military reorganisation was announced. It had been evident for some time that an axe hovered over the Territorials; now it fell, and they were replaced by a smaller Territorial Army Volunteer Reserve. In the Highland District, the 51st Highland Volunteers (T.A.V.R.) inherited a long tradition of soldiering, and their single battalion was soon increased to three, to which The Black Watch contributed three companies. But it was a sad loss when the 4th and 5th Battalions, from Dundee and Angus, and the 6th and 7th, from Perthshire and Fife, departed from the scene; they had provided a vivid part of the Regiment's history and had contributed some fine soldiers to the field, from Colonel Walker in the First World War to Brigadier Oliver in the Second. A small remnant survived until 1969, but then they too were finally disbanded.

The Regular Army was also affected by the reorganisation, and in 1968 the Highland Brigade was combined with the Lowland Brigade to form the Scottish Division. Again the number of regiments was cut, the Argyll and Sutherland Highlanders being reduced to a cadre, but The Black Watch survived once more – not merely survived, but began to flourish again after the doldrums of the 1960s.

Part of the reason came from the relief felt by the Regiment after the changes had been made. Its depot, which had spent the decade wandering between Stirling, Fort George and Aberdeen, finally came to rest at Glencorse with the Scottish Division, and their future was now settled. At the same time, however, the infantry as a whole had come out of the cold. The B.A.O.R. (British Army of the Rhine) was decentralised into Brigade Groups for protection against nuclear attack, so that in Europe an infantry battalion had once more a clear operational role. And during the decade, the Regiment was armed with greater power than it had ever had in its history. In 1959 it received the Self-Loading Rifle, and this was followed by the Ferret scout car, helicopters, and the Saladin armoured personnel carrier. After this last was introduced, a *Red Hackle* correspondent claimed, 'there need be no difference between Infantry, Cavalry and Artillery', and that is probably as good a guess as any at the shape of things to come.

On the 3rd May, 1975 the Queen Mother presented new Colours to the 1st Battalion, some 236 years after The Black Watch was raised. Merely to have survived for close on a quarter of a millenium is no light matter, but to have flourished through the shock of battle, the corrosion of terrorism and the torpor of peace, is a substantial achievement indeed. Each name on the Colours represents a triumph over the violent confusion of battle, but together they contain the progression of warfare from muzzle-loader to machine-gun, and there is implicit in them a story of constant change, preparation and the acquisition of new skills. It is a pleasant paradox that such sinuous versatility should be found in a regiment apparently so encrusted with tradition, but perhaps this book will have served to show the sternly utilitarian purpose of regimental traditions.

There was good reason for Moore to remind the 42nd, at Corunna, of Egypt, for Pipe-Major Roy to play 'Lawson's Men' at Tobruk, and for Wavell to restore the Red Hackle to the 2nd Battalion in India, for in moments of crisis there is a strength to be derived from a history, a tune, or a hackle, which is beyond price. If The Black Watch remains a little more tribal than most regiments, a little more feudal, and a little more punctilious about formalities of dress and behaviour, it is because that strength grows best round some ritual, and in its long life that inward preparation has enabled it to overcome all the crises of war and peace. 'It is not a regiment,' a Colonel of the Regiment has said. 'It's a religion,' and whatever challenge the future may hold, that formula seems proof against it, perhaps against the very passage of time.

# Appendix

SOME STATISTICS OF 19TH CENTURY RECRUITS

AREAS IN WHICH 19TH CENTURY RECRUITS WERE BORN

(1798 as comparison)

(expressed as percentage of total)

| Year Recruited | High- land | 42nd area | Loth- ians | South West | North East | England Ireland | Rest | Total in Numbers |
|---|---|---|---|---|---|---|---|---|
| 1798 | 51 | 9 | 4 | 14 | 13 | 6 | 4 | 330 |
| 1807/24 | 32 | 12 | 10 | 14 | 14 | 8 | 9 | 268 |
| 1825/9 | 12 | 10 | 10 | 50[1] | 3 | 1 | 14 | 291 |
| 1830/4 | 9 | 17 | 27 | 18 | 11 | 4 | 14 | 204 |
| 1835/9 | 21[2] | 10 | 19 | 35 | 3 | 1 | 12 | 445 |
| 1840/4 | 10 | 16 | 20 | 33 | 10 | 1 | 10 | 824 |
| 1848/9 | 6 | 9 | 16 | 51 | 5 | 2 | 10 | 145 |
| 1854 | 5 | 12 | 10 | 20 | 6 | 37 | 10 | 390 |
| 1859 | 5 | 10 | 5 | 30 | 3 | 38 | 8 | 277 |
| 1865/6 | 14 | 8 | 21 | 18 | 20 | 3 | 7 | 147 |
| 1871/2 | 8 | 19 | 20 | 28 | 11 | 2 | 12 | 192 |

[1] Almost all weavers, a third from Ayrshire.
[2] Almost half from Argyll but mostly recruited in Glasgow.

TRADES OF 19TH CENTURY RECRUITS

(1798 as comparison)

(expressed as percentage of total)

| Year Recruited | Labourer Servant | Weaver | Shop Office | Craft | Indus-trial[1] | Miner | Cloth-Worker | Cobbler Tailor | Rest | Total |
|---|---|---|---|---|---|---|---|---|---|---|
| 1798 | 44 | 23 | 3 | 14 | 2 | 0 | 1 | 10 | 5 | 343 |
| 1807/24 | 63 | 14 | 3 | 4 | 2 | 1 | 2 | 9 | 2 | 314 |
| 1825/9 | 28 | 35 | 3 | 10 | 3 | 3 | 4 | 10 | 4 | 271 |
| 1830/4 | 43 | 11 | 10 | 14 | 1 | 1 | 5 | 8 | 7 | 235 |
| 1835/9 | 41 | 12 | 6 | 12 | 3 | 1 | 6 | 12 | 7 | 542 |
| 1840/4 | 38 | 12 | 7 | 12 | 6 | 4 | 5 | 10 | 5 | 780 |
| 1848/9 | 30 | 10 | 8 | 20 | 5 | 10 | 6 | 8 | 3 | 145 |
| 1854 | 38 | 9 | 5 | 16 | 5 | 4 | 5 | 11 | 7 | 266 |
| 1859 | 30 | 2 | 6 | 21 | 10 | 7 | 6 | 11 | 7 | 281 |
| 1864/5 | 40 | 0 | 9 | 19 | 9 | 8 | 1 | 9 | 5 | 172 |
| 1871/2 | 32 | 0 | 12 | 18 | 10 | 10 | 2 | 8 | 7 | 238 |

[1] Includes iron and steel workers, ship-builders, etc.

## FATE OF 19TH CENTURY RECRUITS

(expressed as percentage of total)

| Year Recruited | Discharged[1] Pensioned | Died Killed | Deserted Transported | Bought Out[2] | Transfer | Total in Numbers |
|---|---|---|---|---|---|---|
| 1825 | 59 | 25 | 5 | 2 | 8 | 128 |
| 1833/5 | 25 | 23 | 23 | 25 | 4 | 85 |
| 1839 | 33 | 34 | 9 | 15 | 7 | 120 |
| 1842/4 | 34 | 25 | 15[3] | 16 | 9 | 309 |
| 1848/9 | 29 | 15 | 19 | 6 | 31[5] | 185 |
| 1854 | 33 | 15 | 33[4] | 4 | 15 | 264 |
| 1859 | 29 | 8 | 21 | 22 | 19[5] | 276 |
| 1864/5 | 35 | 6 | 11 | 18 | 25[5] | 231 |
| 1871/2 | 55[6] | 22 | 4 | 12 | 4 | 258 |

[1] Includes: life service (20 years), limited (7 years), pensioned as unfit
[2] Army average in 1847 was 25 per cent
[3] Mostly Reserve Battalion
[4] Recruits at depot before being sent to Crimea or India
[5] Especially, Canada 1852 to 74th, and India 1867 to 92nd
[6] Includes transfer to Reserve.

# Bibliography

Published Works

| | |
|---|---|
| David Stewart | Sketches of the Highlanders (Edinburgh 1822) |
| Anonymous | Journal of an Anonymous Private of the 42nd (London 1822) |
| John Malcolm | Reminiscences of a Campaign in the Pyrenees (London 1822) |
| James Anton | Retrospect of a Military Life (Edinburgh 1842) |
| Tom Morris | Recollections of Military Service (London 1845) |
| Anthony Sterling | The Highland Brigade in Crimea (London 1895) |
| Archibald Forbes | The Black Watch (London 1910) |
| Arthur Wauchope | The Black Watch in the Great War (London 1925) |
| John Gordon | Six Years in The Black Watch (Boston 1929) |
| Eric Linklater | The Man on My Back (London 1941) |
| B.J.G. Madden | History of the 6th Battalion (Perth 1948) |
| Bernard Fergusson | The Black Watch and the King's Enemies (London 1950) |
| Philip Howard | The Black Watch (London 1968) |
| Michael Brander | The Highlanders and Their Regiments (London 1971) |
| W.G. Blaxland | The Regiments Depart (London 1971) |
| Bernard Fergusson | Trumpet in the Hall (London 1973) |
| The Red Hackle Magazine | |

## Unpublished

(Unless otherwise stated, the following diaries, letters and reports are all in the possession of The Black Watch Museum, Balhousie Castle, Perth)

*The Diaries of:*

Private Gunn
Lieutenant McNiven
Colonel Wheatley
Colonel Drysdale
Private MacKintosh
Captain Halkett
Sergeant Cooper
Brigadier-General Stewart
Sergeant Duncan (in possession of diarist)

*The Correspondence of:*

The Marquess of Blantyre
General Dick
Colonel Johnstone
General Cameron

*The Reports of:*

Brigadier Allison
Colonel MacLeod

# Index